# A CURRICULUM FOR PRESCHOOLS

## SECOND EDITION

Carol Seefeldt

*University of Maryland*

Charles E. Merrill Publishing Company
*A Bell & Howell Company*
Columbus    Toronto    London    Sydney

Published by
Charles E. Merrill Publishing Co.
*A Bell & Howell Company*
Columbus, Ohio 43216

This book was set in Optima and Korinna.
Cover Design Coordination: Will Chenoweth.
Text Designer: Laura Wallencheck Gustafson.
Production Coordination: Lucinda A. Peck.
Cover Photograph: Four by Five, Inc.

*Photo Credits*

Larry Crouse: pages 76 and 108; Rohn Engh: pages 11, 63, 68, 90, 98, 130, 139, 141, 143, 162, 166, 178, 270, 286, and 332; Richard Farkas: pages 2, 4, 13, 23, 24, 28, 44, 50, 60, 72, 74, 78, 96, 106, 111, 112, 113, 119, 126, 135, 158, 170, 174, 185, 190, 193, 198, 200, 202, 203, 215, 229, 230, 236, 240, 241, 254, 256, 259, 261, 263, 271, 299, 303, 305, 307, 321, and 336; Franklin County Children Services: page 54; Larry Hamill: page 36; Tom Hutchinson: pages 8 and 87; Lavisa Wilson: page 327.

Library of Congress Catalog Card Number: 79–90122
International Standard Book Number: 0–675–08137–8
Printed in the United States of America
1 2 3 4 5 6 7 8 9 10—85 84 83 82 81 80

*TO EUGENE, PAUL, AND
ANDREA, WHO BELIEVE THAT
WOMAN HAS THE RIGHT
AND THE RESPONSIBILITY TO
PARTICIPATE IN THE WHOLE
OF LIFE*

Statistics show that over one–third of all children under the age of five in the United States are currently enrolled in some type of preschool program. With the current trend of more and more women being employed outside of the home, as well as the research giving validity to early educational experiences, it seems likely that preschool programs will become a reality for many more children and their families.

*A Curriculum for Preschools,* second edition, provides ideas, materials, and methods for establishing a successful curriculum within a preschool center. It is based on the premise that highly trained, skilled, and knowledgeable persons are essential in the staffing of an effective program. Research has verified the disastrous effects of raising children and infants in group situations with insufficient numbers of trained, concerned adults. Conversely, data from programs that were staffed with highly competent adults and well–planned curricula show that children do prosper when given the benefits of a quality preschool program.

This book is designed for use as a text in college undergraduate programs and other training programs preparing persons to work in preschools. The content is concerned with the very practical aspects of working with groups of young children, and may, therefore, be a resource for those currently working in Head and Home Start, day care programs, and other preschool programs.

The early years have been identified as those most important to the education of an individual, and quality preschool programs must, therefore, be educational in nature. Children need opportunities to develop in the areas of language, art, science, mathematics, and social concepts. Every experience in a preschool, whether designed to give physical care or not, must be considered an educational experience.

It is the philosophy of this text that the play of the child is of utmost educational value. It is essential for the development of cognitive structures; it also establishes in the child the pattern of learning how to learn, provides for full exploration of the environment, and gives opportunities to solve problems creatively. Play also allows children to express their individuality and emotions.

The significance of fostering the individuality of each infant and child in group care or a preschool is recognized. All experiences in group living are directed toward building the child's sense of self-worth and dignity. Conformity to routines is not only inappropriate for young children, but it is also physically unhealthy. Ideas for meeting the child's physical needs and suggestions for teaching health and nutritional concepts are developed.

Stressing the idea that the preschool program must not serve to supplant the child's parents and home, *A Curriculum for Preschools* offers suggestions for fostering and facilitating parental involvement and emphasizes involving parents and community in relevant decision making. Working with volunteers and aides from the community and involving the wider community in the preschool are also considered.

*Carol Seefeldt*

# CONTENTS

# INTRODUCTION TO PRESCHOOL EDUCATION

## PART ONE

The concept of preschool is not new to the United States. Our nation was involved in caring for children outside their homes as far back as 1830, when the first child care program opened in Boston. Early programs were provided for children of immigrant parents, assisting both the child and his family to become acculturated and allowing both parents to work. Universities sponsored programs for very young children during the early 1900s; such programs provided socializing experiences for the children, who also served as subjects for research or teacher training.

Government entered the picture in the 1930s with the Works Administration Program, establishing centers for children of poverty stricken families and providing work for unemployed teachers. Again, in the 1940s government stepped in and built preschools for children of women working for the war effort.

Our quickly changing society, the restructuring of the role of women, as well as the research indicating the important effects of early childhood experience, have each contributed to the development of other methods of child care and education to supplement, not to supplant, the role of the family as the basic unit for the care and education of the young child.

# PRESCHOOL EDUCATION

*Teaching the child under six is a lively and bubbling profession. Ever so much is going on.* (Hymes, 1974, p. 3)

1

If you decide to become a teacher of young children, you will be entering a lively, bubbling profession where much is going on. Because so much is going on, many believe that early childhood education is new in our nation.

*Teaching is a lively profession.*

Nothing could be further from the truth! Early childhood education has been present in our country since the early 1800s. Day care centers, or day nurseries, for children of mothers who worked in mills and factories, are reported to have been established as early as 1830 (Fein & Clarke-Stewart, 1973).

Federal aid was available to establish day care centers during and after the Civil War in order to permit mothers to help in the war effort (Ginsburg, 1978). Most of these early nurseries were designed to provide safe and hygienic care for children while their mothers worked.

**THE KINDERGARTEN** Kindergarten programs also have a long history in our country. The first kindergarten program in the United States is credited to Mrs. Carl Shurz who, in 1853, opened a kindergarten on the front porch of her Watertown, Wisconsin, home.

All of these early kindergarten programs were begun by women who had immigrated from Germany and had at one time or another worked with

Friedrich Froebel, the originator of the kindergarten. Froebel believed that children should have the opportunity to grow and live within an environment specifically designed for them. Thus, he created the kindergarten, a garden in which children could grow. He gave children blocks, balls, and other items as gifts and created occupations of paper folding, cutting, and sewing to occupy the children. He wrote convincingly of bringing children close to God through the activities of the kindergarten. His ideas of God and of bringing children to God through the activities of the kindergarten were accepted eagerly in the United States.

Many kindergartens were opened in the late 1800s in poor areas of cities, near factories, or in immigrant neighborhoods. The programs were sponsored by church groups, welfare agencies, and even the Woman's Christian Temperance Union either to aid children of the poor and their families, or to help immigrants become acculturated into the ways of their new country.

Because of the great popularity and success of the kindergartens, public school systems began to sponsor them by the late 1800s (Weber, 1969). Today the majority of states mandate communities to provide kindergartens, and although no kindergarten program is compulsory, in 1977 over 92 percent of all five year olds did attend a kindergarten program (Hymes, 1979, p. 5).

## THE NURSERY SCHOOL

Just as the kindergarten has a long history in our nation, so does the nursery school. The beginnings of the nursery school, like those of the kindergarten, can be traced to another country. In the early 1900s the McMillan sisters opened a nursery school in Deptford, a heavily industrialized slum of London. They named their program a nursery school, using the word *nursery* to represent the love, nurture, and physical care children would receive in the program, and the word *school* to represent the learnings and educational experiences that would accompany the care and nurture (Eliot, 1978, p. 9).

Soon after the McMillan sisters established their school, programs began to appear in the United States. The earliest nursery programs are believed to be those of Abigail Eliot in Boston (1922); Edna White at the Merrill-Palmer Institute in Detroit (1922); Harriet Johnson at Bank Street College of Education in New York (1919); and Patty Smith Hill at Teachers College in New York (1921). It is difficult to list the beginning schools, for many other women were establishing schools for young children at the same time. Although it is not possible to list them all, it is possible to conclude that the nursery schools created in our country in the early 1900s were the work of women who held the "conviction that some definite educational effort is necessary before the age of five" (Eliot, 1978, p. 17).

Eliot (1978) believed that the crucial difference between the nursery school and the kindergarten, as well as the day nursery, was the fact that the nursery school was planned specifically for children ages two through four. The kindergarten offered a planned program for five year olds, and the day nursery, although it enrolled children younger than five, usually had no planned program but offered custodial care only.

Program planning was seen as the key to the nursery school. In a nursery school, children were active, alive, choosing, busy, happy (Eliot, 1978, p. 16). Children under the age of five in these schools were provided with a program designed to give them "a rich and useful experience when they are enabled to live in terms of their own present, and act spontaneously within the limits of their present powers" (Hymes, 1978, p. 18).

In 1924 24 nursery schools were reported in 11 states. By 1930 the number had risen to 262 as more and more parents established programs for their young children (Rothstein, 1979).

Today the census bureau estimates that well over 32 percent of all three and four year olds are enrolled in some type of nursery school program. Some of these nursery schools are run by parents who work cooperatively in the school; others are run by church groups, government funds, or businesses.

## CHANGING SOCIAL FORCES

Even though preschool education is not new to our nation, it has never before reached as many children as it does today. The first kindergartens, nursery schools, and day nurseries were small and enrolled only a few children at any one time. Many of the schools were unique in their community and were more likely seen as isolated attempts to provide early educational experiences for children than as programs serving all children.

Today, however, preschool education is available in every community across our nation. Children from all backgrounds and locations can be found in some type of preschool program. Social changes, as well as changing ideas and theories on the nature of young children's intellectual growth, have contributed to the increase in preschool education.

## Social Changes

Traditionally most infants and young children under the age of six have been cared for by their own mothers within their own homes. That is, if you discount the fact that children of the very poor—whose mothers have always been employed outside of the home—have been cared for by others, and children of the very rich have historically been cared for by persons hired by their mothers.

Today, however, the majority of mothers with children under the age of six are employed outside of the home. Many women enjoy the fulfillment of a career in addition to that of wife and mother, but many more are employed for economic reasons.

Changing family composition has also contributed to the increase in preschool programs. More children under the age of six live in single-parent families than ever before. This means that the parent with whom they live is also the parent employed outside of the home.

The mobility of families has also increased the need for preschools. Since many families live far from grandparents and other relatives, many parents need preschools to support them in their role as parents as well as to help in the care and education of their young children.

## Changing Ideas

Changing ideas have also had an effect on the proliferation of preschool education. During the 1960s the work of Bloom, who wrote *Stability and Change in Human Characteristics* (1960), and that of Hunt, author of *Intelligence and Experience* (1961), led to the idea that enriching educational experiences could increase children's intelligence. The idea that the years before the age of four were critical in terms of intellectual development became widely accepted during the 1960s.

Both Hunt and Bloom pointed out that children reared in nonstimulating, nonverbal environments were likely to score lower on intelligence tests than those reared in more stimulating environments. The concept that an environment, such as that of a good preschool—full of language, experiences, and interactions with others—could serve to increase the intellectual functioning of children born into poverty was supported by many.

The fact that many children of low intelligence were poor became apparent during the civil-rights movement of the early 1960s. Social and economic inequalities that persisted in our country were clearly demonstrated during the movement. This demonstration led to the rationale and base for providing all children, but especially those of poverty, with preschool education. If a child participated in a good preschool program, this experience would foster intelligence and later the child would compete successfully in the social and economic world. In the long run, the child's increased intelligence and ability to compete would permit later success in school and in the job market, and would thus eliminate poverty in our nation.

Head Start, developed under the 1964 Office of Economic Opportunity, is perhaps the most comprehensive child development program designed to ameliorate the effects of poverty on young children. Soon after the establishment of Head Start, serving children ages two through five, the Parent Child Centers were implemented. The Parent Child Centers are designed for children, ages birth through two or three, and their parents. Other programs such as Home and Health Start, as well as several programs under the Elementary Secondary Education Acts, were also implemented in attempts to provide the young with enriching, early educational experiences, and thus eventually eliminate the effects of poverty.

There is evidence that these enriching, early educational experiences can work to increase children's intelligence and school achievement, as well as bring about social and economic benefits for children, families, and communities. The findings of longitudinal studies of low-income children who participated in experimental infant and preschool programs, beginning in 1962, show "without a doubt, that in the main, programs which had deliberate cognitive curricula had a significant long-term effect on school performance" (*The Persistence of Preschool Effects*, 1978, p. 2). These studies demonstrate that investments in early educational experiences do have long-term benefits for children.

These studies also clearly show that fiscal and social benefits can result from early educational programs. Most of the children who had participated in these programs did not have to repeat grades in school, nor were they assigned to special education classes or to other institutions. All of this constitutes a substantial savings for school systems, taxpayers, and children.

## DIVERSITY IN PROGRAMS ————————————————————

The activity in early childhood education is reflected in the diversity of programs available. The many different types of early childhood programs are called by different names and established for different purposes. Some are sponsored by the federal government, others by churches, school systems, parent cooperative groups, industry, or for profit. Among the different preschool programs available today are the following:

*There are many diverse programs.*

**KINDERGARTENS**  Kindergarten programs are usually sponsored by the public school system and enroll five-year-old children. Some public school systems also sponsor prekindergarten programs for three or four year olds. Readiness for reading and school experiences often provide the focus of today's kindergartens.

**NURSERY SCHOOLS**  Nursery schools usually enroll children two through five years of age. Some are run by church groups or civic clubs; others are sponsored by parents. Parent cooperative schools are organized, administered, and run by parents. Parents must volunteer their time on a regular basis to keep the school operating.

Nursery schools might enroll children for half or full days or any combination. Some programs are for two year olds two mornings a week, some for three and four year olds three full days per week. The usual purpose of the nursery school is the same today as it was in the past—to provide for children's social, emotional, health, and educational needs.

## HEAD START

Head Start is a preschool program providing comprehensive services for children ages two through five. The Head Start program offers health, physical, and social services to children and their families. Parent and community involvement are high priorities of the program. The educational program of Head Start focuses on increasing mental processes, self-concept, social and emotional development, as well as readiness for school.

## HOME START

Home Start is based on the same principles of Head Start, but unlike Head Start, which takes place in a center, Home Start takes place in the children's homes. Home visitors work with children and their parents. It is believed that the parent is the most influential educator of her children, and home visitors focus on developing parent skills as teachers.

## DAY CARE PROGRAMS

Day care programs are designed to care for children when parents cannot. Although the prime purpose of most day care programs is to provide for children of employed parents, other parents—for example, those with health problems or those who, for any other reason, need some support in caring for and raising children—benefit from day care programs.

Although most day care programs are designed to provide care-giving experiences for children, most programs usually include a strong educational component as well. A diversity of day care programs is available, including the following:

### Infant Programs

Infants receive care in group situations. Infant day care, while concerned with the physical care of the baby, also provides for the intellectual development of the child. Care givers provide enriching and stimulating educational activities for babies as well as care for their physical needs.

### Hospital and Industrial Day Care

To meet the growing demand for skilled workers in hospitals and businesses, many hospitals, companies, and unions run and sponsor day care centers. Hospitals and factories report benefits for children, parents, and the company when day care services are available where parents work.

Some industries, rather than running a day care program in the factory or business, help parents select and pay for day care services for their children. Vouchers, valid for any child care center the employer might select, are being considered by many industries.

## Franchise Day Care

Business entered into the field of day care in the 1970s by establishing franchises. Many of the beginning franchises did not prove successful in establishing high-standard preschool programs. The cost of quality child care, and the diversity of communities and their needs, negates implementing a single model across all locations economically.

## Private Day Care

A person or a group of persons may establish a child care program for profit. Unlike the franchises, these are single operations, designed to meet the needs of children and families within a given neighborhood or community.

## University Day Care

Since mothers are returning to school in increasing numbers, and students are more socially aware, universities and colleges are establishing day care programs. Children of faculty members, as well as staff and members of the community, often participate in these programs.

## Family Day Care

Family day care is the care of children in the home of a family other than their own. Such care often meets the unique needs of infants, school-age children, children with special needs, and preschoolers. Some children who would not benefit from a large group experience find a family day care home appropriate to their needs. Mothers with young children at home, or those persons who enjoy the company of young children, have found family day care to be a beneficial and profitable experience.

## Day Care for Children with Special Needs

Some preschool programs are designed for children who have special needs. Now that all children, regardless of handicapping condition, are to be provided equality of access to educational opportunities, more and more preschool programs are being developed for children with special needs. Some of these programs are sponsored by school systems, others by organizations or civic groups. All provide special experiences for children with a variety of special needs.

**DIVERSE YET UNIFIED**   "But if the array of names in the United States is confusing, it does indicate one thing. The education of children under six is a wide-open field. It has not settled down"

(Hymes, 1974, p. 3). Early childhood education continues to be a growing, developing field, as well as a diverse one. If the diversity of programs offers a confusing picture, it demonstrates that the field is wide open, filled with opportunities for those who want to work with young children.

Although the programs are diverse, there is a certain unity among all. It does not matter if the program is a parent cooperative nursery school or a day care center run by an industrial company for employees. Whether the program is designed for two year olds or five year olds, there are similarities in all programs of quality that reflect the principles of a democracy.

Living in a democracy means that there must be diversity, but it also means that there are certain unifying factors, for in a democracy, all citizens must possess certain characteristics. Citizens of a democratic society must be autonomous—able to think for themselves, make decisions, and have confidence in themselves. At the same time, a citizen of a democratic society must be able to relate and work with others, demonstrating concern for the welfare of others as well as for that of himself.

All quality preschool programs have the common goal of preparing children to become responsible citizens of a democratic society. Recognizing that citizens in a democracy must have self-confidence and knowledge in order to make wise decisions, and must be able to relate effectively with others, as well as be physically strong, preschool programs of quality have the following goals in common:

1. To provide children with a foundation for learning.
    "At whatever age the child starts school, his beginning school years are critical for what he learns and will continue to learn" (Association for

*The early years are critical.*

Childhood Education International, 1965, p. 1). Every good preschool, whether a day care center, home-based program, or nursery school, offers children a foundation for learning.

Abundant opportunities exist for children to develop their skills as learners, and to find out about their world. Children, in a good preschool setting, can follow their natural interests and develop their curiosity as they explore things in their world within the safety of a secure environment. They can find out how things work, taking things apart and putting them together again, or explore the nature of the earth itself as they play with sand, mud, and water.

Good preschool education also develops children's ability to explore ideas. As children have firsthand experiences with the things in their world, they are building a foundation for thinking. Through firsthand explorations and experiences children are helped to see relationships. They can relate the ideas that come from one experience to those from another. You, as a teacher, can help children to see similarities and differences between experiences and to draw generalizations from them.

Children also have opportunities to communicate their experiences to others through language. Learning to speak so others will understand their ideas and learning to listen to the ideas of others provides children with a foundation for later language usage. Once children have the use of language, they can increase their knowledge by using what others have said or written to increase their own understanding of the world.

2. To build a strong sense of self in young children.

Everyone needs a measure of self-confidence. All of us, especially young children, need to feel we are capable people, people who have skills, knowledge, and abilities. Without a certain amount of confidence in themselves, children will fail to learn. Learning involves taking a risk; there is always a challenge to learning something new. If a child believes she is not capable, she will not be able to take many risks and her learning will be impaired.

Good preschools help children to analyze their own strengths and weaknesses. After experiencing many things—from digging in the sand to painting or reading stories from pictures—children are encouraged to identify things they can do well. "I can climb. When I'm taller, I'll be able to climb to the top."

In a good preschool, children also learn to gain confidence as they learn to control their feelings and emotions. A child grows in confidence when he is able to understand and handle feelings. Plenty of opportunities are available in a good preschool for children to express joy, happiness, anger, sadness, or hostility in positive ways. They can paint, pound the clay, sing a song, dance, play, run, or find other ways to express feelings safely.

Children who are confident are independent. Quality preschool programs let children assume responsibilities they can handle. As children can, they are encouraged to feed, dress, and care for themselves. In preschools for older children, four and five year olds, and even some two and three year olds, assume responsibilities for their school. When children have the skills and maturity, they feel confident as they can clean up after their play, care for the materials of the school, or help in preparing snacks and setting tables.

3. To help children develop physically.

Quality programs plan for children's physical growth as well as their intellectual and emotional growth. Children can not learn self-confidence or anything else if their physical needs are not met. Therefore, preschool programs should provide for the children's physical growth and development through comprehensive plans for medical and dental health care as well as nutrition.

Comprehensive plans for the children's physical safety are part of quality programs. The physical facility of the preschool is checked, and possible safety hazards are removed. You should be trained in emergency procedures and first aid.

Within the safety of the preschool environment are opportunities for children to exercise and develop small and large muscles and gain control over their growing bodies. They are free to run, jump, climb, ride wheel toys, and exercise, in many different ways, their developing bodies. Small muscle development is facilitated as they build with blocks, draw, paint, or put puzzles together.

A balance of exercise and rest is present in good preschool programs. Children need to rest their developing bodies just as they need exercise.

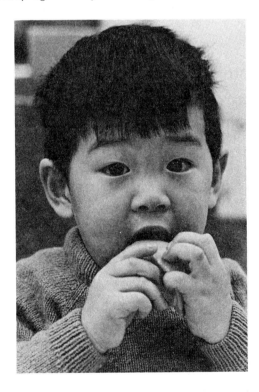

*All good schools provide for nutrition.*

Nutritious snacks and meals are also served to children in a good preschool program. These are planned to balance the children's total diet, as well as to sustain them through the preschool day.

4. To help children learn to relate effectively with others.

Living in a democracy means that children must be able to demonstrate concern for others, and learn to relate effectively with others. Just as children develop an awareness of themselves, developing understandings of their feelings and emotions, they must learn that others share these same feelings and emotions. Preschool experiences are designed to enable children to understand that they must often adjust their own thinking to take that of others into account.

Learning to cooperate, share, and get along with others is not taught at any one time of the day. Children can learn to relate effectively through their work and play with others. You can help them learn to relate with others by making comments such as "This is Jim's shovel; use this one," "If you tell her what you want, she may give it to you," "Jose will sell the cookies now," and "Susan is angry because you didn't let her. . . ." Throughout the day, in connection with all different experiences, you can help children to learn the ins and outs of working with others and of developing an understanding of another's point of view.

UNITY THROUGH PLANNING    In most quality preschool programs, you will find that the following activities take place regularly during the day:

## Arrival Time

This is the time for you to greet the children warmly and personally as they arrive at the preschool or family day care home. During this time, you and parents may have a chance to talk over the plans for the day or share some information about the child.

Arrange activities either on tables or in different areas of the room to attract children to specific play activities. Place open books on a table, thereby inviting children to read; place puzzles or games on another table.

Arrival is a relaxed time. It is the time to hang up coats and ready yourself for the day, but it is also a time to greet friends, talk over the plans for the day, or tell what happened last night. It is a warm, personal time, a time of sharing that establishes the climate of care, concern, and friendliness that will last the entire day.

## Planning Time

When all of the children have arrived, a short period of time for planning is common in a preschool program. Even two year olds can take some time to think about the things they will do during the day or to be informed of the activities that will take place. Start by saying, "Today we will. . . ."

Five year olds, on the other hand, will take a more active part in creating plans. You may even record the plans for the day on a chalkboard or chart as you and the children discuss the activities for the day.

Planning time may be the time for sharing news. Some days you will write a news story on the board; at other times children may share some news in which the entire class will be interested.

Sometimes planning time is a good time to share songs, poems, or read a short story. These activities can set the theme for the day, giving children useful ideas that can be used in their play, or stimulating ideas for creative activities.

## Activity Time

After planning, children move into a block of time often called free play or activity time. This is the heart of the preschool program and is usually 1½ to 2 hours in length. In full-day programs activity time occurs during the morning and again during the afternoon. During this time, whether in the morning or afternoon, children move freely from one activity to another. Some may paint first, and then move to the clay table; others may begin by building with blocks or reading a story, and then move to an art activity. Dramatic play is an important part of this time.

Preschool programs of high quality offer children a number of choices during this time. Every day the following choices should be available:

1. Dramatic play in the housekeeping area, store, office, etc.
2. Art activities for drawing and painting.
3. Modeling activities with clay, salt dough, etc.
4. Building or constructing activities, using blocks, woodworking, junk construction, etc.
5. Manipulative activities, requiring the use of peg boards, puzzles, table games, sorting activities, etc.
6. Reading activities, using books, pictures, class booklets, etc.
7. Exploration and experimentation with math and science materials.

Arrange the choices so children are free to circulate throughout the room, selecting their own activities as well as the children with whom they will work or play. The children will decide what they will do, whether they will do it by themselves or with others, and when they wish to move on to another activity. They are free to use the bathroom, get a drink of water, or even have a snack during this time.

Afternoon activity time is often less intense and may be more restful. In the afternoon children and the day are winding down. The choices may not be as wide and may include many more quiet activities such as drawing, cutting or pasting, reading books, or dramatic play. The activities differ from those in the morning, offering children different experiences as well as more quiet ones.

Following the activity time, children take part in cleaning up. They put materials back, store their work, and put the room in order again.

## Quiet Time

After activity time, which is intense and active, children need a quiet period. This quiet time helps them to rest and synthesize their experiences, as well as share their work with others. During quiet time, children can discuss the work they have completed, tell others how they constructed the block building or achieved a certain effect with the paints.

There may be time for a song, poem or story, or other quiet activity. Sometimes, depending on the length of the day and the nature of the program, a snack may be appropriate.

## Outdoor Activities Time

Children need time outdoors. Large muscle activities, such as running, jumping, or climbing usually occur during this time. Although outdoor activity is really designed to permit children to exercise their growing bodies, it also is planned to give children the same types of experiences found indoors. Make provision for children to take part in dramatic play activities, read a book under a tree, or even draw or paint.

This is the time for children to play active games with others or to dig quietly in the sand or mud. Because of the different resources available outdoors, you can plan science activities. Play with the wind and water, or the opportunity to grow a garden are possible.

In full-day programs a period of outdoor activity can be planned for both morning and afternoon. In half-day programs only one period of outdoor activity may be possible.

## Nourishment Time

All quality programs plan for children's nutritional needs. In half-day programs one snack may be sufficient. In full-day programs breakfast, a snack in the morning and afternoon, and lunch may be served. All menus are planned with children's total nutritional needs in mind.

## Rest Time

Every quality preschool program plans rest periods for young children. Quiet times, to balance the active ones, are necessary. When young children are together in a group, a nap is essential. Two or three year olds may need a nap in the morning and another in the afternoon. Five year olds, on the other hand, may require only one rest period in the morning, or they may also need a nap in the afternoon.

Children's individual preferences and needs for rest are important in planning for rest periods. Whether in a full- or half-day program, children's inner schedules must be respected. Babies will sleep when they need to. Their individual schedules cannot be ignored. Even toddlers and preschoolers have their own inner clocks dictating when rest is needed and how long it is needed.

## Time for Summing Up

The end of the day, whether in a half-day or full-day program, should be a time for summing up or synthesizing the activities that took place during the day. In the same relaxed atmosphere you used to greet the children, help them sort out the events of the day. This may be done as children dress to go home, or it might take place in a group meeting for older children.

The point is that children are helped to view their experiences with clarity, and to begin to evaluate their day and plan for the next. Review the events of the day, chatting informally with children, sharing their impressions of what went well and what things were problems. You can recognize children's progress by discussing with them the day's events.

## _____ SUMMARY

Preschool education is certainly not new in our nation. Day nurseries, offering custodial care for children of working mothers, are reported as early as 1830. Kindergarten programs appeared in the later 1800s, and nursery schools with planned educational programs as well as nurturing care appeared in the early 1900s.

Today, however, many more children are attending a preschool program of one kind or another. The popularity of preschool education today stems from the following:

1. Preschool experiences have proven beneficial for children, parents, and communities.
2. Social changes—that is, the greater mobility of families, the higher incidence of mothers employed outside of the home, and more single-parent families—all contribute to the need of support systems in the form of preschools for children and their families.

Many different kinds of preschool programs, different names and purposes exist. All programs of quality, however, share similar goals and similar programs. The goals focus on children's intellectual, social-emotional, and physical development, with the view of preparing children to become competent citizens of a democratic society. The program similarities focus on providing children with a balance of quiet and active periods, with time for rest, nourishment, and evaluation.

## *REFERENCES*

Association for Childhood Education International. *Basic Propositions for Early Childhood Education.* Washington, D.C.: Association for Childhood Education International, 1965.

Bloom, B. *Stability and Change in Human Characteristics.* New York: John Wiley & Sons, 1960.

Eliot, A. "America's First Nursery School." In *Living History Interviews, Book 1: Beginnings,* edited by J. L. Hymes, Jr. Carmel, Calif.: Hacienda Press, 1978.

Fein, G. G., and Clarke-Stewart, A. *Day Care in Context.* New York: John Wiley & Sons, 1973.

Ginsburg, S. "The Child Care Center Chronicle." In *Living History Interviews: Book 2: Care of Children of Working Mothers,* edited by J. L. Hymes, Jr. Carmel, Calif: Hacienda Press, 1978.

Hunt, J. M. *Intelligence and Experience.* New York: Ronald Press, 1961.

Hymes, J. L., Jr. *Teaching the Child under Six.* 2d ed. Columbus, Oh.: Charles E. Merrill Publishing Co., 1974.

_____. *A Look at 1977.* Carmel, Calif.: Hacienda Press, 1978.

_____. *A Look at 1978.* Carmel, Calif.: Hacienda Press, 1979.

*The Persistence of Preschool Effects.* Washington, D.C.: U.S. Department of Health, Education, and Welfare, 1977.

Rothstein, J. L. "The Government of the United States and the Young Child: A Study of Federal Child Care Legislation between 1935 and 1971," doctoral dissertation, University of Maryland, 1979.

Weber, E. *The Kindergarten: Its Encounter with Educational Thought in America.* New York: Teachers College Press, 1969.

## RESOURCES

Hymes, J. L., Jr. *Living History Interviews.* Carmel, Calif.: Hacienda Press, 1978.

*A Statement of Principles: Day Care.* Washington, D.C.: U.S. Department of Health, Education, and Welfare, 1971.

## PROJECTS

1. Survey the preschool programs available in your neighborhood. You might use the Yellow Pages of the phone book to locate preschool centers. How many different kinds of preschool programs can you find? Who sponsors these programs? What age children are served?

2. Select two programs to explore in depth. Ask to interview the directors of the programs. Ask them what the goals of the program are. How are the goals of both programs similar? How do they differ?

3. Complete your own history of preschool education in your community. Interview older residents or retired teachers to find out about education in the past. Look at old records to find out what provisions for the education of young children were made in your community.

# THE PEOPLE IN
# A PRESCHOOL
# PROGRAM _____

## PART TWO

Much of the curriculum of a preschool develops from interpersonal relation-ships. The curriculum is enhanced when many adults—parents, teachers, volunteers, aides, resource personnel—are available to interact and respond to the young child. Children also learn from one another, and the multiage grouping within a preschool fosters their interactions and extends their learn-ing possibilities.

"It is very easy to persuade ourselves that all we need to do is to buy the toys and materials and sit back and let the children utilize them. There are still institutional settings in which young infants do not have enough people to take care of them, but where they have access to an array of play materials. It has been observed that children fail to play with the toys in such settings" (Caldwell, 1972, p. 103). Children need other children to play with, but they also need the attention of a concerned adult. A good program is one that involves many people working directly with the children, or working for their benefit.

One person alone cannot be expected to have complete knowledge of all of the factors inherent in a good program for young children. Nor can one person assume the duties of physician, dentist, educational specialist, commu-nity organizer, lawyer, and administrator. However, when many people—parents, teachers, aides, volunteers from the community—work together, they can provide for all of the needs of the child.

No curriculum is valid that has not considered what the community and parents want. The experiences the child has in the family and community are important in his life, and should be acknowledged and related to his educational experiences in the preschool. Curriculum content and methods can include those things the parents and community believe important. The values, standards, and goals of the community should be respected and valued in the center.

# WORKING WITH PARENTS _____

*... home and school, parents and teachers, must work together at the continual task of the education of the child. ...*
(Caldwell, 1978, p.1)

*Parent involvement builds continuity.*

The close relationship between parent and child is not discontinued just because a child attends a preschool. The young child and her parents are completely dependent upon one another. The child needs her parents and the parents, to be parents at all, need the child (DesLauriers & Carolson, 1969).

Teachers of young children have always involved parents in the education of children. Throughout the years, early childhood educators have recognized and respected the close physical, emotional, and intellectual relationship between the child and her parents. Today early childhood teachers continue to work with parents. Today's teachers view parent involvement as critical to the success of any preschool program. When parents are involved, children as well as parents and teachers benefit.

## PROVIDING CONTINUITY
Parent involvement helps build a continuity between home and school. When parents and teachers work together, children experience a feeling of continuity. Parents know what is going on in the preschool and can reinforce the teacher's work at home. When parents are involved, teachers understand what goes on at home and can support and reinforce the parents' efforts at school. Parents and teachers are not at odds with one another. They can share their goals, hopes, and dreams and work together to obtain them. As a result, children feel secure, knowing that the important adults in their lives are together.

The need to build this feeling of continuity between home and school did not always exist. Long ago when the teacher was hired by the community, went to the same church as the parents, and usually lived with one of the families, children knew that parents and the teacher were together. If the teacher did not perform or reinforce the values of the home at school, she was fired. "The community not only hired her, but decided what she should teach and even supervised her personal conduct . . . the home and the school were in close communication" (Gordon & Breivogel, 1976, p. 1).

However, today the child's school, home, and teacher may be physically separated by many miles. Teachers usually do not live in the same community as the school in which they teach, and the children may not even live in the area. Busing, while providing for racial balance, further separates home and school. Thus, special attempts must be made by both teachers and parents to build a bridge between home and school.

This bridge serves to provide a continuity for the child and helps preserve his cultural heritage. When you, as a teacher, and parents do work together, you learn to respect each other's background. You will learn to recognize and value the variety of cultural backgrounds the children bring to the school. As you reflect on the children's cultural differences, you can plan ways to use this knowledge to design curriculum and to increase the children's pride in their heritage as well as in the heritage of their classmates. Parents might even take part in designing the curriculum, suggesting ideas for activities or even conducting learning experiences for the children.

Parents could share a holiday observance with the group or teach children a song in their native language. They might read a story or tell about their life as a child. Such activities strengthen the continuity between home and school, and let children know their cultural background and heritage are respected.

## INCREASING ACHIEVEMENT

When parents are involved in the school, and continuity between home and school is present, academic achievement is fostered. It may be that parents know how to continue the learning-teaching process in their own home when they are involved in school, or it may be that children feel confident to learn when continuity is present. Whatever the reason, involved parents and increased academic achievement seem to go hand in hand. Not only does academic achievement increase when parents are involved, but children's self-esteem, motivation to learn, and their language skills also grow (*A Review of Head Start Research since 1969*, 1977).

## SUPPORTING PARENTS

Parenting has always been a difficult job under any conditions, but today's parents seem faced with a lot more pressures than those of the past. Today economic conditions in our nation often require both parents to work outside of the home. An estimated 54 percent of all mothers of children under the age of five work outside of the home (Keniston, 1977). Although research shows that mothers working outside of the home does not harm their children, it also shows that women who go off to work each day are likely to worry about their children (Keniston, 1977, p. 5).

Even when both parents do not work outside of the home, today's parents seem worried about their children. "American parents today are worried and uncertain about how to bring up their children" (Keniston, 1977, p. 3). Living far from relatives and family, most parents are on their own.

Many young children are being reared in single-parent families. Even though research shows that single parents are just as good as two parents, living alone with children to care for does increase a single parent's stress and worry. Four out of ten young children live in single-parent families, which means a lot of parents are in need of support.

Preschools can offer this support, taking some of the pressure and worry of child rearing off the parents. While teaching, you can relieve parents of some of the day-to-day care of young children and help them see the good job they are doing in child rearing. Commenting on the child's progress and her specific strengths, you can give parents feelings of satisfaction with themselves and their children. Parents who have participated in Head Start programs feel a sense of well-being and satisfaction with their job as parents (*A Review of Head Start Research since 1969, 1977*).

Involvement in a preschool program also increases the parents' skills and knowledge of child rearing. Positive interactions between mothers and children seem to increase when parents are involved. All in all, involved parents seem to be more effective parents (*A Review of Head Start Research since 1969, 1977*).

## PARENT INVOLVEMENT IN HEAD START _____

The Head Start program, recognizing that parent involvement is so beneficial for parent, child, and teacher, has mandated several different levels of parent involvement. In Head Start programs, parents are involved in the following ways:

1. They actively participate in the decision-making process. The Policy Council, which consists of over fifty percent parents, makes decisions pertaining to the operation and nature of the total Head Start program.

2. They also participate in the classroom as time allows them, either as employees, volunteers, or observers. They are invited to the preschool to eat lunch with the children, to attend special parties, or to visit at any time.

3. They plan and conduct activities such as family picnics, field trips, and workshops on homemaking, budgeting, legal problems, and child-rearing practices.

4. They work with teachers in developing teaching games and activities for use at home and at school. Teachers also visit the homes of the children, often bringing books, toys, or games the children enjoy.

# ⎯⎯⎯⎯⎯⎯⎯⎯ PARENT INVOLVEMENT IN OTHER PROGRAMS

Not all preschool programs are mandated to involve parents in the way the Head Start program does. All programs, however, can follow the example of Head Start. You could begin by establishing commitment and trust and by communicating with parents informally. All teachers, in any preschool program, should arrange to keep parents informed about the things their child does during the day and about the total program. This, however, is only a beginning. Parents can and should be involved in the activities of the classroom, at home, in group meetings, and as decision makers.

## COMMITMENT AND TRUST

"Young children's dependency on their parents is not qualified, and their vulnerability contributes to their loyalty. Care givers and teachers who pride themselves on providing care which is better than the parents can give or who gain secret pleasure when children do not want to go home exhibit a frightening lack of understanding of young children's needs" (Warren, 1977, p. 11).

While loving, nurturing, and supporting each child, you must never supplant the child's parents. Perhaps parent involvement begins with this basic understanding. Children will sense any attempt to supplant their parents and will be confused and insecure if this occurs.

You must be committed to preserving the close bond that exists between parent and child as well as to establishing open communication and trust between home and school. Communication and trust take time to develop. Sometimes this can be a slow process. Sometimes you will feel discouraged; yet if you are committed to providing the best for young children, you will work, perhaps trying a number of different ways, to establish communication and trust with the parents of all children.

## COMMUNICATING

Parents are busy; merely finding time to complete all of the life support chores for children is a true challenge. Night meetings, classroom observation, or regular conferences between parent and teacher are often not possible. Furthermore, when parents work and are away from their children for most of the day, they should not be expected to attend numerous night meetings or conferences which would take them away from their children still more.

If you are totally committed to establishing communication with parents, you can utilize many daily happenings within the preschool to achieve this goal. For instance, the few moments in the morning when the parents bring the child to school can be used to encourage communication. You should arrive some time before the parents in order to complete any preparations you must make for the day. If you have finished mixing paints, cutting paper, or putting clay on the tables, you will be better able to meet parents in a relaxed manner, giving them your undivided attention.

Parents and children arriving at a preschool in the morning should receive as warm a welcome as possible from the staff. You may wish to inquire how the evening went: "Did the child sleep well?" "Did his cold develop?" "Did she tell you about the squirrel we saw?" Perhaps you may wish to tell the parent of some of the plans for the day: "We're going to bake bread today—we'll save some for you," or "The dentist is coming today to talk to the children." This information can be communicated quickly and informally at this time.

Parents also need to inform teachers of the child's welfare on any particular morning. "Jim was happy to come today; he wants to finish building the fort," or "Angelo was cranky this morning; you might want to watch him closely."

Evenings are another rushed time in a preschool. Parents have dinners to cook or shopping to do, and everyone is exhausted from a day's work. Mothers at Mary Elizabeth Keister's do take time, however, to receive a final report of the day as they pick up their children. The nursery attendant tells the parents about the child's day, his eating and sleeping schedule, the new toy he reacted to. Time is taken to share some complimentary anecdote about the child's day with the parents.

Just as you should be ready to give the parents your undivided attention in the mornings, you should also be prepared to do so in the evenings. The children can be prepared for going home before the parents arrive. Faces and hands are washed, sometimes clean clothes are put on, or in the case of infants, bed clothing is put on. Important items, the children's art work, their paintings, or treasures should all be in order to give to the parents.

*Use the curriculum to communicate.*

## COMMUNICATION VIA CURRICULUM
Activities that are part of the curriculum can often serve to inform a parent of the experiences her child is having at the center. Using the language experience approach with preschoolers insures increased communication between parents and staff. The pictures the children paint, their drawings, or collages all tell a story.

## Language Experiences

Occasionally ask the child to tell you about the story of a painting he has done and write this story on the picture, or on a note attached to it. For the two year olds, or three year olds, who are still exploring the media and usually have no story to tell about their work, you may write a brief note on the back of the painting to tell the parent what the child was singing while he was painting, or the colors the child named, or some other descriptive item.

When working in groups, children often compile booklets. These booklets are generally dictated to you, either by one child or by a group of children. Write the story as the children tell it, and let the children illustrate the story. Some booklets may be completed entirely by you; others are compiled by you and the children together. Examples of booklets that would inform the parents of the activities of the preschool are:

1. *Cookbooks*   Favorite recipes are compiled, duplicated and put in a booklet to send home with the children. The recipes could be those from the preschool's kitchen or those that the children have used themselves in classroom cooking experiences.
2. *Address Books*   The names and addresses of all of the children and staff, and any one else involved in the preschool, are compiled into a very practical address and telephone number book.
3. *Field Trip Books*   After field trips, children dictate the events of the trip, the things they saw, the parts they liked best.

Other individual booklets may be written around such topics as "I Was Frightened When," "My Family," "I Am Angry When," "Things I Do Not Like," or "We Have Fun at Preschool."

You should have working cassette tape recorders and a good supply of tapes ready at all times. You will want to record the first vocalizations of the child, the new song he has learned, his conversation with a friend, or the new word he now uses so that these important occasions can be shared with the parents. Tapes are also valuable for use by the preschoolers. Children may be taught how to use the cassettes by themselves in order to tell their parents, on tape, of some exciting discoveries or important events, catching the excitement of the moment. The tape and recorder can then be sent home with the child for the parents to enjoy later in the evening.

## Photographs

Each preschool should have a good supply of various types of cameras, film, batteries, and flash bulbs. You must be fully trained in the use of each camera, and feel comfortable using cameras. The baby's struggling to roll over for the first time, the first steps of the child, his attempts at the climbing bars are all memorable events and should be recorded on film. Polaroid shots are of immediate reinforcement to the young child, and are of lasting value to his parents.

Snapshots of the children can be used to decorate the school's bulletin boards, or given to parents as gifts. Snaps taken of the children on a field trip, at mealtime, during naps, or at play communicate the activities of the school in a very personal way. When these snaps are mounted on heavy cardboard and made available to the children, they are appreciated and talked over at length.

Slides taken of the events of the day are useful to show at parents' meetings or at community organization meetings. Slides can serve to illustrate the preschool's program, goals, and objectives. Eight-millimeter movies are also valuable for soliciting community support and communicating with parents.

## Attitudes

You must continually demonstrate to the child your respect for her parents. Throughout the day make such comments as "Let's save this for your mother," "I think I'll write that down in a letter to your daddy," and "Won't your parents be proud to hear that you did that?" Such comments serve to reinforce the child's sense of self-worth, dignity, and esteem, demonstrating to her that she's important to staff and parents alike. Guard against making any comment to the child that could be interpreted as a threat or bribe. Comments such as "If you don't go to sleep, I'll tell your mother" have no place in a school that respects and trusts both children and parents.

Attitudes are also shared through activities. Pride in their parents can be instilled in the children through many activities. Stories describing mothers and fathers at work and stories of families can be read to the children. Small-group field trips may be taken to observe mother and father at work if the school is conveniently close.

Props used by the parents at work such as typewriters, pencils, paper, tool chests, pipes, or lunchboxes can be brought to school by the staff to help the child act out her parents' work. This enables her to better understand her parents, their jobs, and her feelings toward them.

## COMMUNICATING IN OTHER WAYS

Communicating through the curriculum is only one means of establishing communication and trust with parents. If you are really sincere about developing a strong parent involvement program, extend communication to the use of the following:

## Bulletin Boards

Place bulletin boards where parents can read them as they bring or pick up their children. Notices of policies and procedures can be posted on the board, children's artwork displayed, or special notes to parents tacked to the board. Many commercial companies offer free materials in the form of handouts that deal with nutrition, child rearing, and health. These can be posted and made available to parents. The school's handbook of policies or newsletter could also be posted on the bulletin board, or a supply of handbooks and newsletters could be placed on a table near the board so these are readily available to parents.

## Newsletters

Parents are often interested in receiving copies of the weekly menu with favorite recipes attached. They need to be informed of upcoming field trips, new activities, or pieces of equipment. A weekly schedule of tentative events can supply such information to parents and provide a focus for conversation between parent and child. When the parent, receiving weekly plans, has some idea of what his two-year-old child is attempting to explain, he can then converse intelligently with the child, providing the words the child needs, or relating some experience of his own to enhance the conversation.

Bi-weekly or monthly newsletters from school are useful communicators of information. Articles dealing with child-rearing practices, building toys, or working with children at home can be included in the letter. News items pertaining to the children, staff, and parents will be of interest to everyone. Curriculum plans can be shared and national news on preschool legislation, licensing, innovative preschool programs, or research may also be disseminated through the newsletters.

## Reporting

Reporting in a preschool must be a two-way process in which parents report to the school and the school reports to the parents. Clearly, when infants and very young children are involved, reporting and keeping accurate records are of critical importance. Health records must be accurately maintained by both parents and school. Records of eating, sleeping, or physical growth and development are not only of lasting interest to the child and his family, but are also important pieces of information for you and parents.

## Cumulative Folders

You should keep a cumulative folder on each child as a positive record of her growth and development. Health records, growth charts, as well as anecdotal records can be placed in the cumulative folder. Record items of importance about the child's development in the cumulative folder. For instance, samples of the child's artwork, clearly dated, should be placed periodically in the folder. Records of his motor development and social-development can be recorded. The date the baby saw herself in the mirror for the first time, or stood by herself, or caught a ball are all important milestones. When entered as part of a cumulative record, the child's rate of growth and her present level of competence can be assessed.

Observational records, in the form of anecdotes, have been used by nursery teachers for many years to record children's behavior and progress. Cohen's *Observing and Recording the Behavior of Young Children,* Almy's *Ways* of *Studying Children,* and Lindberg and Swedlow's *Early Childhood Education: A Guide for Observation and Participation* are valuable textbooks describing the process of keeping anecdotal, observational records.

You and your attendants should have pencil and paper handy at all times. You can then quickly and unobtrusively record descriptions of children's behavior, taking samples from many varied routines and activities. These observational records should be strictly objective. When they are kept over a period of time, they serve to clarify the behavior of the child and give an accurate picture of his growth and development.

## Telephone Calls

You can maintain more frequent contacts with parents through telephone calls. Parents will appreciate hearing from you by phone, especially when you have positive comments to make. The ease and quickness of phoning helps maintain the communication process.

## Conferences

Periodically arrange formal conferences with parents in order to discuss the progress, growth, development, or problems of the child. During these conferences the records of the child can be reviewed. Developmental levels can be discussed and plans for the next year formulated. Although you will encourage the parents to talk, you should assume a leadership role. Be ready to share with the parents the child's cumulative record folder, samples of his works of art in chronological order, the results of any standardized or informal tests, and anecdotal records. A summary statement about the child's growth and development, based on the data, might be prepared for the parents.

During a conference, be as concrete and specific as possible, documenting your evaluations of the child with samples of his artwork, anecdotal records, or photographs of the child. Comparisons with other children or families should be avoided. If problems are present, they should be honestly approached by enlisting the parent's cooperation in their solution. "How do you think we could help . . ." and after listening to the parent's suggestions suggest concrete possibilities for solutions. "We might try to do this and see what happens." Disagreements may arise; however, you can tactfully avoid allowing disagreements to become arguments.

Concluding the conference might be a discussion of plans for the coming year, either in the preschool or in the grade school the child will be attending the next year. Planning for the future ends the conference on a positive note of looking forward to a continued, cooperative relationship between parent and preschool.

## Group Meetings

When children spend their days away from home, it is important for them to spend their evenings at home with their families. Preschools do not need to rely totally on group meetings as their only means of communicating with parents; however, total group meetings are of value for sharing information, clarifying the goals of the preschool, or introducing new procedures.

Most successful group meetings are dinner affairs, or family picnics and parties. Showing movies or slides taken at the school, having holiday parties and summer swimming picnics are popular with children and adults alike. Topics of interest to the total community may be selected by the parents for presentation at large-group meetings. Parents must be fully involved in selecting a topic for the meeting, completing the meeting arrangements, and implementing these plans.

## PARENTS IN THE CLASSROOM

"Juan's mother came to school today and we made tacos!" Involving parents in the classroom is another form of parent involvement. With an extra pair of hands, it is easy to make tacos, take a trip, or plan a special art project; yet involving parents in the classroom offers many more advantages than simply another pair of hands to help out.

When parents work in a classroom, either as paid aides or as volunteers, everyone benefits. First, the children benefit because they get extra attention and perhaps individualized help because there is another adult in the classroom. Children who need help in learning to relate with others, to keep themselves in control, or to develop other skills, find another adult in the classroom beneficial—someone who has time to spend helping them without being distracted by the needs of other children.

When other adults are present, children develop better interpersonal skills. They must now learn the name of someone else, find out what he is like, and discover how best to communicate with that person. All of this leads to developing the ability to understand and relate with others.

Another adult's participation with the class provides the opportunity for the children to learn about the culture and values of other people. Making tacos with Juan's mother might be perceived of as a fun activity, but it could also lead to an understanding of the culture of others. When parents of differing backgrounds work in the school, children learn that all people have the same needs, desires, and dreams, yet they do things differently.

You, as the teacher, will benefit from working with parents in a classroom. You will be better able to establish communication because the parents actually see what is happening. Rather than attempting to explain the rationale behind the program or activity, use events in the classroom to point out the goals of the program or how children learn. The ways things are done at school are clarified as they actually take place.

When parents work in the classroom, their feedback is direct and honest. "Why did you let Susan paint after you called for cleanup? I always taught her to obey." Or, "George doesn't like it when you talk so loud; he's afraid of you and can't hear what you're saying." You can really begin to understand what parents want for their children and develop a better understanding of the parents' values, which is basic to establishing and maintaining communication.

Parents also benefit when they are able to work in a classroom. They can develop a better understanding of their own child. They see their child interacting with peers and other adults, and see strengths not always apparent when the child is at home. As they work with you and the children, they gain new skills in child rearing. They learn new ways to interact with children and teach children.

Parents increase in confidence as they develop skills and understandings. Their self-esteem is fostered; and because of the knowledge they have gained, they feel more in control of themselves and their children. With their sense of power increased, parents can be free to assume the role of partner in the continual task of the education of the child.

## Initiating Parent Involvement

"I wish they'd just let me shut my door and be by myself," said one new teacher in a preschool program that heavily involved parents in the classroom. Working with others is not always an easy job. But with planning and thinking ahead, the task of involving parents in the daily activities of the school becomes less difficult.

First, prepare yourself. Perhaps you could take some time to observe in a classroom where parents are already involved. You could talk with teachers who have worked with parents and ask them for pointers. You could enroll in an in-service training program designed to prepare teachers to work with parents.

You will also want to prepare yourself by finding out about the parents with whom you will be working. If you have knowledge of the cultures of the parents, the things they value, and the way they do things at home, you will have some idea about how to communicate with them.

You might also want to think about being in charge of another adult. It is often uncomfortable to think about giving directions to someone who is older than you or who is from a different culture. Thinking of ways to guide adults, without sounding like a boss, may be useful. "Would you help me with . . . ?" "Terry needs help with. . . . Would you work with him . . . ?" Let the parent know what to do without sounding like a dictator. At other times, however, it is wise simply to state directly and matter of factly what is expected of the parent. "Today I want you to. . . ."

When parents know exactly what they are to do, the need for giving directions is minimized. You might think ahead of the things parents could do. Parents can work at several levels in the classroom. They could:

1. Create learning materials for use in the classroom or at home.
2. Work as a teacher of a child or of the group, telling a story or teaching a game or a song.
3. Supervise on the play yard, at lunch, or during naps.
4. Help out with paperwork, filing, and record keeping.
5. Maintain classroom supplies, repair library books, and keep cupboards in order.

Whatever job the parents are asked to do, it must be meaningful. Busy work destroys the value of parent involvement. "Nothing will turn parents off quicker than if what they are asked to do is Mickey Mouse or if they are uninterested in what they are doing" (Morrison, 1978, p. 141).

Preparation of the parents is also required. Parents must know what they can and cannot do, and should have the opportunity to become acquainted with the school, its policies, and the way things are done at school. This type of information can be relayed through an orientation session, training programs, or printed materials. Many programs use a combination of techniques, involving parents in group meetings, preparing printed materials describing the school and how to work with children, and giving parents time to observe in the classroom before working with children.

Parents also need to understand the ethics of working with children. Although you will serve as a model, make it clear that adults who work with children will not gossip about the children to others, or compare children with one another. What happens in school is confidential and is not to be told to a neighbor, clerk, or letter carrier.

# HOME VISITS

"...the whole adult population is friendly, and the nursery holds them by strong ties through the love both places have in common for their children" (McMillan, 1919, p. 177). Home visits are not new to early childhood. Since the time of Margaret McMillan, and even before that time, teachers of young children have visited in homes as a means of involving parents in the educational process of the child.

Teachers who work in nursery schools, day care centers, kindergartens, and other center-based programs, usually conduct several home visits a year. In Head Start, home visits are a required task of all teachers, and at least four visits to the home of each child are suggested.

McMillan believed these visits opened "doors of new truth" (1919, p. 177). In a way, home visits do open doors, for so much can be learned about a child and his family by visiting in the home. When you visit in the home, a new relationship develops between you and the parents.

The dynamics of the relationship changes. Instead of being perceived as a power figure, you are a guest. As a guest in a home, you are in a low power position. You must wait for the parents to invite you in, offer you a seat, and encourage you to stay. You are the one in unfamiliar surroundings, and the parent gains in power. Under these conditions parents may feel more comfortable and better able to communicate with you, sharing ideas, feelings, or asking questions. All in all, home visits can help parents be more responsive to you and your ideas, and better able to talk about problems or worries.

Home visits are also important for children. They feel it is wonderful that you care so much about them that you visit in their homes.

Recognizing the values of home visits, a number of early childhood programs are based entirely in the home. In these programs, which include the models of Gordon's Home Visitor Approach, Levenstein Verbal Interaction Project, and Home Start, the teacher visits in the home and works with the child and his parents. Based on the idea that parents are the most influential educators of their own children, the visits are designed to bring educational experiences to children and at the same time increase the parents' effectiveness. Focusing on the parent increases the educational opportunities for the child in the program, for the siblings in the home, and for those children yet to come.

*A home visit by the teacher can be a rewarding event for everyone.*

## Conducting a Home Visit

"The home visitor's prime responsibility is to build the relationship between a home and a classroom. She is a liaison person sharing information in both directions (Gordon & Breivogel, 1976, p. 22). There is no one right or wrong way to go about conducting a home visit, but the goal of the visit always includes building a bridge between home and school for the benefit of the child.

Usually the first home visits are get-acquainted visits. Calling ahead to arrange the visit, plan to use the first visit to establish rapport with the parents. At times the visit will not even take place in the home but under the trees in the back yard, on the porch, or on the porch steps. If you bring a toy, book, game to play, or something for the parents, you will help ease shyness on your part and that of the parent. This will give you something to focus attention on and to talk about, thereby helping both you and the parent to get over feelings of shyness.

Once rapport has been established, you can work to develop goals for the children. When working in a home-based program, the establishment of goals becomes a critical part of home visiting. Once goals are established, you can then plan ways to fulfill them. Home Start suggests that the goals could be obtained in any number of ways, including the following:

1. Help with a household chore, demonstrating how this activity could be used as a learning experience for children.
2. Introduce a game or activity for you, the child, and the parent to play together.
3. Support the parents by listening and chatting with them as they discuss their concerns.
4. Make a toy, game, or household item, involving the children in the task.
5. Play a game, read a story, or spend time with the child, with the parent observing.

Evaluating the progress you and the child have made and planning for the next visit can also take place. Some visits might be made to conduct conferences with the parent about the child's progress in school or in the program. During others you might share information with the parent, bringing him literature on the local library or how to receive services available in the community, as well as other information about children's growth and learning.

While visiting in the children's home, you must be continually aware of the ethics of the teacher-parent relationship. Information you receive while in the child's home is confidential, to be used only by you and the school's staff to improve the quality of life for the child.

## PARENTS OF CHILDREN WITH SPECIAL NEEDS
"While there is an interest in parent education in general, there is a great deal of emphasis in particular on the education of parents of handicapped children" (Morrison, 1978, p. 175). Children with special needs are found in today's preschools. Public Law 94-142, providing for a free and appropriate education for all persons between the ages of three and twenty-one, also affords protection to the parents of children with special needs. Under the law, parents of children with special needs have the right to:

1. Give consent to the evaluation of their child.
2. Examine all records kept on the child.
3. Be given notice, in their language, of any meeting that will take place concerning their child.
4. Participate in the development of their child's individualized educational program.
5. Participate in meetings about the child, which are to be held at a time and place agreeable to the parents and in the parents' native language.

Even if the law did not protect parents' rights to become fully involved in the educational program of their children, you would still want to establish positive working relationships with all parents. There are, however, some things you should understand when working with children who have special needs.

Parents of handicapped children may have a long history of working with professionals. These professionals, perhaps because of a heavy workload or an inability to communicate in plain language, may have made parents wary of all professionals. With this history, it is hard for parents to trust teachers who say, "We want to work with you in the education of your child." Sometimes you will have to be a little more persistent in establishing effective relationships, trying any number of techniques to establish communication and trust.

Some awareness, and if possible, an understanding of what it means to have a handicapped child must also be developed. Love (1970) describes a series of emotional stages parents go through when they find out that their child has a handicap. First there is a stage of grief, then denial of the abnormality, followed by feelings of hostility, hopelessness, and many times despair. Some parents have been known to withdraw completely from any association with family, friends, or neighbors.

Many times parents will feel inadequate. They may even feel it is their fault for having a child with a handicap. With all of the emphasis that is placed on the relationship between the diet of the mother, pollution, smoking, and the health of the infant, it is easy to see how a parent could feel responsible for having an impaired child.

The preschool program can help the parent of a child with a handicap to cope. This is not a simple task, but an awareness of the parent's needs and their attitudes can help you. All of the methods of establishing communication between home and school can be used. In addition, parent group meetings have been found to be especially useful in helping parents to cope.

When parents meet together in a group, they can share their common feelings, fears, and hopes and gain the support of others. Just recognizing that they are not alone is helpful; valuable advice, tips on how to work with a handicapped child, and practical know-how is also shared and is very useful. In a group with parents who also have had a child with special needs, some of the feelings of hostility, fear, or distrust are dissipated.

# INVOLVING PARENTS IN DECISION MAKING _____

True, successful parent participation comes only as parents are involved in the decision-making processes concerning the goals, objectives, policies, and procedures of the school. In this way, parents become totally committed to the goals of the school, and cooperation and open communication result.

All schools receiving federal funds, some receiving foundation grants, and cooperative preschool programs all require parents to be actively involved in making decisions. Church-oriented, industrial, or private centers should also strive to involve parents in decision-making roles.

Valid decisions must be based on information, knowledge, and understanding. It follows that the staff should continually work to strengthen the communication process. Parents, who do have the right to make decisions about the welfare of their children, should be aware of all aspects of the program.

## ESTABLISHING A POLICY BOARD

Whether a program is administered by a board of directors, a social service agency, or an individual, it will seek legal advice on incorporation. Incorporation requires the designation of a board of directors to establish policies and procedures under which the program will operate. Usually any policy-making board will be comprised of at least 50 percent parents.

## DECISIONS PARENTS MAKE

Among the many decisions the policy board will be asked to make are:

1. Do we need a preschool program in the community? Whom should the school serve? What ages should the children be? How many children should the school enroll?
2. Where should the school be located? What facility can meet the program goals and objectives?
3. What should be the goals and objectives of the program? What philosophy of child development should be implemented? How should services be evaluated and what types should the program offer? How long should the school be open?
4. What staffing patterns should be followed? Who should direct the school? What qualifications should be established for aides, teachers, volunteers, directors, and other personnel?
5. What personnel procedures should be established? What should comprise job descriptions? Salary levels? Working hours? Benefits and career ladders?
6. How should the school meet licensing requirements? What standards should be maintained?

Parents directly involved in establishing the policies of a preschool center from its inception continue to shape and formulate the program as it develops. Running a preschool is an ongoing process; thus, the role of the policy board is ever-changing. Established programs consistently seek new policies and procedures in order to broaden their services, perhaps to reach more children or to extend the types of services to the children and families already being served.

Specific ongoing committees on such aspects of the program as funding, research and evaluation, or service or program development may be necessary. These committees become more effective as they expand to include representation from parents and other community agencies.

SELECTING POLICY BOARD MEMBERS Selecting from among themselves, parents with children currently enrolled in the program may elect a specific number of representatives to the policy board. Some provision for rotation of membership may be made, and the board, itself, may establish the length of term for each representative.

In order to assure direct community involvement and participation in the preschool, the remaining members of the policy board may be chosen from the community at large. Increased support and awareness of the preschool's goals and objectives are obtained when board members represent major community, civic, professional, or service organizations. Others who have demonstrated a concern for the children of the community may be selected.

Although staff members should not serve on policy boards as voting members, they should participate in board meetings as observers, advisors, and consultants. They have important information to share and contribute as the board weighs decisions. Personnel of the school should be invited to attend all meetings of the board and allowed to participate in all discussions, establishing, expanding, and protecting communication between center, child, and parent.

# IT'S UP TO YOU

In 1919 Margaret McMillan told her teachers, "Our task is new. It has never before been attempted" (p. 174). Today working with parents is not new. The benefits of involving parents in the education of preschool children have been demonstrated over and over; yet today's teachers are still faced with challenges. "Teachers face new problems as they move toward new relationships" (Gordon & Breivogel, 1976, p. 14). Developing relationships has never been easy in the past or now. Humans are complex and their interactions are complex.

Working to develop skills of relating with parents is worth it. If you want to become a teacher of young children, you must also learn to work with parents. You might begin by developing your own confidence. Start by deciding what area you are most confident in. If it is talking with parents informally, holding a group meeting, or visiting in a home, begin with that area. Build on your own skills; as you gain confidence in relating with parents, try things that are new to you.

It is not always necessary to develop skills of involving parents by yourself. Ask other teachers to help you or ask for training from the school staff. Perhaps the principal or director of the school will work with you and assume some of the responsibilities for working with parents.

There is no best way to reach and work with parents (*Persistence of Preschool Effects,* 1978). To date one approach seems to be as effective as another; the important thing is that parents are involved. As you develop your techniques and program, think about what would be best for each specific child and her family, and what you are most comfortable with, and use these ideas as your guide.

## REFERENCES

Caldwell, B. M. "Some Precautions in Establishing Infant Day Care." In *Perspectives on Infant Day Care,* edited by Richard Elardo and Betty Pagan. Orangesburg, S.C.: Southern Association for Children under Six, 1972.

————. *Working Together: A Guide to Parent Involvement* by A. J. Coletta. Atlanta: Humanics Limited. 1978.

DesLauriers, A. M., and Carolson, C. *Your Child Is Asleep: Early Infantile Autism.* Homewood, Ill.: Dorsey Press, 1969.

Gordon, I. J., and Breivogel, W. F. *Building Effective Home-School Relationships.* Boston: Allyn and Bacon, 1976.

Keniston, K. *All Our Children: The American Family under Pressure.* New York: Harcourt Brace Jovanovich, 1977.

Love, K. D. *Parental Attitudes toward Exceptional Children.* Springfield, Ill.: Charles C. Thomas Publishers. 1970.

McMillan, M. *The Nursery School.* New York: J. M. Dent & Sons, 1919.

Morrison, G. S. *Parent Involvement in the Home, School and Community.* Columbus, Oh.: Charles E. Merrill Publishing Co., 1978.

*The Persistence of Preschool Effects.* Washington, D.C.: U.S. Department of Health, Education, and Welfare, 1977.

*A Review of Head Start Research since 1969.* Washington, D.C.: U.S. Department of Health, Education, and Welfare, 1977.

Warren, R. M. *Caring: Supporting Children's Growth.* Washington, D.C.: National Association for the Education of Young Children, 1977.

## RESOURCES

Coletta, A. *Working Together: A Guide to Parent Involvement.* Atlanta: 1977.

Honig, A. *Parent Involvement in Early Childhood Education.* Washington, D.C.: National Association for the Education of Young Children, 1975.

Hymes, J. *Effective Home-School Relations.* Sierra Madre, Calif.: Southern California Association for the Education of Young Children, 1974.

Wilson, G. *Parents and Teachers.* Atlanta: Humanics Limited, 1974.

## PROJECTS

1. Visit a Head Start program. Ask the teachers what techniques they use to establish trust and communication. What evidences of parent involvement do you observe? What types of activities are planned for parents?

2. Interview parents of preschool children. Find out what kinds of activities they expect the preschool program to plan for their children. Try to interview parents who both work outside of the home as well as single parents. Ask these parents how the preschool can be more responsive to their needs.

3. Identify a home-based preschool program in your area, or ask a teacher in a preschool program to let you accompany her on a home visit. Observe how the parents put the teacher at ease, what the teacher does to put the parents at ease, and how the visit is conducted.

4. Attend a group meeting of parents, a parent-teacher conference, or a decision-making meeting. Describe the type of parent-teacher communication you observed. Which of these activities do you think helps to establish effective teacher-parent communication?

# INVOLVING THE COMMUNITY _____

*What the best and wisest parent wants for his own child, that must the community want for all of its children. . . .*
*(Dewey, 1900, p. 19)*

3

Preschool programs, working as integral parts of the community, help to insure the future of society, which depends on the physical, mental, emotional, and social development of its children. Members of a community hold the interest of its children in common and consciously communicate this interest among themselves and with others in the larger community.

Communities have long participated in providing care for children. The WPA of the 1930s established preschools designed to meet the specific needs of the community by providing employment for teachers. At the same time, the centers furnished educational care for young children of unemployed or underprivileged families. During World War II over three thousand preschools were organized for children of working mothers. Industry also set up preschools in great numbers for their female employees.

Today early childhood education is meeting the needs of the total community by providing early educational experiences for children under the age of six. Programs, such as Home Start, Head Start, and Parent Child Centers, are efforts of the community to effect change in the economic, social, and educational life of child and family. Early childhood programs also provide for the needs of the community by caring for children of working parents or those in single-parent families. These programs provide for the needs of all children, giving experiences that foster social, emotional, physical, and intellectual growth.

Today's preschool programs, which have on the one hand been given part of the responsibility to meet the needs of the community, must, on the other hand, commit themselves to totally involving the community in their programs, holding the community ultimately responsible for its children. The preschool "program has a responsibility of serving as a bridge to the larger community in which the child lives. There must be deliberate planning which draws into the program persons from the community, both children and adults, who offer special interests, skills, or knowledge to the children and their families"(*Day Care: A Statement of Principles,* 1971, p. 10).

## PLANNING FOR INVOLVEMENT

The establishment of a preschool program is an attainable goal for a community group or organization to set for itself. Many communities have united around the common concern for children, and have succeeded in either establishing adequate preschool and day care facilities or in becoming involved in established programs.

Involving the community in preschool programs requires specific, careful planning and programming along with a commitment on the part of the preschool staff and parents that community involvement is critical to the success of the program. Plans should be made to:

1. Acquaint yourself with the community. As a teacher, you must either become aware of the nature of the community in which the school is located, or you must work in a vacuum.

2. Acquaint the total community with the preschool program—its goals, objectives, methods, and programs.

3. Involve the community in the life of the center. Open the program to volunteers, visitors, parents, and the community at large. Plan many opportunities for all to participate in the program, including the involvement of persons from the community on policy-making boards.

## Acquainting Yourself with the Community

Every neighborhood has its special features. In any given community, there are resources for children and families, as well as cultural factors that are helpful to understand. A knowledge of the community will help you develop an understanding of the children so that you will be able to plan learning experiences.

Learning experiences are only effective when they build on the children's background of experiences. When you know the community, you have insights into the experiences the children bring to school, and have some foundation for planning. You might see if the community has provided spaces for children's play. If spaces are limited, you might plan space and time for large muscle, active play times in the preschool. If children have plenty of play space, the program may not need to use valuable space for large-muscle activities.

Look for resources in the community that might be used to expand services to children and families. Are there libraries, zoos, police and fire departments, and other community services? What church and civic groups are available? Are health, social services, and neighborhood centers in the community? How could these be used by the preschool program or by families? Could any of these places provide the focus for a field trip? Could representatives from these agencies visit the children at school?

Other things you might want to identify as you observe the community that will help you to understand children and their families are (Adair & Eckstein, 1969):

1. What is the predominant income level, language, race, culture of the community?
2. Is it an industrial and/or residential area? What shopping facilities are available?
3. What are the special features of the area? Are there parks, market areas, museums, historic locations, bridges, patterns of transportation?
4. What celebrations will take place in the community? Will there be neighborhood fairs, craft shows, camp meetings?
5. What is the social climate of the community? Do people seem friendly or are there tensions in the community between different groups?

## Acquainting the Community with the Preschool

Once you are acquainted with the community, you can work to acquaint the community with the preschool. If the community has decided to establish the school, it is already acquainted with the program and has a say in running it.

On the other hand, if the community has not been involved in establishing the program, you will want to publicize the school. Publicity is a continual process and performs an important role in involving the total community in a preschool program.

Newspapers are usually eager to obtain articles of human interest that have broad appeal. All children possess a certain quality that arouses sympathy, interest, and concern in adults; thus, editors strive to include articles featuring children as often as possible. The preschool, with its infants, toddlers, and young children, is a perfect source of human interest stories.

A staff member, parent, or volunteer might be selected to be responsible for keeping the press informed about the program. Initial topics of interest to newspapers include 1) the need for the preschool, 2) board meetings when plans are being formulated, 3) the search for facilities, 4) the preparation of play yards and rooms for the children, 5) biographical information about the personnel of the school, and 5) opening day at the preschool.

Training in preparing news items for publication may be available from the newspaper office itself or from a volunteer with reporting skills. Newspapers often assist the school in developing a form for writing up news items for press release. Publicity releases are generally required to include all of the facts relevant to the story and the names of as many people involved in the program as possible. Including the names of the people involved, giving each some identification, helps "sell" the story to the newspaper.

After the school is functioning, newspaper publicity can serve to acquaint the community with current theories and practices in early childhood education. An astute publicity agent can demonstrate, through newspaper articles, the value of many of the routines and programs of the school. Pictures of the children playing in water, with an accompanying explanation of the concepts the children are formulating, is appealing to the public and, at the same time, educational. Candid shots of the children serving lunch to themselves, dressing to go outside, or napping can serve to illustrate other segments of the program.

Many types of publicity other than newspaper items are valuable. TV and radio stations are also interested in items concerning young children. Listing the center's phone number, hours of service, and other information in the Yellow Pages of the phone book, both under "Preschools" and "Day Care" or "Child Care," is a simple way to publicize the school. A small pamphlet, describing the program, staff, and services of the school, can be prepared and distributed to those inquiring about the preschool or to community groups.

A speaker's bureau, available to community groups, churches, PTA's, or any other group wishing to learn more about the preschool, may be established. Teachers, aides, volunteers, and other staff members are given training in talking before groups about the program. Using slides, movies, or snapshots as they talk, the speakers further publicize the preschool and facilitate community involvement.

Perhaps the most effective means of publicizing the preschool program is through personal contact. Each parent, staff, and board member should be adequately informed about the total program in order to describe it positively and accurately to anyone who may be interested.

## Involving the Community in the Preschool

With representatives from the community involved in decision making as they participate as members of policy boards, and the community informed and aware of the school through coverage provided by the media, other types of community involvement in the preschool develop. Provisions can be made by the staff to allow visitors to observe the program in action, arranging schedules to permit them to observe the children at work and play, during meals, or at resting time, without interfering with the daily routine. Children usually welcome the attention of another adult; if visitors to the center are planned for and arrangements are made so as to create minimal distractions, children have no difficulty adjusting to them.

Before outsiders visit the school, the director, publicity chairman, or volunteer in charge will want to describe the program to them, identifying places where quiet should be maintained, rooms where visitors can have contact with the children, or parts of the school where no visitors are permitted for health or safety reasons (perhaps the kitchen or infant nursery). If the visitors have no concept of a child-centered program or little understanding of how children learn, some prior information about the program may be useful or necessary in order for them to benefit from their observations.

# VOLUNTEERS

A professional artist volunteers her time in a preschool one day a week, working with children in the morning and introducing new techniques to the staff in the afternoons. Once a year the artist unobtrusively captures each child as he plays by sketching his portrait in charcoal. A ninety-year-old grandfather comes to another school regularly. He sits in the play yard telling stories to the children about the old days, fixing a bike now and then or catching a ball with the children. A teenage boy stops by the preschool on his way home from school and spends his time with the children at the woodworking bench.

Volunteers bring a bit of the outside world into the preschool while providing an additional pair of hands to hold a child, tie a shoe, tell a story, or blow a nose. Volunteers give each child one more opportunity to establish a personal relationship with another human being. Some volunteers, such as a speech therapist who works with individual children or screens a group of children for hearing problems, will have specific skills and talents to share with the children. Other volunteers bring a willingness to assist in any way possible and give of themselves to the children.

Involving elderly volunteers in a classroom is especially beneficial for teachers, parents, and older persons. For many older people, working with children is useful and enriching in and of itself. Children express love and affection for the elderly. "They're good and wonderful," "They love you," "You can sit on their lap," and "They'll talk to you" are typical of the comments children give when asked how they feel about older people (Jantz et al., 1976).

On the other hand, children also describe older persons as sick, tired, wrinkled, and sad. When older persons are involved in the program, they will help dispel some of the myths children hold toward older people. The stereotyping children do of the elderly may simply be the result of a lack of contact between the young and the old. It is difficult to dispel conventional notions about a group of people when there is no contact with the individuals who make up that group. As children come to know the elderly in a variety of satisfying roles and lifestyles, they do learn to question existing ideas of old people as unhappy, inactive, or sick members of society.

*Elderly volunteers are special.*

When volunteers are obtained from the immediate community, they may help to interpret the customs, traditions, and values of the neighborhood to the preschool staff. At the same time, such volunteers will interpret the goals, objectives, accomplishments, and needs of the preschool to the community.

Volunteers who work directly with young children should, of course, enjoy the company of young children. Parents are excellent volunteers and should be invited to participate whenever possible in the school's daily activities. Although parents may not have much free time, they occasionally may be able to spend an hour, part of an unexpected holiday, or a half day at school.

Volunteers working directly with young children in the preschool can:

1. Be assigned to work with a special child, a shy child, an overly aggressive child, or a child from a single-parent family.

2. Assist in the playroom under your direction.
3. Escort children to or from school, or to some special community event.
4. Accompany you and the children on field trips.
5. Help during medical and dental examinations.
6. Tell or read stories to children.
7. Talk to the children about anything or everything.
8. Sing with the children.
9. Supervise outdoor play.
10. Assist before or after meals, helping children to wash before eating and to get ready for naps.

Other volunteers are also necessary. These may be persons who do not desire to work directly with young children, yet who are very concerned about their welfare. These volunteers can:

1. Explain health and social services to the parents of the children in the preschool.
2. Provide transportation for parents.
3. Baby-sit while parents attend school meetings.
4. Fix plumbing at the school.
5. Take over the yard work, keeping bushes trimmed and grass cut.
6. Paint the school.
7. Build or find equipment.
8. Serve as public relations officers.
9. Organize money-raising events.
10. Assist as kitchen, nursing, or social work aides.
11. Establish a clothing exchange.
12. Set up a library for children, staff, and parents.
13. Conduct English classes, sewing classes, and the like for parent or community groups.
14. Write newsletters.
15. Recruit children for the preschool or parents for policy boards.
16. Take pictures of the children.
17. Volunteer barber or beautician services.

In a large preschool program, volunteers are often recruited by an administrator or staff person in charge of volunteers. Smaller programs may utilize your services and that of other teachers to recruit volunteers. Parent volunteers can be recruited at meetings, or on an individual basis as you visit their homes. You can enlist neighborhood volunteers through both organized publicity and personal contact. Word of mouth is a most effective means of recruitment. As you talk about your work to your church circle, your friends and neighbors, or your beautician, you help draw volunteers from the larger community.

National organizations with local affiliation regularly provide volunteer services. You could contact these organizations. They include the Chamber of Commerce and Jaycees, National Association of Manufacturers, Lions, Kiwanis, Rotary Clubs, National Alliance of Businessmen, League of Women Voters, National Council of Jewish Women, American Association of University Women, Young Women's Christian Association, National Council of Negro Women, Junior League, Boy Scouts, Girl Scouts, Camp Fire Girls, schools, colleges and universities, churches and religious groups, as well as labor unions.

The National School Volunteers Program, Retired Senior Volunteers Program, and other organizations of older persons might be available to work with children in the classroom. The National Retired Teachers Association is another organization of elderly persons especially interested in children.

## SELECTION OF VOLUNTEERS

Once volunteers are recruited, they must be interviewed, screened, and assigned. When the volunteer is to work directly with you in the playroom, it is wise to meet with the volunteer in order to share ideas and philosophies. The two of you must establish communication and understand and respect one another's goals and objectives. A volunteer who indicates during the initial interview that she believes children must be physically punished might serve the preschool in a capacity other than working directly with children. Or a volunteer who indicates that she believes in free play and dislikes routine might be assigned to the group having the most extensive free-play activities.

Health regulations may also be considered in screening volunteers. Certain local health regulations may necessitate physical examinations of volunteers working with children. Physical disabilities of volunteers may require their assignment to play groups where physical exertion is not required.

## TRAINING OF VOLUNTEERS

During the orientation and training period, the role of the volunteer must be clearly defined. Ambiguity results in frustration, apprehension, and worry. A vague assignment, "help out wherever . . . ," leaves the volunteer to direct herself, either overstepping her responsibility or not asserting herself enough. In order to gain the feel of the program, volunteers might benefit from observing in the preschool during orientation, before beginning to work with the children.

A volunteer manual to be distributed during orientation may include the purpose and goals of the center, a listing of the staff and policy board members, the services the center offers, rules and regulations, sample programs, schedules and forms, and job and work schedules and descriptions.

Continual training is a necessity for volunteers. They may be invited to meet occasionally with the staff during regular staff training meetings, or they can reserve some time to meet with you and the director to discuss their continuing role in the classroom. Additional training may be given through workshops, discussion groups, observations of other programs, and movies. Field trip procedures, dos and don'ts of handling behavior problems, safety precautions, and procedures for activities to conduct with the children are topics for discussion.

Much of the training of the volunteers will be your direct responsibility, for you will supervise and direct the volunteer in the playroom. By commenting on the volunteer's strengths and pointing out more efficient and effective ways of working with children, you provide on-the-job training.

During orientation and training it can be made clear to the volunteers that their role is of great importance to the school and the children. It should be stressed that the preschool expects regular attendance from the volunteers, trusting them to give of themselves in a responsible manner.

## THE ROLE OF THE TEACHER
You also will need training, support, and assistance in working with volunteers. The teaching staff may be helped to achieve the skills necessary to work in a supervisory capacity. Delegating authority or giving directions to others with possibly more education is not an easy task. Training can build your confidence as well as provide you with the necessary skills.

You can learn to develop flexibility in working with others, preparing for changes in scheduling, leaving room for the volunteer's ideas. Volunteers may bring with them special projects they wish to try, or they may want to work with the children in different ways. Training in interpersonal relationships, communication, and supervision may be useful.

Volunteers will want to be recognized for the work they do, and their efforts should be reinforced. Write an occasional note of thanks to the volunteers and remember to relay the appreciation of the children. For example, you may say, "John is so happy on the days you work with us," "You really do have a way with Eloise, no one else seems to be able to relate so effectively with her," or "Mr. Smith told me how much Janet likes you."

At the end of the year formal recognition should be given to the volunteers. A certificate can be prepared, or a scrapbook containing the children's artwork and photos can be presented to the volunteers. You might plan a volunteer luncheon, dinner, or evening program to which representatives from the mayor's office, the agencies concerned with children, and parents are invited.

## ———————— INVOLVEMENT WITH COMMUNITY AGENCIES

In order to foster still more complete community involvement, the preschool—staff, parents, board of directors—should become involved with other agencies and organizations within the community. Involvement with other agencies concerned with the welfare of young children is necessary to obtain, coordinate, and facilitate services for children and families to insure a quality life for all.

*Teachers must identify and learn to use the resources of many community services available.*

The preschool is only one institution within a community affecting the lives of children and families. Churches, schools, courts, health and welfare agencies, and recreational programs all influence the quality of children's lives. Early childhood educators committed to involving the total community will relate to all of the existing community services and agencies. By becoming informed about the services these agencies can and will provide for children, and how to obtain these services, the preschool can help to develop ways of cooperating and coordinating efforts between agencies. Referral services can be used by the staff to assist individual families and children in obtaining the services they require.

You alone can work to improve the quality of life for children and families. Teachers should take the responsibility to advocate for children. "Children don't vote, we adults have to vote for them" (Edelman, 1978, p. 19). Children, who cannot speak for themselves, need concerned adults who will speak for them. As one teacher, you can speak for children by:

1. Telling others about your job. Tell your neighbors, friends, relatives, clerks at the store about your job. Tell them how many children benefit from the services of the day care center or preschool. Have at hand facts about the neighborhood, so you can also tell people how many more children are in need of preschool services.

2. Keeping informed on the issues and legislation concerning children. Join an organization concerned with legislation and the welfare of children. The National Association for the Education of Young Children, the Day Care and Child Development Council of America, and the Children's Defense Fund are organizations that alert citizens to current issues and legislation for children.

3. Voting for officials and policies benefiting young children. Use your right to vote to strengthen families and improve the quality of life for children.

4. Writing letters to those persons designing policy for children, or telling them your views of services for young children and the benefits of early educational experiences for children and families.


**ADVOCACY DOES WORK**   When one person decides that he can effect change for children, a lot can happen. Citizens, over the past decade, have done much to improve the quality of life for all children. A group of concerned parents in Pennsylvania banded together to obtain education for thirteen retarded children. Their action led to the decision in Pennsylvania affirming the right of all citizens to a free and appropriate education. Today all handicapped citizens between the ages of three and twenty-one are afforded the right to a free and appropriate education under the 1975 Public Law 94-142. Without the action of the concerned citizens, this right to education for all, including those with handicaps, may not have occurred.

## Licensing and Standards

You, as a teacher and a citizen, can become involved with the licensing and regulation of preschool programs. "There is an urgent need for child care workers to understand the role of regulation. There is an urgent need for licensing personnel to understand the role and problems of early childhood personnel" (Lorber, 1978, p. 14). Often persons in charge of licensing early childhood programs are not familiar with the nature of young children or of effective methods of working with children. You can work with the licensing agency, talking with the representative of the agency, communicating why certain things are important for the growth of young children and the essential components of a quality program for young children.

Minimally, all preschools should follow the Federal Interagency Day Care standards and any other local or state guidelines. The guidelines a preschool adopts for licensing should be available and familiar to each member of the staff as well as to the parents and board of directors. These can be used as resources in planning and developing programs, or as helps in evaluating the progress of a program.

Often, however, the guidelines themselves are minimal. Licensing has been described as the "cop on the beat" in terms of protection for children (Lorber, 1978, p. 14). Licensing standards are essential for the protection of young children and must be raised, as well as supported, by all early childhood educators. In many areas of our country, there are more stringent licensing guidelines for animal kennels than for preschools, so you can understand the need for raising and supporting standards for schools for young children. "I therefore advocate that child care workers and licensing representatives talk together, work together with one common goal: early childhood programs which insure growing, developing, learning children in a safe, secure environment" (Lorber, 1978, p. 14).

## Child Abuse and Neglect

"As citizens and as professionals we all have a role to play in protecting children" (Ferro, 1975, p. 63). Child abuse is not new in our nation, nor does anyone actually know the true extent of the problem. We do know, however, that many young children are subjected to physical, sexual, or emotional abuse or neglect. The Child Abuse Prevention and Treatment Act of 1974 was passed to provide means of preventing child abuse. The act provides for research and demonstration projects, the creation of the National Center on Child Abuse and Neglect, and other activities including the training of teachers and the creation of Parents Anonymous chapters across the country.

Since you will come in contact with young children on a daily basis, you have an obligation to become knowledgeable, sensitive, and aware of the problems of child abuse and neglect. In order to help you understand your role in child abuse, Chapter 5 presents a discussion of the characteristics of children who may have been abused and procedures to follow in reporting suspected cases of child abuse.

Frequently teachers are concerned with individual children; however, the problems of child abuse extend to the total community and all children. The issue of corporal punishment in schools, for instance, is an area in which teachers should become involved (Ferro, 1975, p. 64). The recent Supreme Court ruling suggesting that corporal punishment was acceptable in schools adds urgency to the problem. Even though the Child Abuse Prevention and Treatment Act does not address corporal punishment in schools, you might work to have your preschool, or local school system, rule corporal punishment unacceptable.

Children are also abused and neglected in institutions. Involvement with institutions in the community caring for children is another form of advocacy for children. Through involvement you can help formulate policy and programs for institutions and work to see that institutions "ostensibly created to help children or adults, instead—for whatever reason—do not exploit, abuse, and neglect the very persons they were established to help" (Ferro, 1975, p. 64).

## Children's Defense Fund

The Children's Defense Fund is one group effectively promoting benefits for all children. The CDF, a nongovernment, nonprofit organization of persons, organizations, and agencies is dedicated to advocacy on behalf of children. The CDF has established the following priorities (Children's Defense Fund, 1974):

1. The right to education for children excluded from school.
2. The elimination of classification and labeling of children.
3. The right to treatment and education for institutionalized children.
4. The right to care and treatment for children by juvenile justice systems.
5. The right to adequate medical care and the delivery of health services for children.

6. The protection of children when used as subjects for medical and drug research.

Acquainting yourself with the work of the CDF, as well as with other organizations involved with advocating for children, is another way of protecting children. Through the publications of these organizations, you can keep current on the issues facing children and the legislation being debated or introduced. The National Association for the Education of Young Children, The Association for Childhood Education International, and the Day Care and Child Development Council of America are examples of other organizations concerned with the welfare of all of the children in our nation.

# IT'S UP TO YOU

Involving the community presents a challenge for all teachers of young children—a challenge that must be met. Without an involved community the preschool stands alone. When a community becomes involved in a preschool, everyone benefits. Children have the attention of volunteers, and resources for children and families are available. Teachers find the support of community agencies and members reinforcing, and the community benefits by becoming aware of the needs of children and families.

Community involvement does not end with the daily activities of a preschool. You have a responsibility to advocate for all children. "In a simpler world, parents were the only advocates children needed. This is no longer true. In a complex society where invisible decision makers affect children's lives profoundly, both children and parents need canny advocates" (Keniston, 1977, p. 211). Knowledgeable of the community, and of the needs of the children and families within the community, you can become one of these canny advocates for children.

## REFERENCES

Adair, F., and Eckstein, E. *Parents and the Day Care Center.* New York: Federation of Protestant Welfare Agencies, 1969.

Children's Defense Fund. *Report of the Second Year Activities of the Children's Defense Fund of the Washington Research Project.* Washington, D.C.: Children's Defense Fund, 1974.

*Day Care: A Statement of Principles.* Washington, D.C.: U.S. Department of Health, Education, and Welfare, 1971.

Dewey, J. *School and Society.* Chicago: University of Chicago Press, 1900.

Edelman, M. W. "Expanding Roots." *Childhood Education* 52 (1978): 19–21.

Ferro, F. "Protecting Children: The National Center on Child Abuse and Neglect." *Childhood Education* 52 (1975): 63–67.

Jantz, R. K.; Seefeldt, C.; Galper, A.; and Serock, K. *Children's Attitudes toward the Elderly.* Final report. College Park, Md.: University of Maryland, 1976.

Keniston, K. *All Our Children: The American Family under Pressure.* New York: Harcourt Brace Jovanovich, 1977.

Lorber, M. "Regulations: A Challenge to All National Association for the Education of Young Children Members." *Young Children* 33 (1978): 13–14.

## RESOURCES

Keniston, K. *All Our Children.* New York: Harcourt Brace Jovanovich, 1977.

Steiner, G. *The Children's Cause.* Washington, D.C.: The Brookings Institution, 1976.

The following organizations may be contacted for information on children. They each disseminate information on the legislative process and current legislation affecting children and families.

Association for Childhood Education International
3615 Wisconsin Avenue, N.W.
Washington, D.C. 20016

National Association for the Education of Young Children
1834 Connecticut Avenue, N.W.
Washington, D.C. 20009

You may also want to contact the following organizations for information on child abuse, legislation, and child advocacy.

Administration for Children, Youth and Families
Box 1182
Washington, D.C. 20013

National Center on Child Abuse and Neglect
Department of Health, Education, and Welfare
Washington, D.C. 20201

## PROJECTS

1. Identify the agencies within a given community that are serving children and their families. Describe the types of services each agency provides and how these services may be useful to the preschool.

2. Attend a volunteer training session, observe volunteers working within a center, or attend a volunteer recognition meeting. How do the volunteers perceive their role in the center? What services do the volunteers give to the preschool?

3. You have been given the responsibility for publicizing the preschool's program. Write a news release for the local paper around some happening in the school. Include a description of the photographs you would like to submit with your story.

4. Review the licensing and standards guidelines utilized in your community. How could these guidelines serve as a resource for the school's program? How does the school strive to meet these guidelines? Could the school exceed these minimum standards to build a better program?

# *THE ROLE OF*
# *THE TEACHER*_____

*Children in a child care center need more than an ordinary teacher, they need a "mothering" teacher. (Murphy, 1972, p. 5)*

A beautiful new building, two acres of play yard, hills and trees, beautiful books and toys, and all of the equipment in the world cannot alone produce a quality preschool program. Without a highly skilled, trained teacher who understands children and who knows how to utilize the facilities available, superior care and education will not result.

Every person who works in a preschool and comes in contact with the children can be thought of as a teacher. Through their very actions, the cook, janitor, bus driver, volunteer, aide, teacher, social worker, physician, and nurse all teach the young child. Young children imitate and model themselves after those people they come in contact with, and especially those people they respect and look up to. Some people, however, have primary responsibility for working with the children in the capacity of a teacher.

Whatever the program chooses to call the people working directly with the children—nursery attendants, care givers, teachers—these people have the major role in the day-to-day living experiences of the children. "[It] is a role that encompasses more than education. Special knowledge and understanding of the children, plus skills that will enable the child to profit from the group experience and educational opportunities, must be blended with nurturing qualities that create an environment in which children can feel confident, secure, and protected" (Child Welfare League of America, 1966). Piaget claims that the teacher of young children must have a depth of understanding, knowledge, and skills:

> The more one wishes to appeal to the spontaneous activities of small children, the more psychological initiation is required. The fact that it is much easier to deal with very young children within a framework of games or exercises entirely governed by the teacher, and the less training the latter has, the less he understands how much he is losing through his lack of psychological knowledge. (Piaget, 1969, p. 99)

Today, as a teacher of young children, you can take advantage of innovative training programs designed to develop the skills necessary for your position. For example, the Child Development Associate program provides on-the-job training for child care workers.

In order to be an effective teacher, you need an understanding of human growth and development, knowledge of the ways young children learn, and understanding of how to foster mental and physical health in young children. As parental and community involvement is critical to the functioning of a preschool, you should also know how to relate to parents and the broader community. Knowledge of curriculum content, concepts to be developed, and materials, methods, and resources available for developing those concepts is also necessary.

Lists describing the qualifications and characteristics desirable in teachers of young children often appear unrealistic; however, teachers in preschools, according to a survey of school directors, are more effective and enjoy their positions more when they have (Chambers, 1971, p. 407):

1. A basic liking for children.
2. Empathy for children and the ability to accept them at their present levels of development.

*Teachers must like children.*

3. Flexibility.

4. Lack of prejudice.

5. Intellectual curiosity without being overly intellectual.

6. A good education with much practical experience.

7. An understanding of and liking for parents.

8. The ability to fulfill their own needs apart from the children.

9. Interests and investments outside of child care.

10. The capacity for further growth as persons.

The number of caregivers and the number of children is an important variable in quality preschool programs. The size of the staff required will vary according to the size of the building, availability of regular volunteers, and local licensing standards. Those preschools serving a large number of children with special needs, or those focusing on infant care, will require a high teacher ratio. In smaller programs the director may serve as an extra teacher, eliminating the need for a full-time additional staff member.

The National Day Care Study, *Children at the Center* (1979), suggests that smaller groups of children and higher care giver ratios (fewer children per care giver) are associated with more desirable behavior and higher test score gains on the part of the children. When there is a high care giver ratio, teachers devote less time to managing children (commanding and correcting), and children show more task persistence and more interest participation in preschool activities (*Children at the Center*, 1979, p. 14). This study suggests that with a maximum group size of fourteen, there should be one care giver per seven children; with a group size of sixteen, one care giver per eight children; or for a group size of 18 children, one care giver per nine children.

There appears to be a consensus among educators and psychologists that preschools serving infants should provide a single nurturing person for each infant and young child (Willis & Ricciuti, 1975). Language, cognition, emotional security, and behavior attainment are all fostered by the presence of a single teacher who builds positive, reciprocal relationships with an individual child. Thus, the teacher of infants and toddlers should be given primary responsibility for the same few children and relate to these children on a continual basis.

# THE TEACHER'S RESPONSIBILITIES _____

Mature enough to give the mothering love young children require, while at the same time emphasizing to the child the importance of his mother and father, knowledgeable about curriculum content and methods, and competent in combining love, security, protection, and physical care with educational experiences for the child, you will be responsible for planning and carrying out the daily program and for fostering relationships between the children, parents, community, and the center.

## THE DAILY PROGRAM

Although the preschool's director, educational supervisors, and policy boards may be directly involved in formulating the type of educational program to be developed in the school, you are the person who will implement the program, changing it to meet the needs of individual children, and planning for daily experiences and activities.

You must develop goals and objectives for the individual children in your group based on the overall goals of the program. You will decide what story will be read, where the group will go on a field trip, what social studies concepts are appropriate for the children, and what equipment will be placed in the available space.

Before children arrive at the preschool, you have the responsibility of arranging the playroom and yard for maximum benefit to the children. Materials may be readied for art activities, toys not currently attractive to the children stored, and others, presenting more challenge and stimulation to the group, placed in the room.

You must also decide how to provide for a balance of activities during the day, week, month, and year. You must schedule both quiet and active times, provide for room for individuals to be alone or for small groups of children to work together, and allow time for children to laugh together, enjoying one another's company, growing in social skills.

Evaluation of the daily program and the growth of individual children within the program is also your responsibility. Program evaluation may be informally conducted as you record instances of children using new vocabulary words, of their increasing independence and self-assurance, or of their successes in mastering the equipment and materials.

Situations can be structured in order to observe and record the growth of individual children. As the children are playing with blocks, you might ask a child to hand you two, three, or four blocks, the red truck, or the blue car, noting the child's ability to comprehend concepts and follow directions. If you have been working on developing the concept of the interdependence of living things on one another, you may unobtrusively sit down with an individual child and ask him questions about what frogs eat, what insects eat, or what he eats, to determine the extent of his understanding of the experiences provided. Formal testing may also be your responsibility in evaluation of the program or of individual children.

## RELATIONSHIPS WITH CHILDREN

Fostering each child's self-concept, supporting each in his attempts to relate to others, you are responsible for facilitating the children's social, physical, emotional, and intellectual development. Each child must be provided with the attention, challenges, and successes he needs to become a participating member of the group. You must know each child so well that you can anticipate his needs and wants, organize the program to meet these needs, show interest in the things he finds interesting, and demonstrate an appreciation of his accomplishments. In this way, you help each child to feel secure and confident, interested and able to reach out and relate to other children and adults.

## RELATIONSHIPS WITH SPECIAL NEEDS CHILDREN

You have a special responsibility to form effective relationships with children who have special needs. One Head Start teacher, when she found out that a deaf girl was to be assigned in her class, describes the stages she went through and how she finally developed the sensitivity, skills, and knowledge necessary to relate with the child. She stated:

> At first I was overwhelmed with the responsibility of teaching a deaf child. Why I didn't even know one thing about hearing impairments! I didn't know who in the world could help me either. I didn't even know how I really felt about having her in my class. I guess at this point I was mostly frightened.
>
> First, I found out all I could about hearing impairments. I spent a great deal of time in the library, finding and reading all I could about hearing impairments and young children. I was lucky to be near a college for the deaf, and I used every resource they had to offer. Armed with at least some information, I was then able to examine my own attitudes about the child.
>
> Next, I met with the girl's parents and found out all I could about the child from them. After all, they're the ones who knew Kathy the best. I

asked about her likes, dislikes, abilities—all the things she could do well, as well as all about the things she needed to learn. The parents really made me feel more comfortable and were willing to share their knowledge with me.

At about this time I enrolled in a class for manual interpreters. I know there's some controversy about manual interpretation, but knowing at least a little signing permitted me to communicate with Kathy, and begin our relationships. (White, 1979)*

This teacher, although perhaps not realizing it, followed the advice experts give (Baun & Lasher, 1978). In preparing to meet the needs of a child with special needs, you are encouraged to:

1. Examine your own attitudes and feelings about working with children who have special needs. Children could be limited by your misconceptions or stereotypes about specific handicaps. Then, too, if you understand your own feelings about children with special needs, you will be better able to convey attitudes that support growth and acceptance.
2. Meet with the child's parents. After all, the parents know their child better than anyone else.
3. Locate and utilize all possible resources. Find out all you can about the specific handicap and the specific adaptations that must be made to provide the least restrictive educational environment possible for the child.
4. Consult with experts in the field of special education to begin to prepare yourself to work with the children. Developing specialized skills may be necessary. A therapist, physician, or psychologist might help you gain the skills needed.

In order to build confidence in the children, and support children's growth and development, you must also feel confident. As you gain knowledge about the handicapping condition, about the adaptations you must make, and as you gain the skills necessary to relate effectively with the child, your confidence will grow.

### RELATIONSHIPS WITH PARENTS

Although the preschool may have a staff member responsible for planning and conducting parent meetings and developing parent involvement, you are ultimately responsible for the quality and extent of parent involvement in the preschool. It is you who continually reminds the children of the importance of their parents, and it is you who makes contact with them, either formally or informally, establishing the necessary rapport between parent and preschool.

You are also responsible for most of the reporting to the parents, either through daily, informal contacts, or through planned formal conferences. In

*Reprinted with permission from Ms. Sadie White.

turn, it is you who learns from the parents about the child and his family—how they function as a unit, the things they do together, their specific needs as a family.

## RELATIONSHIPS WITH THE COMMUNITY

Again, you will assume the primary responsibility of informing the community about the preschool's program. You will help the director or supervisor recruit volunteers, speak to community groups concerning the school, and obtain support of existing community agencies. You will refer children to the dentist, physician, and other health personnel and sometimes assist in examinations and treatment. You will relate to the social worker and psychologists, observing children and families with problems, obtaining data for the specialists, and seeking advice on specific children in your care. Other resource personnel will relate directly to you, planning with you to improve the program of the preschool.

You are also the logical person to relate to the various community agencies, making arrangements for services to be provided for individual children and families. Participating on policy boards of supporting community agencies and attending the policy board meetings of the preschool are also your responsibilities.

## ——————————————————— THE AIDE—ANOTHER TEACHER

The teacher's aide or teaching assistant is a valuable member of the preschool staff. Although she may not possess all of the formal qualifications of a teacher who directs, plans, implements, and evaluates the total program, she does possess the same characteristics of the teacher. The aide must demonstrate affection for young children, enjoy being with them, and understand children's needs and how to meet them. She shares the concern of the teacher about obtaining continuing education to enhance her skills and capabilities of working with children.

Although the aide will work under your direction, she is often indistinguishable from a teacher. Both of you are involved with the children, working with them individually or in groups. Both help the children clean up messy activities and both assume the responsibility of eating with the children, of supervising outdoor play, and of keeping the room neat and orderly.

Chosen from the community, the aide brings with her a knowledge of the cultural traditions of the community. She serves as a resource person to the preschool, interpreting the values and goals of the community to the staff who may not live nearby. Perhaps the aide is even a neighbor of the children, helping to make them feel more at home. In areas where English is the second language, an aide, speaking the language of the community, is invaluable.

In turn, the aide helps to promote community involvement in the preschool, relaying the program's goals and objectives to the neighborhood

*Aides are valuable additions.*

and describing the activities and purposes of the center to her friends and neighbors.

You must assume the major responsibility for working with and training aides. Even when orientation programs are provided and continual training is available for aides, you must demonstrate specific techniques of working with young children. The practical experience of the aide observing you during the daily activities of the preschool gradually equips her with the skills she will need to become a teacher herself.

Aides must know exactly what they can and cannot do in the program, and generally you will be responsible for relaying this information. In some programs, aides may not assume total responsibility for a group of children at any time because of legal restrictions, or take a group of children from the school without a teacher present. You can help aides function effectively by defining the tasks for the day and describing exactly how they should be accomplished.

You and the aide working with you will develop your own working relationship. There should be time to determine the specific responsibilities and tasks each of you will assume for the day, week, or month. Often, when a teacher and an aide are responsible for a small group of children, they attempt to do too much for the children, leaving nothing for them to do for themselves. The things the children can learn to do for themselves, such as cleaning up, dressing, or feeding themselves, can be identified, and the adult's role in these experiences described. Responsibilities such as housekeeping chores, toilet supervision, or setting up cots for napping can be divided between you and the aide during the planning times.

Aides may assist in preparing materials for the day and in arranging the playroom and yard for planned activities. You and the aide will share in the responsibility of supervising and observing children during indoor and outdoor play times. It may be that the aide will assume primary responsibility for the maintenance of equipment and arrange for equipment repair and replacement.

If legal restrictions permit, the aide may be responsible for some group activities. She may lead the children in finger plays or songs, show them slides or movies, or lead them in a discussion of some important topic. Plans may be made for the aide to continue her education so that she may obtain promotions, eventually qualifying her to assume the status of a teacher.

Relating to individual children, the aide is another listening ear. "[She is] another lap to sit on and much more" (Bruner, 1966, p. 16). The aide is that other person ready to motivate children to learn, to give them security that permits them to explore and experiment, developing their own sense of individuality and importance.

—————————————————————————— IT'S UP TO YOU

The people who work with children are no doubt the most important factor in a preschool program. The program will only be as good as you and the other teachers make it. Teaching young children is a large responsibility, but one that brings rewards and pleasures.

It is your responsibility to develop relationships with children, parents, and the community. You will be responsible for planning the program and for evaluating the children, the program, and the teaching staff. In addition, you will also be in charge of working with aides, directing, guiding and often training them as you work with them.

The aide, another teacher, also has responsibilities to the children and the program. As the aide obtains training and skills, she assumes more responsibility for the group. Often the aide comes from the community, and is a valuable resource for the preschool, translating the community's goals and values to the preschool.

Even though you will have a lot of responsibility as a teacher of young children, you have the pleasure of working with them and seeing them grow and develop. Children are a joy to be with, their enthusiasm is catching, and their joy of life is contagious.

## REFERENCES

Baun, S. J., and Lasher, M. G. *Are You Ready to Mainstream?* Columbus, Oh.: Charles E. Merrill Publishing Co., 1978.

Bruner, C. "A Lap to Sit on and Much More." *Childhood Education* 52 (1966): 9–11.

Chambers, G. S. "Staff selection and training." In *Day Care: Resources for Decisions,* edited by E. Grotberg. Washington, D.C.: Office of Economic Opportunity, 1971.

Child Welfare League of America. *Guide for Establishing and Operating Day Care Centers.* New York: Child Welfare League of America. 1966.

*Children at the Center.* Cambridge, Mass.: Abt Associates, 1979.

Murphy, L. B. *More than a Teacher.* Washington, D.C.: U.S. Department of Health, Education, and Welfare, 1972.

Piaget, J. *Science of Education and the Psychology of the Child.* New York: Viking Press, 1969.

White, S. "All about Kathy." Unpublished manuscript. College Park, Md.: University of Maryland, 1979.

Willis, A., and Ricciuti, H. *A Good Beginning for Babies: Guidelines for Group Care.* Washington, D.C.: National Association for the Education of Young Children, 1975.

## RESOURCES

Hess, R. D., and Croft, D. *Teachers of Young Children,* 2d ed. Boston: Houghton Mifflin Co., 1975.

Hymes, J. L., Jr. *Teaching the Child under Six,* 2d ed. Columbus, Oh., Charles E. Merrill Publishing Co., 1974.

Schickedanz, J.; York, M.; Stewart, I., and White, D. *Strategies for Teaching Young Children.* Englewood Cliffs, N.J.: Prentice-Hall, 1977.

## PROJECTS

1. Observe a teacher and an aide working together in a preschool. How do they each relate to the children? What duties does each complete? How do they relate to each other?

2. Interview a teacher in a preschool. How does she define her responsibilities to the children, the parents, and the community? How does she perceive her role? How does she carry out responsibilities? What aspects of her position does she indicate she enjoys most? What does she find to be most frustrating?

3. Observe a teacher with a small group of young children. How does he meet individual needs while assuming responsibility for the total group? How does he maintain control of the situation and the children?

4. Ask to see the teacher's plans for the day, week, or month. How do these plans relate to the goals of the preschool? What type of planning does the teacher do? How complete should plans be when working with young children?

# CHILDREN IN THE PRESCHOOL_____

*Young children are a special
breed.* (Hymes, 1974, p. 36)

**5**

All children—no matter whether they are rich or poor, boys or girls, black or white—have similar characteristics and needs (Hymes, 1974). All young children, regardless of their background or heritage, find that a preschool program fits them. In a preschool they find an environment designed to meet the special needs of young growing bodies and minds. In a preschool children's needs for nurturance, love, affection, and companionship are also met.

*Children are a special breed.*

Some children may come from single-parent families, others from homes in which both parents work outside of the home. These children find a day care program or preschool meeting their needs for care and at the same time fulfilling their need for early educational experiences. Other children who live in cramped apartments or crowded homes with little space for play and freedom find opportunities to explore, run free, and play in school. Only children, or those without friends their own age, find playmates and their need for companionship fulfilled by a preschool program.

Preschool programs are also beneficial for children with special needs— those with speech or hearing handicaps, or those who are emotionally or mentally retarded. Still other children in preschools may come from deprived homes and families lacking the essential requirements for raising children— families who have been deprived of opportunities for acculturation and improvement of social functioning (*Child Welfare League of America Standards for Day Care Service,* 1966).

There are suitable preschool programs designed to meet the needs of children of all ages. Some day care programs are designed for infants only a few weeks of age, and others begin when children are eighteen months or two years of age. Generally, the children are three to five years old; they are the ones who benefit most from a group experience. Three to five year olds enjoy being with others, and require opportunities to learn to live with, work with, and learn from others.

———————————————————————————————————— **INFANTS**

Caring for infants, however satisfying, is an enormous responsibility in a preschool. The human infant is extremely vulnerable, completely dependent on the adults around him for his physical welfare, as well as for his intellectual, social, and emotional development.

Any program caring for infants must provide specific safeguards in addition to the usual components of a preschool to insure the positive, healthy growth and development of the child. Impersonal care of an infant, or emphasis on physical care only, can have damaging and irreversible effects. Infants raised in the unstimulating, impersonal environments of institutions are not only intellectually damaged, but retarded in their social, emotional, and physical growth patterns as well.

Education and care giving cannot be separated (*Child Welfare League of America Standards for Day Care Service,* 1966). Each care-giving experience, in effect, is a teaching experience. As the child is fed when he is hungry or changed when he is wet, he begins to feel that the world is a safe, secure place he can trust. If, on the other hand, the infant's needs are never met when they are important to him, he begins to learn that the world is unsafe, full of discomforts—a place he can neither trust nor feel secure in (Elkind, 1978).

During the first year of life, the infant is building a sense of trust or security through each satisfying physical and emotional experience. This implies that his needs are being met as he demands—holding him securely, cuddling him often, feeding and clothing him properly, and giving him sufficient attention.

As you feed or change the baby, talk to him, call him by name, sing to him, and always respond to his beginning attempts at communication—smiling back when he smiles, laughing, and even cooing back in response to the baby's coos and gurgles (Willis & Ricciuti, 1975).

Every time you cuddle the baby, hold him, fondle him, pay attention to him, you are teaching. Your very presence provides the sensory stimulation the young child needs to develop intellectually. Food and clothing are, of course, essential to the infant; the person who cares for him is just as important.

Infants are individuals. No two babies are alike in their needs, growth, or development. In one year they change from completely helpless creatures to the possessors of teeth, with the ability to understand language, communicate desires effectively, and move about with surprising agility. In that year there is a wide range of normal growth and behavior; with so much learning and grow-

*To care for a tiny baby is satisfying.*

ing taking place, it seems apparent that the baby needs more than simple physical care.

The growth and development of the infant depends, in part, on his environment and the adult encouragement he receives, in addition to his genetically determined developmental and maturation rate. Children who are around adults—who have adults who talk to them, read to them, play pat-a-cake, sing nursery rhymes—grow into children who are verbal and competent communicators. Those children who do not experience verbal interaction with an adult grow to be retarded in their language ability. Likewise, muscle development depends, in part, on the baby's opportunities to practice rolling over, crawling, or pulling himself up. Children raised in cribs for the first year of life demonstrate retarded physical development; in the restrictive environment of the crib they are unable to practice and obtain the skills involved in mobility.

When caring for babies, encourage each child in his attempts to walk, talk, sit, and handle objects. The infant, once he is able to reach and grasp an object, needs many things to play with, and once able to creep, the freedom to explore his environment safely.

# TODDLERS

When a baby begins to walk, usually around a year of age, until the age of three or so, she is often called a toddler. At this point the child's developing autonomy provides the key to understanding his behavior. The toddler wants to do for herself. She wants to control her body—walking, climbing, jumping; she wants to master the objects in her environment—pushing her stroller instead of riding in it, buttoning her own buttons, putting her shoes on. Saying "No" to everything, trying to have power, to be a person, to grow up makes being a toddler difficult, and living with a toddler an adventure. From her first birthday through her third, the toddler will learn social skills and toilet control. She will develop an amazing vocabulary and a rather complete language system.

Discovering and asserting herself, the toddler demands a preschool program without rigid scheduling or routines. She is in a "dart, dash, and fling" age and must have the freedom her developing body requires rather than being restricted for long periods of time to a playpen, highchair, or other confinement. The environment can be arranged to satisfy the toddler's sense of autonomy. For example, giving her many finger foods and having her feed and handle a cup herself help her to feel independent. You can, by helping the toddler put her toes into the tip of the sock and giving an unobtrusive assist in getting the sock over the heel, give her the feeling that she has taken major responsibility for dressing herself. Letting the child participate in real-life tasks, such as washing off table tops, sweeping up scraps, helping to set the table, assists her in learning about her environment while fostering her feelings of autonomy. Toys and equipment can be selected for the toddler that allow her to play with and use them without adult assistance or guidance (Hildebrand, 1975).

The toddler's language ability, as the infant's, grows and develops through a combined verbal exchange with interested adults. The more adult stimulation of the child's language, the more advanced her language will become.

Toddlers do benefit from being with other children. Although they are more likely to engage in parallel play, they do enjoy the company that others provide, do practice communicating with other children, and begin to develop social skills.

Many opportunities in the preschool should be given the toddler to make choices so that she may better develop the type of control the adults around her desire. A young child, having the choice of when she goes to the bathroom, what she will eat, or how she will play may be more willing to submit to an adult's desires in the area of toilet training, social development, or physical control.

# PRESCHOOLERS

Growing in self-awareness, learning social communication, developing healthy attitudes toward his own development, mastering physical skills, and forming concepts related to physical and social reality, the preschooler, between the ages of three and five, is ready for new experiences, new responsibilities, and acquaintance with the wider world.

The preschooler is fully capable of living with others and learning to control aggressive and impulsive behavior in order to become part of the group. Although he is still self-centered, he now desires other children to play and work with.

*Preschoolers learn to work with others.*

A sense of initiative—of being someone who has an idea and can carry it out—develops during the preschool years. The child now needs time to plan, the freedom to carry out his plans and ideas, and someone to help him enjoy his finished product. The plans may include such activities as smearing peanut butter on the blocks to see if they'll stick together, but they *are* plans. These plans show themselves in the child's art activities, language, music, song, dance, and play.

The preschool should strive to structure the child's experiences with the world of ideas. Taking the child places, acquainting him with other people and things in the environment, and bringing in people for him to meet are all important activities. Concepts of time, space, weight, distance, measurement, and the beginning use of symbols are rapidly developing at this time.

Language, out of bounds at four years of age, becomes a tool for the child to express his ideas, to gain social access to a group, and to control himself and others. The child's natural interest in words and language during the preschool years makes this a logical time to introduce many experiences with language, poetry, and literature.

Large and small muscles are developing continually, but the preschooler reaches new measures of control and develops new skills of skipping, hopping, and climbing, as well as the ability to manipulate small objects and items.

The preschool child can take the responsibility for himself and his behavior and participate in making decisions about himself and his activities. For this reason, his day should include many opportunities to explore and exercise his judgment in making choices and decisions. Developing initiative, the preschooler also needs to participate in adult activities—helping adults in their tasks, taking responsibility for routines, cooking, caring for his clothing, and helping in housekeeping chores.

These are the years in which to try everything. The child needs materials to work with and time and freedom to do what he wants with the materials. Wood, paint, clay, and scrap materials are necessary; dress-up clothes and housekeeping equipment are important and treasured. Children who are given the opportunities to experiment and explore materials and to observe life around them can act out their observations in make-believe play. They can ask questions and be given answers based on their experiences and have the opportunity to develop into real people, with good ideas, ready to go on growing and becoming.

*Table 1* ———————————————————————————————————————

|  | birth to 6 months |
|---|---|
| THINKING | Baby discriminates mother from others, is more responsive to her |
|  | Baby acts curious, explores through looking, grasping, mouthing |
|  | Recognizes adults, his bottle, discriminates between strangers and familiar persons |
|  | Shows he is learning by anticipating situations, responding to unfamiliarity, and reacting to disappearance of things |
|  | Uses materials in play such as crumpling and waving paper |
|  | Looks a long time at objects he is inspecting |
| LANGUAGE | Baby coos expressively, vocalizes spontaneously |
|  | Baby vocalizes over a sustained period of time to someone who is imitating his sounds |
|  | Baby babbles in word-sounds of two syllables |
| BODY EXPRESSION AND CONTROL | Baby develops his own rhythm in feeding, eliminating, sleeping, and being awake—a rhythm which can be approximately predicted |

|  | Baby quiets himself through rocking, sucking, or touching |
|---|---|
|  | Adjusts his posture in anticipation of being fed or held (in crib, on lap, at shoulder) |
|  | Balances his head |
|  | Baby turns to see or hear better |
|  | Baby pulls self to sitting position, sits alone momentarily |
|  | Coordinates his eye and hand in reaching. Baby reaches persistently, touches, manipluates |
|  | Retains objects in hands, manipulates objects, transfers from hand to hand |
|  | Baby engages in social exchange and self-expression through facial action, gestures, and play |
| SOCIAL PLAY AND RESPONSIVENESS | Baby imitates movements |
|  | Gazes at faces and reaches toward them, reacts to disappearance of a face, tracks face movements |
|  | Responds to sounds |
|  | Smiles to be friendly |
|  | Opens mouth in imitation of adult |
|  | Baby likes to be tickled, jostled, frolicked with |
|  | Makes social contact with others by smiling or vocalizing |
|  | Quiets when someone approaches, smiles |
|  | A mutual exchange goes on between adult and child through smiling, play, voice, bodily involvement |
| SELF-AWARENESS | Baby smiles at his own reflection in the mirror |
|  | Looks at and plays with his hands and toes |
|  | Feels things about himself through such actions as banging |
| EMOTIONS | Baby shows excitement through waving arms, kicking, moving whole body, face lighting up |
|  | Shows pleasure as he anticipates something, such as his bottle |
|  | Cries in different ways to say he is cold, wet, hungry, etc. |
|  | Makes noises to voice pleasure, displeasure, satisfactions |
|  | Baby laughs |

**6 to 9 months**

| THINKING | Baby shows persistence in doing things |
|---|---|
|  | Becomes aware of missing objects |
|  | Makes connections between objects—pulls string to secure ring on the other end, uncovers a hidden toy |

|  | Increases his ability to zero in on sights or sounds he's interested in<br>Baby's attention span is prolonged<br>Baby shifts his attention appropriately, resists distraction |
| --- | --- |
| LANGUAGE | Baby babbles to people<br>Says "da-da" or equivalent<br>Notices familiar words and turns toward person or thing speaker is referring to<br>Shows he understands some commonly-used words |
| BODY EXPRESSION AND CONTROL | Baby sits alone with good coordination<br>Manipulates objects with interest, understands the use of objects—rings a bell on purpose<br>Practices motor skills, crawls, stands up by holding on to furniture<br>Uses fingers in pincer-type grasp of small objects<br>Increases his fine-motor coordination of eye, hand, and mouth |
| SOCIAL PLAY AND RESPONSIVENESS | Baby cooperates in games<br>Takes the initiative in establishing social exchanges with adults<br>Understands and adapts to social signals<br>Shows ability to learn by demonstration |
| SELF-AWARENESS | Baby listens and notices his own name<br>Makes a playful response to his own image in mirror<br>Begins to assert himself |
| EMOTIONS | Baby expresses some fear toward strangers in new situations<br>Pushes away something he does not want<br>Shows pleasure when someone responds to his self-assertion<br>Shows pleasure in getting someone to react to him |

### 9 to 18 months

| THINKING | Baby unwraps an object, takes lids from boxes<br>Recognizes shapes in a puzzle board<br>Names familiar objects<br>Baby becomes increasingly curious about surroundings, sets off on his own to explore farther than ever before<br>Becomes more purposeful and persistent in accomplishing a task |
| --- | --- |

| LANGUAGE | Baby jabbers expressively |
| | Imitates words |
| | Says two words together |
| BODY EXPRESSION AND CONTROL | Baby stands alone, sits down, walks with help |
| | Is gradually gaining control of bodily functioning |
| | Throws a ball |
| | Becomes more aware of his body, identifies body parts |
| | Stands on one foot with help |
| | Walks up and down stairs with help |
| | Needs adult as a stable base for operations during his growing mobility and curiosity |
| SOCIAL PLAY AND RESPONSIVENESS | Baby plays pat-a-cake, peek-a-boo |
| | Responds to verbal request |
| | Imitates actions |
| | Stops his own actions on command from an adult |
| | Uses gestures and words to make his wants known |
| | Focuses on mother as the only person he will permit to meet needs |
| SELF-AWARENESS | Baby becomes aware of his ability to say "no" and of the consequences of this |
| | Shows shoes or other clothing |
| | Asserts himself by "getting into everything," "getting into mischief" |
| | Wants to decide for himself |
| EMOTIONS | Baby shows preference for one toy over another |
| | Expresses many emotions and recognizes feelings in other people |
| | Gives affection—returns a kiss or hug |
| | Expresses fear of strangers |
| | Shows anxiety at separation from mother, gradually masters this |

18 to 24 months

| THINKING | Child says the names of familiar objects in pictures |
| | Explores cabinets and drawers |
| | Begins to play pretend games |
| LANGUAGE | Child uses two-word sentences |
| | Has vocabulary of twenty to fifty words |

|  | Begins to use "me," "I," and "you"<br>Follows verbal instructions<br>Listens to simple stories |
|---|---|
| BODY EXPRESSION AND CONTROL | Hand coordination is increasingly steady—child can build tower of many blocks<br>Climbs into adult chair<br>Runs with good coordination<br>Climbs stairs, using rail<br>Uses body actively in mastering and exploring surroundings—an active age |
| SOCIAL PLAY AND RESPONSIVENESS | Child scribbles with crayon in imitation of adults' strokes on paper<br>Likes parents' possessions and play that mimics parents' behavior and activities<br>Follows simple directions<br>Controls others, orders them around<br>Tests, fights, resists adults when they oppose or force him to do something<br>Child is able to differentiate more and more between people |
| SELF-AWARENESS | Child recognizes body parts on a doll<br>Identifies parts of his own body<br>Child takes a more self-sufficient attitude, challenges parents' desires, wants to "do it myself"<br>Child's sense of self-importance is intense—protests, wants to make his own choices |
| EMOTIONS | Child desires to be independent, feed self, put on articles of own clothing<br>Shows intense positive or negative reactions<br>Likes to please others, is affectionate<br>Shows some aggressive tendencies—slaps, bites, hits—which must be dealt with<br>Shows greater desire to engage in problem solving and more persistence in doing so<br>Develops triumphant delight and pride in his own actions<br>Becomes frustrated easily |

24 to 36 months

| THINKING | Child can name many objects<br>Begins to grasp the meaning of numbers |
|---|---|

| | Child's memory span is longer |
| --- | --- |
| | Child's ability to reason, solve problems, make comparisons develops |
| | Child grasps the concepts of color, form, and space |
| | Begins to respect and obey rules |
| | Shows strong interest in investigating the functions and details of household objects |
| LANGUAGE | Child uses language as a way of communicating his thoughts, representing his ideas and developing social relationships |
| | Child enjoys using language, gains satisfaction from expressing himself and being understood |
| | Understands and uses abstract words such as "up," "down," "now," "later" |
| BODY EXPRESSION AND CONTROL | Child can jump and hop on one foot |
| | Child walks up and down stairs, alternating his feet at each stair |
| | Begins to notice the differences between safe and unsafe activities |
| | Expands his large-muscle interests and activities |
| | Tries hard to dress and undress himself |
| SOCIAL PLAY AND RESPONSIVENESS | Child tests his limits in situations involving other people |
| | Says "no" but submits anyway |
| | Shows trust and love |
| | Enjoys wider range of relationships and experiences, enjoys meeting many people other than parents |
| | Likes to try out adult activities, especially around the house, runs errands, does small household chores |
| SELF-AWARENESS | Child becomes aware of himself as a separate person, can contrast himself with another |
| | Expresses preferences strongly |
| | Expresses confidence in his own activities |
| | Expresses pride in achievement |
| | Values his own property |
| EMOTIONS | Child strives for mastery over objects |
| | Child can tolerate more frustration, more willing to accept a substitute for what he cannot have |
| | Shows strong desire for independence in his actions |
| | Gradually channels his aggressive tendencies into more constructive activities |

| | |
|---|---|
| | Uses language to express his wishes and his feelings toward others |
| | Shows a developing sense of humor at surprises, unusual actions, etc. |

**36 to 48 months**

| | |
|---|---|
| THINKING | Child shows curiosity and wants to investigate everything new; he questions everything |
| | Shows more and more interest in the wider world, and needs to experience new places and things |
| LANGUAGE | Continuing to increase his vocabulary, the child can now engage in a conversation and is able to tell stories from pictures or books |
| | Enjoys listening to stories and repeating simple rhymes |
| | Has an estimated vocabulary of around 750 words and speaks in 3- or 4-word sentences |
| BODY EXPRESSION AND CONTROL | Child is more sure on his feet and is fast developing good control over his body |
| | He needs room to run, jump, and climb, but still requires adult supervision |
| | He can dress himself fairly well but may need help undressing |
| | Makes crude designs with paints and crayons |
| SOCIAL PLAY AND RESPONSIVENESS | Child likes to be with other children and is beginning to learn the give-and-take of play |
| | He will be testing social situations and still needs adult assistance |
| SELF-AWARENESS | Child is developing a sense of himself and what he can do |
| | He wants to please others, often asking, "Is this right?" He needs to feel secure and accepted and likes to participate in adult tasks such as helping to set a table or stirring a cake |
| EMOTIONS | Child is less negative but can still be easily upset and forced to tears or temper tantrums |
| | May fear separations from his family and have other fears—of the dark, large animals, or strangers |

**48 to 60 months**

| | |
|---|---|
| THINKING | Child expresses ideas in artwork and language |
| | Counts, names colors, and recognizes that people can |

| | gain meaning from the printed word—a period of rapid intellectual growth |
|---|---|
| LANGUAGE | The silly, out-of-bounds talk of the four year old, with the use of "bathroom" words, grows into mature, social conversation<br><br>The child can listen to stories, has over a 2,500 word vocabulary, and uses language for social control |
| BODY EXPRESSION AND CONTROL | Very active, the child has good body control<br><br>Child can catch and throw a ball, skip, and is capable in climbing, running, and jumping<br><br>Child can respond to music, keeping time with his body |
| SOCIAL PLAY AND RESPONSIVENESS | Child is social, needing company of others<br><br>Child can relate to others, sharing ideas, and beginning to cooperate<br><br>Is responsive, with the five year old almost conforming to the wishes of others<br><br>Group play abounds |
| SELF-AWARENESS | Child uses the word "I"<br><br>Child thinks for himself and seems to know right from wrong<br><br>Four- and five-year-old children take responsibility for their own actions |
| EMOTIONS | Four year old's emotions are close to the surface<br><br>Five-year-old child controls his emotions, expressing them in acceptable ways |

Reprinted with permission: *Day Care: Serving Infants.* Washington, D.C.: U.S. Department of Health, Education, and Welfare, 1971.

## CHILD GROWTH AND DEVELOPMENT

# CHILDREN WITH SPECIAL NEEDS _____

"Children with special needs are found everywhere—in well-to-do families and those struggling in poverty, in the homes of young adults who are just embarking on the challenges of parenthood, and in those of middle-age parents completing their childbearing years. They come from every race and ethnic group" (Fallen & McGovern, 1978, p. iii). Because children with special needs are found everywhere, in all neighborhoods and parts of the country, many will be in attendance in a preschool program. Today you are mandated under law to design educational experiences for all children—those with special needs, those who have been abused, as well as those who have special gifts or talents.

## HANDICAPPED CHILDREN

Public Law 94-142, the Education of All Handicapped Children Act of 1975, mandates that all children with special needs have access to free and appropriate educational experiences. These experiences are to be planned to meet the unique requirements of each individual child, whether he is retarded, hard of hearing, health impaired, emotionally disturbed, or learning disabled.

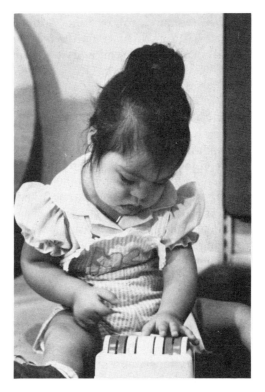

*Handicaps can range from minor problems to more serious physical or mental disabilities.*

Early childhood educators have always been concerned with meeting individual needs. Young children are very individualistic, and it is nearly impossible to ignore this individualism. Early childhood educators have always maintained that the individual's level of development must be considered in planning any preschool experience; thus the mandate of Public Law 94-142 is not entirely new to early childhood educators. "It is rather a reaffirmation of the tenets their programs have followed since their inception. Teachers must strive to meet the needs of all children in their groups" (Dickerson & Davis, 1979, p. 29).

Now, however, educators recognize that some children may need more than others. "'Basically, this child is like my other children, only more so,' says a mother of a child with a handicap." (*Day Care: Serving Children with Special Needs*, 1972, p. 8).The "more so" is what Public Law 94-142 is all about.

Children who are hearing or visually impaired, have a language or learning problem, are retarded, are orthopedically impaired, or who are emotionally disturbed may be enrolled in a regular preschool classroom. It is believed that such children will be better able to develop their full potential when their special needs are not used as an excuse to restrict their educational opportunities.

When describing children with special needs, take care not to use labels. If children are described in terms of their deficits, "He's the blind child," or "Oh her, she's the one who's disturbed," labeling becomes restrictive, as well as derogatory. It is a source of pride for teachers in programs serving children with special needs when the children with the needs cannot be readily identified by visitors (Galinsky & Hooks, 1977, p. 249). "In most of the programs people were talked about in reference to their strengths: 'See that child . . . she's wonderful with any art material' or 'He is the most lovable little boy.' This positive attitude toward people did not prevent care givers from helping children when they needed help, but they did so in an atmosphere charged with optimism" (Galinsky & Hooks, 1977, p. 249).

Even though labeling of children is discouraged, it may be helpful for beginning teachers to know something about children with specific conditions. If, as a teacher, you would be asked to work with a child with a special need, you would have to do a lot of homework to find out all about the individual child, as well as a lot about the nature of the special need. The following descriptions are only a brief introduction to the nature of special needs, and are not a basis for planning or teaching:

## Visual Impairments

Children with visual problems are usually able to work and learn effectively within the regular classroom. Visually impaired children find many of the activities of the preschool suited to their needs, and they can take part without help in story times, and art and play activities. Reynolds and Birch (1977) suggest that the most important consideration when working with a visually impaired child is remembering that the child cannot see. Because of the visual impairment, the child will not learn by looking or through imitation (Reynolds & Birch, 1977, p. 614).

You should touch and systematically and deliberately introduce the child to the preschool environment. The child should find consistency in the environment; things should be in a place and left there so she can orientate herself in the room. Touching, as well as communication with words, is helpful as children organize their world (*Day Care: Serving Children with Special Needs*, 1972).

## Hearing Impairments

Children with hearing impairments find the preschool environment suited to their specific needs. With the use of hearing aids many do have some hearing, and can participate in most of the program's activities. You will have to find out how to assist the child with the hearing aid, as well as to learn about his special needs.

Children with hearing difficulties will play, build, create, and enjoy the company of others just like other children. Remember that these children must learn by watching you and others, instead of by listening. You can learn to use manual interpretation or any other communication system the child is being taught.

When talking with the child, remember to be certain he is facing you and watching you. You can increase communication by placing yourself at the child's eye level and by using gestures and facial expressions (*Day Care: Serving Children with Special Needs*, 1972).

## Physical Disabilities

Many children with orthopedic handicaps can get along fine in the regular classroom. First see what adaptations will be required in the physical plant, both indoors and out, and what possible hazards the child will be facing. Understanding the nature of the condition lets you decide what changes to make in the physical plant, as well as in the program.

Maybe special equipment can be obtained. A back support for a chair, or tables specially designed for children in wheel chairs, and other modifications of furniture can be of help to the child with a physical handicap.

## Mental Retardation

Children who are retarded are often placed in regular preschool classes. It is your responsibility to provide practical educational experiences from which the child can profit, and at the same time maintain the regular program for all of the children. Mentally retarded children may need specific experiences in:

1. Social experiences—interacting with others.
2. Self-help skills—dressing, feeding, body care.
3. Sense training—recognizing colors, textures, etc.
4. Speech and language experiences—listening and speaking.

Retarded children may need more concrete experiences than other children. Instead of telling the child about something, tell and show her at the same time. Break down tasks into small steps so the child, mastering one step at a time, can eventually achieve success.

## Emotional Problems

Everyone has a time when he loses control. All children, as all adults, reach a point when they either feel like crying, screaming, or hitting, or actually do lash out at others. Some children have difficulty with control all of the time, and it does not take any special frustration to set them off. Children with emotional problems have always been in regular preschool classrooms, and the placement of such children in preschools is very beneficial.

All of the activities of the program facilitate children's learning to take control. When a child needs special help, assign a volunteer to help her maintain control, or arrange for the child to achieve support through providing a more structured environment, or by limiting choices.

## Speech and Language Impairments

All young children are learning to use language, so it is difficult to diagnose those children who have special problems with language. Nevertheless, children who do have delayed speech, or other language impairments, benefit from a preschool experience.

The verbal nature of the majority of preschool activities, as well as the enriching language activities of stories, poems, and songs, is profitable for these children. Remember to spend more time speaking and listening to these children, or arrange specific activities for them in language.

*The American Humane Association's yearly national study of child maltreatment (1979) shows that neglect may be a more extensive problem than the more easily recognized cases of physical abuse.*

ABUSED CHILDREN    Some children in preschools are abused. The attention on child abuse, as a national problem, has led to the mandate that teachers be responsible for reporting cases of suspected abuse. Authorities suggest that the abused child may exhibit the following characteristics (Fontana, 1973):

1. Cries for no apparent reason.
2. Is afraid of people and things.
3. Does not want to go home after preschool is over.
4. Is not always dressed appropriately for the season or weather.
5. Is withdrawn and unresponsive.
6. Lashes out at others; is aggressive and starts fights.
7. Is sleepy, tired, and in generally poor health.
8. Has evidence of injuries—repeated cuts and bruises, black eyes, facial cuts, etc.

Of course, there is a danger in jumping to hasty conclusions about a child. Pizzo says, "My own child has attended a day care program bruised from numerous falls or dressed improperly for the weather—and what I call clean, other people might surely label dirty!" (Pizzo, 1974, p. 2). Nevertheless, you are mandated to report *suspected* cases of abuse, and the things to look for are patterns of behavior, not one single characteristic. Each preschool program has a procedure for reporting suspected cases of child abuse. Familiarize yourself with this program. In most states, the local office of the Department of Child Welfare, part of the Department of Public Welfare, or Public Health, is the place to contact. Remember that your report is confidential, and no one will know who made the report (Pizzo, 1974, p. 2).

**GIFTED CHILDREN**   Children are gifted in different ways. Some may be gifted in getting along with other people or in leading others. Some may be highly intelligent or highly creative. Dorothy Sisk, head of the Gifted and Talented Program of the U.S. Office of Education, believes the gifted and talented are (Sisk, 1969):

1. The intellectually gifted, who are able to gather and use a great amount of knowledge on a broad range of subjects.
2. Those gifted in one academic area, for example, mathematics or science.
3. Creative-productive thinkers.
4. Those with leadership ability.
5. Those who are talented in the visual or performing arts.
6. Those with psychomotor or kinesthetic ability.

Identifying the gifted child is difficult, for all young children are growing and changing. What may seem like a special talent one day, appears the next as a spurt in maturation or development. Still, programs for the gifted and talented have been mandated, and you should be prepared to identify those children who are gifted or talented, and to plan appropriate educational experiences for them.

Sisk (1979) suggests that in identifying the gifted child three criteria can be used:

1. Standardized test results.
2. Anecdotal information—observations of teachers and others in regular contact with the child.
3. Committees making the final selections.

Once the gifted have been identified, special programs should be planned. There is no one right or wrong program for the gifted, nor any one right or wrong method for teaching them. "Teachers should value creative thinking and be flexible in their instruction. Good teachers of the gifted are comfortable with different ways of doing things" (Sisk, 1979, p. 528).

# IT'S UP TO YOU —————————————————————————————

Young children are a special breed, and it takes some time to get to know all young children, including those who have special needs. You must begin to develop an understanding of the nature of all young children, and be aware of the developmental stages all children pass through. With this information you can then begin to learn about children with special needs.

You may want to spend some time observing children of different ages and with different needs. Relate your observations to descriptions of child growth and development given in textbooks or in your classes. Try to think of children you have observed in the various stages of development. As you become aware of the different stages of child growth and development, begin to think about what this means for teachers.

A knowledge of young children, a true understanding of the nature of young children, is absolutely essential for all preschool teachers. With this information you can then go on to plan programs for all children, and to meet the needs of each child.

## REFERENCES

*Child Welfare League of America Standards for Day Care Service.* New York: Child Welfare League of America, 1966.

*Day Care: Serving Children with Special Needs.* Washington, D.C.: U.S. Department of Health, Education, and Welfare, Office of Child Development, 1972.

*Day Care: Serving Infants.* Washington, D.C.: U.S. Department of Health, Education, and Welfare, 1971.

Dickerson, M. G., and Davis, M. D. "Implications of P.L. 94-142 for Developmental Early Childhood Teacher Education Programs." *Young Children* 34 (1979): 28–32.

Elkind, D. *A Sympathetic Understanding of the Child.* 2d ed. Boston: Allyn & Bacon, 1978.

Fallen, N. H., and McGovern, J. E. *Young Children with Special Needs.* Columbus, Oh.: Charles E. Merrill Publishing Co., 1978.

Fontana, V. *Somewhere a Child is Crying.* New York: Macmillan Publishing Co., 1973.

Galinsky, E., and Hooks, W. H. *The New Extended Family: Day Care That Works.* New York: Houghton Mifflin Co., 1977.

Hildebrand, V. *Guiding Young Children.* New York: Macmillan Publishing Co., 1975.

Hymes, J. *Teaching the Child under Six.* 2d ed. Columbus, Oh.: Charles E. Merrill Publishing Co., 1974.

Pizzo, P. "Child Abuse and Day Care." *Voice for Children* 7 (1974): 1–3.

Public Law 94-142. The Education of All Handicapped Children Act. Washington, D.C., 1978.

Reynolds, M. C., and Birch, J. W. *Teaching Exceptional Children in All of America's Schools.* Reston, Va.: The Council for Exceptional Children, 1977.

Sisk, D. "Need for Gifted Programs." *Educational Leadership* 36 (1979): 527–28.

Willis, A., and Ricciuti, H. *A Good Beginning for Babies: Guidelines for Group Care.* Washington, D.C.: National Association for the Education of Young Children, 1975.

# RESOURCES

*Infant Care.* Department of Health, Education, and Welfare Publication No. Ohds 77-30015. Washington, D.C. 20402.

*Your Child from One to Six.* Department of Health, Education, and Welfare Publication No. Ohds 77-30026. Washington, D.C. 20402.

# PROJECTS

1. Observe an infant. Record the baby's responses to others and to things in the environment.

2. Observe preschoolers at play. Note how they relate with one another and how they use language to communicate with one another. What social and physical skills do they have? What skills are they just developing?

3. Observe in a preschool center serving children with special needs. Try to identify these children without the help of the teachers.

   Note:
   a. The physical adaptations in the room and play yard designed to meet the needs of the special children.
   b. How the special children interact with peers, and the reactions of peers to the children.

      c. How the teachers interact with the special children.

      d. Any special adaptations the teachers use when interacting with the special children.

4. Examine your own feelings about children with special needs. Did you ever know a person with a handicap? How did you feel about that person? Do you believe all children should have the opportunity to the same educational experiences? Why? Why not?

# THE PLAY
# OF THE
# YOUNG CHILD _____

## PART THREE

All curricula for young children must be centered in their play activities; the play of the infant and the child is of utmost educational value. Young children require freedom and time to play, indoor and outdoor space to play in, and things to play with. Play is essential for the development of cognitive structures in the child, establishing a pattern of learning how to learn. Play provides the opportunity for the child to learn about himself and his world. It fosters the child's sense of personal worth and dignity while he is developing self-control, social skills, and responsibility for his actions.

# INDOOR PLAY _____

*Play is the way the child learns what none can teach him. It is the way he explores and orientates himself to the actual world of space and time, of things, animals, structures and people.*
*(Frank, 1957, p. viii)*

When is the young child learning? Must he be sitting still at a desk or table? Do children learn with pencil and paper? Or do they learn while running down a hill, flying a kite, collecting acorns in a cup, or splashing with water? Young children must play in order to learn. No other activity is as valuable to the young child. A curriculum that limits the time the child spends in play is one that limits the child's opportunities to learn.

*Children are always learning.*

Play, in our culture, has often been thought of as unproductive and unrelated to intellectual pursuits—something that should be reserved for after school or work. For the young child, however, play *is* work. The 1930 White House Conference on Child Health and Protection concluded that "with the young child, his work is his play and his play is his work" (Ritchie & Marvin, 1954, p. 206).

There is now clear evidence to support the theory that the play of the child is, indeed, his work—a very necessary type of work. Play fosters the total development of the child and is intimately related to his intellectual and cognitive growth and development. Piaget closely binds the play of the child to the growth of intelligence. He indicates that play provides the child the means for practicing and consolidating all he knows. Play, he believes, leads the child to question his concepts of reality (which are often inaccurate concepts), and to rethink them, revising them to fit reality (Piaget, 1962).

Children do learn while they play. They learn what the world is like, what will happen when sand is mixed with water, how leaves feel, and what turns the wheels on their bike. They find out about themselves and their capabilities. They can paint a picture, read a book, climb a fence, string beads, or put a puzzle together. They learn what it might be like to be an adult, dressing up and assuming the role of mother, father, or teacher; or what it would be like to be a baby again, completely dependent on someone bigger than they. Children learn to carry out their plans and ideas through play.

## PLAY IS COGNITIVE

Play begins in a child's sensory impressions of her environment and continues, as she grows, to be based on active sensory experiences. In order for the child to generalize, to form a concept, she must have related perceptual experiences. As she uses her senses to touch, taste, hear, and smell, she is accumulating a background of perceptual experiences which will, in turn, form the foundations of concepts.

Russell suggests that a child has more basis for understanding the facts of her environment and generalizing about these facts in the form of concepts if she has had abundant sensory experiences—touching, tasting, feeling, climbing, breaking, reaching, twisting, kicking, and getting hurt (Russell, 1956).

Play with objects, mud, water, or sand provides the opportunity for children to develop concepts of weight and volume. Playing with blocks fosters concepts of number, balance, and shape. Piaget believes that the child's growing "awareness that objects have many properties, that they can be viewed along different dimensions, and that they can be classified in a variety of ways" is a product of the child's activity with them (Almy, 1968, p. 345). Through activity with objects—"touching, lifting, holding, arranging, sorting, and so on—the child begins to take note of similarities among the objects he encounters. In like fashion, he comes to pay attention to differences in objects that are alike in some respects and different in others," (Almy, 1968, p. 354). In these activities, Piaget sees the beginnings of true conceptual thinking.

## PLAY IS RICH WITH LANGUAGE

The playing child is a verbal child. Children often talk to themselves or others during play. They sing, hum, chatter, and make up nonsense rhymes. Frequently, they use words in connection with experiences, naming the objects they play with. In this way, words help to order experiences and build a framework for future references. As children grow, communication with other children becomes necessary. As nonverbal communication is limiting and inefficient, words must be utilized for full understanding to take place.

Playing together, children must find a way to communicate their ideas, gain the cooperation of others, and respond, in turn, to the ideas of others. Children under pressure to speak in order to be able to play with other children quickly develop the necessary language.

## PLAY IS EXPERIMENTING AND EXPLORING

To the young child, a great many stimuli are genuinely new and attractive, and he explores these stimuli through play.

Infants play with sunbeams and shadows in attempts to comprehend them, just as toddlers play with dirt and water in order to learn about their world.

Children try things out as they play, making mistakes, learning for themselves. Turning the wheel on an upside-down bike around and around, the child forms initial concepts of wheels and axles, and if the child notices a bike rolling down a hill by itself, he may spend the next hour finding out how many other things will roll down the hill by themselves. Through play, children can explore their world, finding out how it works.

PLAY IS RICH IN SYMBOLISM    Make-believe play, or symbolic play, is highly cognitive. In symbolic play, children form images which they hold in their minds throughout the play activity. A block may become a truck or a child may become the mother or father until the play activity has terminated. Sutton-Smith sees the child's symbolic play as possibly encouraging cognitive growth.

> Beginning with the representational play of two year olds, there develops a deliberate adoption of an "as if" attitude towards play objects and events. The child having such an attitude continues to "conserve" imaginative identities throughout the play in spite of contraindicative stimuli. This cognitive competence is observable both in solitary play, social games, and in the children's appreciation of imaginative stories, yet it is not until five to seven years of age that children can conserve the class identities of such phenomena as number, quantity, space and the like, despite contraindicative stimuli (Sutton-Smith, 1967, p. 360).

Children, engaged in symbolic or dramatic play, are also highly verbal. They use language to elaborate their symbolism: "You be the daddy. Now pretend this is your razor. I'll pretend to be the mother, but you can't come in until you ring the bell." This language adds to the cognitive value of symbolic play.

PLAY IS CREATIVE    All through the child's play, imagination and creative responses are prevalent. Especially in dramatic play, the child imagines complex themes, creating adventures, real-life roles, and situations. As she works with materials—playing with clay, mud, wood, paint, and paper—the child begins to create products.

Problems are solved creatively during the child's play. How will the mother act? How can this material be used? How can these bars be climbed? And since it's only play, the child can risk the new and unknown, making mistakes if necessary.

# INDOOR SPACES

"Play is the heart of the nursery school curriculum" (Read, 1966, p. 63). Play is also the heart of the curriculum in any preschool. Children need sufficient time, space, and an abundance of materials. Most authorities indicate that from forty-five to fifty square feet of indoor space per child is desirable (Hymes, 1974, p. 38). The more space available, the more possibilities for children's play and learning.

The physical environment of the school influences the type of program that is possible, as well as the behavior of the staff. When spaces are limited and children crowded into a small room, you may tend to become more restrictive of children's choices and their play (Prescott & Jones, 1971). Children, themselves, when crowded together, tend to argue more, are more aggressive, and engage in fights more frequently.

Ideally, each playroom should provide the means for a variety of learning experiences, room for large- as well as small-muscle activity, and have its own bathroom and water source. When playrooms open up to the out-of-doors, activities can be extended outside. Routines—eating, resting, napping—when conducted in the child's own playroom, are less frustrating and produce less tension.

When adequate spaces are not available, you can build, even from the most meager physical facility, a world in which young children can play freely. Realizing that a stationary, circular bamboo bar in the middle of a playroom in a Head Start center located in an abandoned resort hotel would require extensive renovation procedures to remove, the teacher decided to make the most of it by turning it into an attractive library room. The inside of the bar became the "library" with a carpet scrap covering the floor and makeshift shelves lining the inside walls. A rocking chair, a table, and a few small chairs completed the inside. The top of the bar, much too high for the children to reach, became the teacher's desk where her records and papers were kept, and the outside of the bar, dominating the room, became a wall for displaying the children's artwork.

Another teacher, extremely short on space, designed a pulley system for drying children's paintings. A rope, attached to a pulley, was lowered to the center of the room and children clipped their wet paintings to it. When the space was required for the next activity, the pulley was raised, and the paintings were lifted to the top of the room for drying.

Top spaces were used effectively at one preschool. The teacher securely attached long ropes and wide long ribbons to the ceiling of the room. One of the ropes, which extended down to the children's reach, was used in the housekeeping area. An assortment of hats—army, navy, flowered—were clipped to the rope with clothespins. Another rope, in the manipulative game area, held cellophane bags of matching materials, and one in the library area was used to display attractive book covers and art prints. These ropes allowed the teacher to provide additional materials for the children without taking up valuable floor space.

## FURNITURE

Young children need little in the way of stationary furniture. When space is limited, the situation is improved by removing as much furniture as possible. Children, who often play on the floor and move around the room freely, rarely need to be seated at the same time. If lunch is served in the room, folding tables can be set up and chairs brought in. Cots for sleeping can be chosen for their folding and stacking qualities. There is no need for a teacher's desk in any playroom.

Furniture selected for a playroom for young children should have flexibility of use. A shelf can be used as a divider as well as a storage area; a table can be a puppet stage when turned on its side. One teacher found that an old upright piano covered with a cardboard sheet served as a room divider, a space for displaying pictures, as well as a musical instrument.

When space is limited, you can rotate furniture, removing some pieces as they lose appeal and adding those that challenge the children or meet their new play interests. Tucking storage shelves against the walls, under windows, or placing them back to back, and arranging the furniture in the room to allow the most space for children's free play can help to maximize the amount of space available.

Children with special needs may require different types of furniture. Children who are visually impaired or blind may need to have the furniture in the playroom remain in the same place, so they can develop a sense of security and learn their way around. The use of textures on the furniture, floor, and walls can also aid the visually impaired child to orientate herself in space (*Day Care: Serving Children with Special Needs,* 1972).

Children with physical impairments may require that the room be equipped with wheelchair ramps, handrails and nonslip floor coverings. Special chairs, benches, or step platforms might be arranged for children with specific physical handicaps.

Good housekeeping practices are necessary when space is limited. Young children should be able to take at least partial responsibility for materials and toys in the room, as well as for their own belongings. Shelves, tables, chairs, and other furniture should be selected to permit the children to handle it themselves. Furniture should be appropriately sized for the children, and they should be able to work doors on cabinets. A cubbyhole, shelf, or some place in the room for each child to place his personal belongings is desirable.

## PLATFORMS

Evans describes the use of platforms in a small room to expand space. A raised platform offers visual variety and provides two levels for activity. The space under the platform can be utilized for storage (Evans et al., 1971). Adding platforms to the room reduces the children's need for large-muscle activity; the very act of getting up on and climbing down from a platform requires release of energy. Children enjoy housekeeping, water play, office play, and other special activities on a platform.

## ROUTINES

In coping with limited space, you will have to analyze your routine. How could the group be subdivided? Could the children play outdoors more often? Would a change in scheduling allow for more space? Would additional staff members or volunteers help or hinder the situation?

## LARGE ROOMS

How wonderful to have a large room! Yet an oversized room for young children can present problems. If you have a large room, you must decide how best to divide the space in order to build closure for certain activities. One part of the room could be equipped with large-muscle toys, blocks, wheel toys, and boxes. Other furniture within the room could be arranged to close off areas for quiet play.

## ———————————————————————————————— INFANTS

Infants play! And infant play is essential to the development of a healthy, intelligent child. Until around the third or fourth month of life, when the infant's eye-hand coordination is developed enough for her to reach and grasp an object, play consists of looking. Individual babies, of course, react differently to visual stimulation; however, it has been reported that infants as young as two weeks of age do respond to visual patterns (Stechler, 1964).

The nursery room of a preschool can provide the visual stimulation that babies require. Ideally, the nursery is located in a quiet area of the school, away from the activity areas and traffic patterns. It is an attractive, bright, cheerful, and relaxed room. Cribs are arranged informally, rather than lined up institutionally against one wall, and there are no more than five or six cribs in any one room. Rocking chairs, either brightly painted or covered with interesting and colorful cushions, invite the adults to relax.

Printed crib sheets, safely constructed mobiles above each crib, and pictures on the wall are all a part of the nursery room. Other visual stimulation is provided by the older children's artwork on the walls, flower arrangements, dry seed pods, and living green plants on table tops.

Mobiles, hung above cribs or from light fixtures, can be easily made from magazine pictures, scraps of material, old costume jewelry, or other interesting household items tied to a clothes hanger with a string. A shiny aluminum pie pan, aluminum foil, or bright paper crushed into a ball and hung where it can twist and turn in the breeze will also catch a baby's eye and amuse her for many hours.

Perhaps the most stimulating sight for the baby is the face of her mother or nursery attendant, for this face responds to her actions—it means comfort, food, and attention. While dressing, changing, or feeding the baby, coo, talk, hum, and sing, thereby offering the baby sounds as well as something to see.

Infants also play with themselves and become intrigued with the sight of their own hands waving in front of their eyes. By the third or fourth month of life, the baby begins swiping with his hands at hanging rattles, glasses, her mother's hair, or at any other object that catches her eye. Now, objects and things take on increasingly important roles in the infant's play.

Between the ages of four and seven months, the infant can handle an object, shake things, bang them, and put them in her mouth. At around eleven or twelve months she becomes aware of objects and things as separate from herself. Before this, when an object disappeared from the child's sight, it ceased to exist for her. Now, she begins to look to see where the object has gone and to anticipate its return. Realizing that objects and things are independent of herself, the baby is appreciative of her ability to act on them.

Objects and toys for infants to play with must be carefully selected to insure safety. Toys should be checked for any possible removable parts, sharp edges, or anything that might be dangerous when mouthed by the baby. The toys should be washable, for the child finds out about her world by putting everything she reaches into her mouth. Many household items can be used as toys if they are safe for the baby to touch, bite, cuddle, chew, or throw.

Infants also need objects and toys that promote their discovery of casual relationships. Toys that offer a variety of textures, shapes, and colors are important. Something soft can be made from a piece of terry cloth or a sponge that is soft yet sturdy enough not to be eaten. Pieces of netting tied together to form a puff ball give the baby something rough to work with. Something smooth could be an empty juice can with no sharp edges, or a set of inexpensive plastic bracelets. Round shapes could be empty wooden spools, and rectangular items could be discarded plastic containers, boxes, or clean pint milk cartons.

Cradle gyms, either commercial or put together with scrap materials, are excellent toys for the young baby. A satisfactory cradle gym can be constructed from discarded wooden spools, bracelets, an assortment of plastic beads, or other objects securely suspended on a piece of strong elastic which is hung across the crib. The older baby, six months of age or so, is able to grasp and pull at the gym; thus all objects must be safe for her manipulation and securely attached to the elastic.

The older baby is capable of combining objects and toys in her play. She can be presented with a block inside of a box, or a box with tissue paper inside, provided you watch the baby closely so that no paper gets eaten. Several objects can be placed in a plastic dish, box, bowl, or bucket for banging together and for taking in and out. Occasionally a baby's toy can be loosely wrapped in paper and placed in front of her. She will delight in unwrapping the package and finding her toy. This activity fosters the baby's memory of the toy, even when wrapped and out of her sight, and encourages her problem-solving skills of getting the paper off the toy. Nesting toys can be made from discarded boxes covered with washable plastic paper, empty boxes with lids, pie pans, coffee pots and glass parts and sharp metal parts removed, or plastic reels from tape dispensers.

All of the baby's senses are involved as she learns about the world through her play. Toys that stimulate listening should be found in the nursery room. Rattles, either purchased or constructed from empty containers with a bit of rattle material inside and securely taped closed, give the baby something to hold, shake, and listen to. Wind chimes, music boxes, a string of bells hung where the breeze can blow them, old keys tied together, or an empty spice box containing a few marbles, beans, or rice also make lovely sounds for the baby.

A wall mirror, close to the floor, allows the baby to play with her reflection after she has learned to crawl or raise her head while on her stomach. Other mirrors, higher on the walls, can be provided for you to hold the baby up to, allowing her to play while being held. A mirror that is attached to the baby's crib, and safe hand mirrors for the sitting-up baby to handle and play with can also be provided. Mirrors near dressing tables give babies the pleasure of watching themselves being dressed or bathed. You can begin to see when the baby recognizes herself by asking "Where's the baby?" "Do you see Carmen?" or "Pat the baby." "Find your ears, nose, mouth." What better way can a child begin to learn who she is, what she can do, and what she looks like than by playing in front of a mirror with someone close to her!

Babies play and learn by touching and feeling. They first learn by touching themselves—pulling on their toes, tasting them, finding their fingers and hands. Later, babies want to touch others—pulling their hair, poking at eyes and glasses. Water play gives babies another experience in touching and learning about their environment. They can be bathed in a small tub with a very small amount of warm water. Older babies enjoy splashing in the water, feeling it, hitting it with their hands, and kicking it with their feet. A squirt of mild soap suds can be added occasionally. Floating objects such as rubber toys and rings enhance bath time. Older babies should be given time to splash in water more frequently than just at bath time.

The six to nine month old is quite active and needs space in which to safely crawl, creep, and explore. Eventually, she will require pieces of stationary furniture on which to pull herself to an upright position. Before a year, some children are extremely mobile—able to walk by clinging to furniture, able to climb on top of things, and able to crawl away with lightning speed to get something interesting. Provision for these capabilities within the nursery playroom must be made.

Bounce chairs, canvas swing seats, playpens, and baby seats are useful and effective additions to the baby room. The older baby, for short periods of time, enjoys being free to creep, crawl, and pull herself up on something. She also enjoys the safety of the playpen and takes pleasure in being able to sit in a swing or chair where she can observe the activity of others.

Babies should periodically be taken from the nursery room to other areas of the center. Very young infants can be carried, while older babies can be taken in strollers to observe other children at play. One center put a baby in a seat inside a playpen in the toddler or preschool room. This procedure allowed the baby the pleasure of observing older children, the older children the learning experience of watching a baby, and kept the baby far enough away from the curious reach of the toddlers.

Infants in Israel are exposed to a greater variety of stimuli in the kibbutz than those infants raised in conventional settings. In a typical day, the kibbutz infants see more people and are moved about more than are other children. An infant who spends many hours watching others at play and work, the kibbutz teachers claim, does not need exciting mobiles and toys to "stimulate" her (Gewirtz, 1971).

The infant room of a center, as every other playroom, must be designed to meet the individual needs of each baby. Therefore, the room should be suffi-ciently large and planned with an eye toward flexibility. Some babies want to be held and cuddled for long periods of time; others enjoy the challenge of being placed on a blanket on the floor where they can try to raise their heads, roll over, and see the world from a different angle. Some babies like to sleep

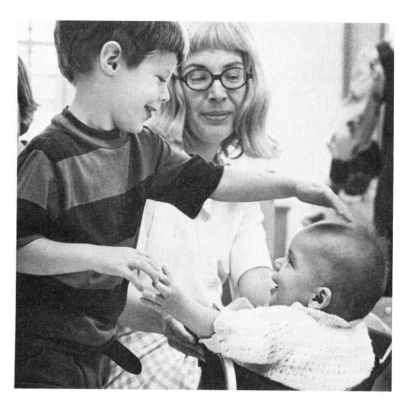

*Babies should be allowed the pleasure of seeing other children.*

under a blanket; others kick off coverings. Some babies are awake for long periods of time; others sleep the day away. Some babies enjoy being near the bustling sounds and sights of other children and adults; others need to be alone in a quiet, serene atmosphere. (Moveable screens can fence off the world for these babies when necessary.) You must be able to meet the needs of each individual baby while structuring an attractive, interesting, and comfortable room for her to play in.

# TODDLERS _____

From the time the baby can walk, until around three years of age, he is often considered a toddler. Highly mobile, the toddler is still unsteady in certain physical aspects, unsure of social skills, and inexperienced in communicating. Toddlers are rambunctious, totally active, curious, and surprisingly quick. They need playrooms where they can safely experiment with their world, using their rapidly developing physical, social, and intellectual skills.

The toddler must be free to use all of his senses as he plays. He cannot be restricted to a playpen or even to one playroom. The entire center, the yard, and even the neighborhood become his playroom. Explorative play abounds as he seeks to learn more about things and how things will react to his actions. He explores the properties of objects and their uses. Blocks are piled up and knocked down over and over again; sand, mud, and water are played with for hours on end. The toddler continues to explore his own body, and his mother's or teacher's body, with concentration. Perhaps this interest in the body accounts for the appeal of games like "peek-a-boo," "where's baby," and "so big."

Motor development, with new skills emerging daily, necessitates the toddler's physical, active play. Equipment and space for large-muscle activity must be a part of the toddler room. Wooden and cardboard boxes give the children something to push and pull and get in and out of. Rocking boats and free-standing stairs, either commercial or homemade, are useful. Wooden planks, in connection with the boxes and stairs, can be arranged to form a type of bridge for the toddlers to crawl under or jump across. Cutting the ends from grocery cartons and placing them in a row provides a tunnel for the children to crawl through or play in. When space permits, wheeled toys can also be used inside. Large wooden trucks, airplanes, and cars, or a wooden, bench-type stool with casters can be sat on and pushed around the room.

Something to climb on is also important in the toddler room. Climbing frames can be purchased, or climbing gates and units constructed. Certain pieces of old furniture such as tables, chests, or chairs might be safe as a climbing apparatus. A blanket over a card table or clothesline is something else to crawl in and out of. Old tires, arranged in a row on the floor, make stepping stones for the children to cross. Much of this large-muscle equipment can be stored on a porch or in the hallway and brought into the room when active play is taking place.

Toddlers seem to enjoy pulling something in back of them. Oatmeal cartons, spools, or shoe boxes attached to strings or ropes make excellent pull toys for these children. Small wagons, doll carriages, and strollers for the children to push or pull can be included.

The use of small muscles during play is also essential in the toddler's development. Unit blocks, nesting blocks, small cardboard boxes, and pieces of wood for building foster the use of small muscles. Art materials are a must. Paper and crayons to draw with, modeling materials, and painting equipment will be put to good use in the toddler playroom.

Using a shoe box and some old-fashioned, wooden clothespins, demonstrate to the toddler the art of placing the clothespins around the edge of the box; this activity can keep a toddler occupied while giving his small muscles exercise. A button box, with buttons too large to be stuffed in ears or noses, or a box of nuts and bolts both encourage small-muscle development as do peg-boards, large beads to string, and small blocks. Discarded paper towel tubes of various sizes, jar lids of different sizes, and spools and plastic cups and dishes are also handled and sorted by the toddler with pleasure.

Extremely simple puzzles can be completed by the older toddler. If appropriate puzzles are not purchasable, they can be easily constructed from heavy cardboard. A single circle, square, triangle, or other shape that is cut from a frame is enough of a puzzle for the young child. Shape boxes, with the shape of a circle, triangle, rectangle, or square on each side of the box, and blocks or

*The toddler uses all her senses as she plays.*

cardboard pieces matching the cut-out shapes, is another type of puzzle. The child matches the solid form to the shape of the hole in the box and drops the solid form into the box.

Many books, magazines, and pictures belong in the toddler room. Books illustrating the baby's day or a single concept, such as a number book, animal book, or book of boats should be provided, as well as a place in which to read them. Toddlers often fall in love with tiny books, such as the original Peter Rabbit books, that they can carry around tucked in their pockets or hand while playing house or store.

Water and sand play should be available indoors on a daily basis. A dishpan on a chair is all that is really necessary for water play. However, a water table, with room for more children, is preferable. Plastic aprons keep the children from becoming too soaked as they pour and splash in water. Sand play, with dry or wet sand, can be offered to the children in a discarded plastic wading pool or large dishpan. Empty plastic containers, spoons, and boxes are added to the sand and water.

Mechanical things fascinate the toddler. A busy box with locks and keys, door knobs, light switches, hooks and eyes, and chains and bolts attached to it is of constant interest. An instrument panel with knobs and switches to turn on and off can sometimes be found in a junk store or town dump.

Although toddlers enjoy being with one another and need each other's company, they are not yet able to play *with* one another. They often treat one another as objects—tasting, biting, pulling, or pushing. Even though toddlers essentially play alone, the room should be large enough for a small group of them to play side by side or to work together on the same activity.

Toddlers are searching for autonomy and must be allowed to do things for themselves. They should be free to explore and find out about their world safely. Arranging a toddlerproof room with sturdy furniture and unbreakable toys and equipment allows children the opportunity to explore independently, with a minimum of adult restrictions and interference. Even when materials and equipment are selected for safety, durability, and flexibility, however, the toddlers need close adult supervision to protect them from danger.

Space for the young child to hang up his own clothes—coats, sweaters, aprons—with hooks low enough to reach, fosters his sense of autonomy. Toddler-sized washstands or small benches at the sinks permit the children to reach the faucets easily. They can then take major responsibility for washing themselves, paint brushes, or other equipment.

If at all possible, the toddler playroom should be large enough for many play activities to take place at the same time. Space for several art activities, for a few pieces of large-muscle equipment, an open floor space for active block play, and room for table activities should be available. Toddlers will be more comfortable, and routines eased, if eating and sleeping can take place in the playroom.

Introducing language as the children play, helping them through difficult social situations, and challenging them with new equipment and ideas, you are the most important resource in the toddler's playroom. Help children use language to relate to one another: "If you ask for the shovel instead of grabbing it, John will give it to you." Or, "Tell her you would like to play with the truck." As the toddler strings beads, count the number of beads on the string; while he is painting, name the colors he is using; and when children are playing in a box, add the words "in" and "out" to their play. You must also meet the individual needs of each young child in the playroom.

# PRESCHOOLERS

The preschoolers' rooms are resplendent with a wide variety of materials, supplies, and equipment. Now, the children need space to begin to learn to play cooperatively, to construct large, complex block buildings, or to play house, office, store, and post office with several other friends. The wider world of the community, neighbors, mathematics, science, and literature assume greater importance to the preschooler. Centers of interest, flexible and ever-changing with materials openly displayed, invite children to try things for themselves.

**CENTERS OF INTEREST** Efficient and effective use of space in a preschool usually results when each playroom is organized into centers of interest. Centers of interest are areas of the room that are clearly defined with either actual dividers or suggested boundaries. They contain materials and equipment organized to promote certain types of play—creative, dramatic, or manipulative—and provide a balance between quiet and active, solitary and group play. Centers of interest, in ordering the play environment, foster children's involvement in their play and encourage them to work at an activity for the maximum length of time with minimum distraction and interference from children engaging in other activities.

Children's decision making is encouraged, for a room with choices clarified by centers of interest demands that children select for themselves the area in which they want to play and then decide when they wish to move on to another center. Children also participate in deciding which centers to include in the room. Their interest in a restaurant, for example, may be demonstrated by their playing restaurant at a table. Picking up on this interest, you can provide tablets and pencils with which to write orders, dishes, a tablecloth, or a check-out counter.

Although each school contains toys, materials, and equipment selected to foster certain types of play, all centers should be flexible. Children may combine two centers, such as the housekeeping area and the store, or the block and the wheel-toy area, moving furniture and equipment to create new centers of interest.

Playrooms for any age child may be organized into centers, for each age group profits from an orderly environment. Children who will be spending four or more years in the same center will demand new, increasingly complex centers and challenges each year. A block center, with simple square and rectangular blocks for the two year olds can be extended to include road maps, cars, blocks of more varied shapes, and road signs for the five year olds. The housekeeping area for the fives may include paper and pencils, shopping lists, newspapers, and magazines, while the same area for the threes could be limited to kitchen and dress-up equipment.

Clearly delineated areas lead to organized, meaningful play. Centers of interest that are arranged with concern for traffic patterns help to negate the need for discipline. Locating the housekeeping and art areas near the water source allows children to wash a brush or obtain water without traveling the length of the room, dripping water or paint on others as they go. If the place for block building is out of the way of other children, block structures are less likely to be knocked over, limiting arguments over who knocked over what.

The library corner and the manipulative-toy area, in which quiet activities are pursued, should be grouped together; the areas requiring more active, noisy responses, such as the block and woodworking centers, should be located in another part of the room.

A variety of dividers has been utilized in nursery schools and preschools to define areas of play. Low, moveable shelves, extended from the wall instead of against it, store materials for the center while forming a boundary. Tables, cabinets, or other furniture may define specific areas. Low, folding screens may be purchased or two pieces of cardboard, joined together, may serve as a folding screen to set off one area of the room.

Temporary dividers may be constructed from brown kraft paper wrapped around two discarded wrapping-paper rolls: the cardboard rolls are planted in gravel-filled coffee cans or set in plaster of paris. This temporary divider forms an acceptable visual screen that can be carried to any part of the room. Pictures and props can be mounted on it, and it can be discarded or replaced with ease.

Brown kraft paper or a discarded sheet, tacked into a corner of the room, creates a space for a house, store, or post office. Large cardboard packing boxes serve equally as well as a "store" while blocking off other areas of the room. Smaller cardboard boxes can be stacked to form a wall with the open side serving as cubbies and the other side as a wall divider.

Centers can be frequently changed, especially where space is in demand, with not every center available all of the time. Some can be removed as children lose interest in them and others added to offer the children new and challenging learning opportunities. Some centers, although changing in complexity, should always be present. These include an area for construction (including art materials and woodworking), for science activities, for block building, and for manipulative types of equipment and games. Housekeeping and library areas should also be continually present.

*Art activities are always available.*

## Art Center

Perhaps the most popular area, the art center of interest provides a variety of materials with which the children can experiment, explore, and create. Each day the children should have a choice of whether to draw, paint, model, or cut and paste. At every age level, self-selection of art materials is desirable.

Materials are arranged on tables or low shelves that are easily accessible to the children. Painting easels are complete with fresh paints, a variety of brushes, and paper. All types of drawing materials—crayons, marking pens, chalk, even pencils for five-year-old children—are stored on open shelves for children's selection. A junk box, with every type of material imaginable, is often kept in the art center. Clay and other modeling materials should be available.

Scissors, including left-handed scissors, can be stored point down in empty egg cartons. Several types of paste should be available—the strong white glue in squeeze bottles, library paste in individual plastic jars, and even mucilage. They are all used by young children in a variety of art projects.

Art activities often spread out over several tables, the floor, the wall, and easels. All painting activities should be located near a water source if possible. Clay, when oilcloth-covered boards are handy, can be taken anywhere in the room. Crayons, or cut-and-paste materials can be arranged on any table or floor space.

## Library Area

A center of activity and excitement, the library corner includes more than a shelf of books. It is an area where there are many things to do (including reading books) and beautiful things to see. It should be located away from possible distractions and be separated in some way from the other activities. Every library center should have provisions for bookshelves and at least one table and

*Dramatic play flourishes.*

a few chairs. In an overcrowded room, you may substitute pillows, sample carpet squares, small footstools, or discarded nail kegs for chairs. If space permits, a small rocking chair adds appeal to the library area.

A wide variety of children's books selected to meet the needs of the particular group of children is available. Some of these can be displayed standing on a table, others on the library shelves. Any arrangement of books that makes them difficult to see and select should be avoided. In addition to the usual selection of children's books, some old catalogs (seed, flower, auto, toy), newspapers, and picture news magazines should be provided.

Even the two-year-old children enjoy "wishing" through a catalog, naming the items they see. The four and five year olds play games with catalogs: "I'm looking at a toy in my catalog. It's red, and rides." The other child tries to find it in her catalog, or guess what toy or object the child is looking at.

Homemade books, books of stories dictated by the children, photograph albums, and stories you write about the children or events at the center are always favorites. Pictures cut from used books or magazines and placed on the library table encourage the children's language development. When children are able to spread the pictures out on the floor or carry them around with them, the pictures are discussed and matching, sequencing, and guessing games often evolve.

Some preschools are fortunate to have listening stations or tape recorders with listening earphones attached. Favorite stories can be taped for individual children to listen to while turning the pages of a book.

*Playing in the kitchen is fun.*

Flannel boards with cutout figures representing story characters, puppets, and other story props are also found in the library area. On one library table, a branding iron surrounded with books on cowboys stimulated the children to find a picture of a branding iron and someone to read about branding to them.

Five year olds begin to utilize reference books and materials. Although a complete set of encyclopedias need not dominate a library area, a central library within the school, serving all of the children and teachers, should contain at least one set. Dictionaries and other reference books should be available. Occasionally, specific reference books from the center library can be selected for use in individual playrooms. Picture dictionaries, useful for naming items and fostering vocabulary development, should be in each playroom.

Selected books that belong to the preschool may be organized as a take-home library for the children. A simple check-out sheet can be mounted above the books with a black and a red crayon attached. The children can place a check by their name in red when they take out a book, and a check in black when they return it.

Children should be free to take the library books wherever they wish. They might take them outside to read under a tree, or in the housekeeping area to read to a doll. The library should be recognized as a treasured area of the playroom. Children should never be exiled to the library for having done something wrong; those with no particular goal in mind for their work should not be told, "Well, why don't you just go and read a book if you have nothing better to do?" Rather, the library area should be reserved for quiet reading, thinking, listening, and discussion and sharing of ideas.

## Housekeeping Area

The dress-up corner, doll corner, housekeeping area—whatever its name—the children find this area of the playroom continually appealing. It is here that dramatic play flourishes, and here the children find a link between their home and their preschool. Children are free to find out how it would feel to be the teacher, doctor, or parent; they explore the roles they may one day assume. As each housekeeping area should be representative of the homes of the children, housekeeping areas may vary according to the region and culture of the neighborhood.

Keeping a variety of hats (soldier, sailor, fireman, delivery man), ties, and a man's jacket or two with the sleeves rolled into cuffs could motivate boys to participate in housekeeping play along with the girls. Discarded electric shavers, a razor without blades, and empty cans of shaving cream receive a great deal of attention from boys. Some of the props in the housekeeping area should reflect the world of work: briefcases, felt hats, hard hats, metal lunch boxes, tool chests (complete with assorted pipe wrenches and other tools), canvas tool aprons, and large rubber boots all add to the complexity of the play.

Vocational aspirations can be fostered in the housekeeping area by providing props suggesting various occupations. Firefighter props may be of interest after a visit to the fire station. If a plumber visits the preschool and the children observe him work, representative tools can help them reenact the plumber's work later.

Furniture for the housekeeping center can be purchased or constructed from heavy cardboard boxes, wooden crates, and odds and ends. The usual equipment includes the kitchen with table, chairs, stove, cabinet, sink, and refrigerator; the living room with sofas, chairs, end tables, and magazines; and the bedroom with dressers and a bed. A variety of sturdy dolls of all sizes and representing the ethnic characteristics of the children, doll clothes, and some doll furniture should be available.

A trip to the local junk shop, Goodwill, or thrift sale furnishes the housekeeping corner beautifully. Parents and neighbors are often willing to donate their discarded items for this area of the children's playroom. Pots and pans, egg beaters, dishpans, coffee pots, measuring spoons, cups and saucers, tablecloths, irons, and broken radios can be obtained through donations or for very little cost. Broken alarm clocks, toasters, sweepers, and other "real" items can be processed to remove potentially dangerous parts.

Dress-up clothes are also easily obtained without expense. A lacy half-slip with an elastic band is just right for going to a formal dance, having a wedding, or becoming a queen; and a piece of lace curtain can be a tablecloth, veil, or queen's train. Hats, purses, wallets, shoes without high heels, earrings, and jewelry complete the outfits. Clothing and apparel of the culture of the families should be included.

Water play is one activity that should be allowed in the housekeeping area. Small dishpans can hold soapy water for washing dishes and pitchers can hold water for "cooking." If water is not readily available in the housekeeping area, children are very ingenious in secreting it to their play kitchen. When provisions are made for water play, you can assume control and keep mess at a minimum.

At the University of Maryland's Center for Young Children, five year olds actually cook in the housekeeping area. Simple recipes, with words and illustrations, along with the appropriate food items, are kept in the housekeeping area.

Although various types of clothing have been suggested for the boys and girls in the housekeeping area, both boys and girls will want to try out the role of mother and father, regardless of their sex.

Caring for children and the home is appropriate for both males and females. Many times, boys whose parents object to their playing with dolls or dressing up find the freedom to try these things out in the preschool; consequently, they spend a great portion of their time in the housekeeping area.

The housekeeping area can be conveniently located anywhere in the room. A corner provides the feeling of closure for the children, or low shelves or a rack of clothing can suggest separation; however, the area should be open enough so that you can observe and supervise the children's play. Children often extend their housekeeping play to other parts of the room, leaving for work or shopping, or continuing the play theme out of doors or in the "store."

## Manipulative Area

Sometimes thought of as the area for cognitive development in which educational types of materials are housed, the manipulative game area is of high value and interest to the young child. In this area you can arrange pegboards, nesting blocks, beads, puzzles, table games, and other small-muscle equipment and materials. Number concepts, shape and size concepts, abstract reasoning, observational skills, language, and attention span are strengthened through the games and materials found in the manipulative area.

Each age group should have a variety of items in this area providing stimulation and challenge commensurate with the developmental level. Games should be arranged for easy access to the children. If space is limited, you can use a rotation system in displaying the materials so that children are given the experience of all types of equipment.

Even the two year olds can be given responsibility for caring for the manipulative toys. All of the children can take care of puzzle pieces and keep game parts together. Pegs should be kept with pegboards and dominoes stored in their box. As children see the adults around them caring for equipment, picking up puzzle pieces, and keeping things in order, they tend to copy these behaviors.

Single-concept wooden puzzles, such as the items used to set a table or four pieces of fruit, are advisable for the younger children. Wooden puzzles of increased complexity, both in number of pieces and in design, are challenging to the older preschool children. Various levels of development found within any age group necessitate a selection of puzzles covering a wide range of difficulty. Puzzles made of foam rubber, plastic, or heavy cardboard are also appropriate in this area. The fives, as they approach their sixth birthday, may begin to enjoy cardboard puzzles of twenty to fifty pieces.

Pegboards are useful for almost every age group. They can be purchased or made from acoustical tiles. Providing a box of rubber bands with the pegboards invites children to wind the bands around the pegs to form designs and exercise small-muscle control. Older children may enjoy a set of cards, each with a pictured design of pegs on it, to copy as they work with pegs.

Construction sets, small plastic blocks, wooden blocks or tiles, Tinker toys, and erector sets should be available. Children build or play other games with the bright colorful pieces.

A few sets of regular decks of cards offer the young children many manipulative and mathematical experiences. Cards can be sorted by the children into a black and a red pile, according to number or suit. Children may also take the cards into the housekeeping area to play with.

Materials for sorting and classification should also be placed in the manipulative area of the room. Things to string—beads, macaroni, washers, and bottle caps with holes in them—and shoestrings, pipe cleaners, and other things to string things on can also be found in the game area.

Fours and fives may be ready to begin to play simple table games, either by themselves or with adults. Commercially available games such as "Candy Land," "Cherry Tree," or "Chutes and Ladders" offer experience in counting and facilitate learning to cooperate as a group. The children may not be interested in the rules that come with the game; they make up their own rules as they go along. You may introduce games to the children, showing them the main idea or theme, and may occasionally play the game with the children.

Many matching games can be purchased or made. Commercial bingo and lotto games are inexpensive and readily available. You may want to construct additional matching games. A bingo game using children's names as the objects to match is very popular with older children, as are bingo games made of old calendars and pictures of fruits or vegetables cut from seed catalogs.

Storage for all of these items is difficult. Puzzle racks keep puzzles neatly stored, but they are hidden from the children; boxes of games stacked one on top of the other only allow the top game to be visible. A few "display" items may be placed on nearby tables or a game set up on the floor.

## Science Area

Another active area of the room is the science corner. Not merely a place to deposit fall leaves and old seashells, it is an area in which children can actively explore many varied materials. Most items in the science area should promote activity on the part of the children.

One teacher arranged a pitcher of water and some small cups on a table next to some instant coffee, tea leaves, dirt, sand, beans, sugar, and salt. She gave the children the problem, "What will dissolve in water?" Children poured water from the pitcher into the cups and stirred bits of matter into the water with popsicle sticks. These five year olds recorded the things that dissolved and those that did not. The teacher later led a group discussion to help the children clarify their experiences.

Balancing scales, widely used in the British schools, should be found in the science area, along with a number of things to weigh and balance. Magnets, compasses, prisms, magnifying glasses, a number of different kinds of mirrors, and colored cellophane also are good things to work with.

Machines to take apart, clocks, pencil sharpeners, instrument-panel boards, radios with tubes and electrical parts removed, and screwdrivers and wrenches can be made available for those children who are curious as to how things work. One group of children worked continually for days until they finally and successfully dismantled an alarm clock.

Another group of children became fascinated with molds, and the science area was taken over by cups of molding bread, fruit juice, cookies (which never did grow mold), milk, dirt, rotting logs, and paste. With a magnifying glass, microscope, and many reference books, the children explored molds for weeks. A volunteer from the science department of the local high school brought her high-powered microscope and some prepared slides so that some of the children were able to see the molds. All of them enjoyed the experience.

Plants and animals can be cared for in the science area, and room for collections of seeds, dried flowers, leaves, shells, and rocks can be arranged. All materials and activities in the science area should change frequently, depending on the maturity and interests of the children.

## Block Area

Blocks are essential for children of all ages. First appearing in the Froebelian kindergarten, they have remained the most important investment a preschool can make. Large hollow blocks, unit blocks, colorful painted blocks, blocks made by stuffing empty milk cartons with newspapers, and purchased cardboard blocks should be found within each playroom.

Building with blocks fosters the language skills of the children; in order to build with one another, they must communicate their plans and ideas. Experience with numbers—"We'll need a double block here," or "Bring two more blocks"—occurs as the children build. Small muscles must be carefully controlled in order to balance the top block while large muscles are used to pull the large hollow blocks into position.

By the time the children reach the age of five, block building culminates in large, complicated structures. Maps of the neighborhood are built; replicas of the airport and farm develop. Older children need an unlimited supply of blocks for these structures. Often, they want to save their building for continued play the next day or even for the entire week.

Additional props for block play such as stop signs, traffic signs, sets of plastic farm animals, toy cars, trucks, and airplanes may be useful for older children. An adult should be ready to help mark signs for cities, garages, airports, and streets.

Ideally, blocks should be stored on open shelves with a place for each type of block. Storing all rectangular blocks on the same shelf, for example, fosters classification skills in children. Blocks can be successfully stored in wagons, boxes, or storage bins with casters on the bottom.

A piece of indoor-outdoor carpeting serves to keep the children comfortable while working on the floor and eliminates much of the noise of falling blocks. There should be adequate space in the block area for expanding buildings. Block play may be very noisy and active, so the block area is best located away from the more quiet areas of the room. If wheel toys are kept near the block area, additional types of play are stimulated, and woodworking near the blocks is convenient for the children.

Block play does require your observation and supervision. Do not direct building, but offer suggestions regarding safety and sharing.

## Office Corner

When parents work in "the office," children are often confused as to exactly what the job entails. The establishment of an office corner, perhaps following a trip to the office of one of the parents, helps the children to clarify what happens and, at the same time, promotes many academic learnings.

An old, but workable, typewriter can be obtained from the Goodwill for a few dollars, or may be given to the preschool by an office, school, or church. Unrepairable telephones (obtained by calling the public relations office of the local telephone company), paper supplies, receipt books, bookkeeping forms, and anything that looks official and has space for writing complete the equipment in the "office." Old calendars—desk, hanging, and appointment—are most valuable. Pencils, scissors, staplers, and most impressive of all, rubber stamps and stamping pad are ideal for playing office.

A clock, briefcase, and office clothing can be near the area. Through play in the office corner, children can gain an understanding of office work. By typing everyone's name and address, or dialing the phone, or writing on the calendars, children learn the alphabet and numerals. Although younger children enjoy playing office, this area is usually reserved for five year olds.

*An office corner is valuable.*

## Audio-Visual Area

In this age of multimedia, no preschool is considered complete without some type of media center where children can learn to operate a variety of audio-visual equipment. A slide projector is easily managed by the children with a minimum of direction and supervision. If you start filmstrip projectors, they can also be managed by the children. Many filmstrips that illustrate favorite stories or factual information are available. A single-concept, 8-mm loop projector, although less common, is another piece of equipment very young children can handle effectively.

A closed-off area of the room that can be semidarkened serves as the audio-visual area. It may be established during one unit of work and need not be present all of the time. Children quickly lose interest in the thrill of manipulating the machines if no real purpose is served. Machines, films, and slides may be available from the local library or school board on a loan basis.

## Water and Sand Area

An indoor water and sand area is essential for each playroom. Babies enjoy splashing in their bath, toddlers love to pour, slosh, and splash, and older children endlessly experiment with the properties of sand and water. Concepts of floating and sinking, evaporation, weight, volume, color, and optics are developed through water and sand play. Such play also has a soothing effect on children, providing an excellent release for tensions.

You may want to select a place indoors for water play that is near to the source of water. Some centers are equipped with low sinks and utilize these for water play. Most preschools, however, have a table and dishpan for water play. Any container and any surface can be used. A tub placed on two crates, a dishpan, an old bassinet, or a plastic wading pool on the floor are all fine containers for water. You may want to use sheets of plastic or newspaper for protection. Children can assist both in the filling and emptying of containers and in the mop-up that follows play.

Coffee pots, squirt bottles, spoons, funnels, plastic glasses, cans, and walnut shells are enjoyed in water play. If children lose interest, a bit of detergent added to the water initiates different types of play—washing doll clothes, blowing bubbles, washing dishes. Food coloring added to the water also serves to stimulate interest.

Sand in a sand table, tin tub, bassinet, or old wading pool should be available at all times indoors. Young children simply run their hands through the sand, pouring it from one container to another, but older children begin weighing sand and molding it into shapes and buildings. Water must be handy for building in the sand. If you object to sand indoors, or live in Florida or other areas where the entire outdoors is sand, substitute rice, beans, dried coffee grounds, or sawdust for indoor pouring and measuring.

## Music Area

A quiet part of the room that is away from the other activities can be established as the music center. Here, a child can go to listen to a record, operating the phonograph by himself, or can play with whatever musical instrument he desires. A piano, autoharp, drum, guitar, shakers, and other rhythm instruments can be on hand. Children, assuming responsibilities, can be taught to handle and experiment with musical instruments without damaging them. They can use instruments in quiet ways so as not to disturb the other children. Bells of assorted shapes and sizes, rhythm sticks, triangles, and tambourines are enjoyed.

## Other Areas

As the seasons change, as field trips are taken, and as children have new experiences, the centers of interest within the room also change. Following a trip to the beauty or barber shop, an area with a chair, rollers, shower hat, cape, mirror, and magazines may be set up in the room. Similarly, a "post office" or a "store" may be established. These centers of interest serve the children in acting out specific experiences they have had. They are established as the children's interests dictate or for the development of specific concepts as you see necessary. Props can be added and removed and, eventually, when the interest in the specific center itself is removed, a new area is established to replace it.

# IT'S UP TO YOU

Without a concerned, interested, and competent adult, even the most fully equipped, spacious playroom is inadequate to provide for the needs of young children. The adult, whether a teacher, volunteer, parent, or aide, is responsible for establishing a relaxing atmosphere within the playroom and for creating a place where children are free to develop socially, gaining knowledge, skills, self-confidence, and emotional maturity.

You, as the teacher, must select and arrange the materials for the children, maintaining a balance between materials that stimulate manipulative, dramatic, social, creative, and physical play. By keeping the materials in order and the room uncluttered through careful selection of equipment, and by establishing centers of interest, you unobtrusively set limits for the children's play and establish order.

You must set the example in caring for the materials and the room. "If shelves are running over with scraps of paper, broken crayons, discarded pegs, and bits of chalk, children cannot perceive or respect the educational purposes of these materials. They will not care how things are kept because you obviously don't care either. If, on the other hand, you prepare table materials and shelves in advance and faithfully involve all adults and children in the upkeep and order of these materials, children will learn the habits of helping to put things away and maintaining their room," (Galambos, n.d., p. 7).

Understanding the nature and value of play, you will want to provide a background of experiences for the children to act out. In order for children to play fully and freely, they must have rich experiences with people and things. Taking many trips in the neighborhood and wider community acquaints children with the roles of adults and the world around them. Caring for pets within the center, cooking, living together, and talking to visitors are other examples of experiences giving children a foundation on which to build creative play.

Children's play must be rich with language. Without directing or interrupting the play, introduce language through questions and comments. Talking in complete sentences, expand on what a child has said. To the boy playing with the doll and saying "dolly," you may reply, "That is a good doll; did you feed her today?" To the child digging in the sand and saying "wet sand," you may respond, "Yes, your sand is wet, and now you can really build with it." (Cazden, 1966, p. 131). The teacher should also label things for children as they play with them. The child who cries for the "digger thing" can be given the shovel as she is told, "Here is the shovel. Do you want the shovel to dig with?"

Number and concept words can also be introduced as the children play. "Let's count your acorns; how many do you have?" "What colors are you using in your painting?" "Is your suitcase heavy or light?" And as the children climb up and down, under and out, you can verbally describe their actions.

Questions may stimulate children to more complex play. Asking children as they play "What will you do with the water?" "How much money do you need in the store?" "Where can I buy a ticket?" may motivate them to extend their play activities. You can also structure problems for children to solve through play, challenging them to develop creative thinking. You may add a plank to the hill and demonstrate how it can help the children move equipment to the top of the hill; or you may allow the blocks to fall and then help to rebuild the structure, pointing out the need for balance.

As children lose interest in a certain activity, you must know whether or not to help them conclude the activity or to extend and continue the play. One teacher, as the children lost interest in water play and began aimlessly and recklessly splashing one another, rather than concluding the play, brought out a basket of toys and objects and asked the children, "What do you think will float?" In this way, she involved them in a problem that held their interest, stimulated conversation, and extended water play for another thirty minutes.

You may also develop children's social skills as they play. The child looking longingly at others playing house may be handed a basket of cookies and asked if he would like to be the cookie man. He can be helped to knock on the pretend door to sell his cookies to the children playing house. Another child may be taken by the hand and introduced to a group of children; or you may sit with a child as he first attempts to relate to others, helping him with physical support in an uncomfortable situation. The overly aggressive child also receives guidance during play. You may send a quick look across the room, saying with your eyes, "Not so loud, or wild, or pushy." You may sit with the overly active child, put an arm around his shoulder, give him a pat on the back, letting him know that you are available to help him control his exuberance. Direct teaching may also be helpful as you describe to individual children exactly how to relate to others in certain situations. You can say, for example, "When you push into the boat, you hurt the other children, so they don't want you to come in. If you would ask them to let you in, they would not be upset. Let's try."

Matterson (1968), in describing your role during free play indoors, says that in the playroom you are rather like a waiter who anticipates and provides for needs, offers suggestions when necessary, and never attempts to direct or force the person he serves. As a teacher of young children, you structure the environment with choices; anticipate when children need new materials, equipment, and challenges; and know when to remove toys no longer interesting to the group. Although you do not directly interfere with the children's play, you do offer suggestions to them, introduce language, and assist individuals in relating to others.

You can enhance the quality of children's play by (Smilansky, 1968):

1. Providing experiences for the children to dramatize—taking them on a trip to an airport for instance.
2. Introducing language as children play. "This is the baggage, take it to the clerk."
3. Entering into the play situation by taking on the role of one of the players. "I'll be the passenger; you take my ticket."
4. Extending children's play with the use of questions. "What will you do now?"

In these ways, "you can make the children aware of different play possibilities and of experiences and memories from which they can draw. They can act as they want without having to face all of the problems of self-expression alone and unaided" (Butler, Gotts, & Quisenberry, 1978, p. 68).

## REFERENCES

Almy, M. "Spontaneous Play: An Avenue for Intellectual Development." In *Early Childhood Education Rediscovered,* edited by J. L. Frost. New York: Holt, Rinehart & Winston, 1968.

Butler, A. L.; Gotts, E. E.; and Quisenberry, N. L. *Play as Development.* Columbus, Oh: Charles E. Merrill Publishing Co., 1978.

Cazden, C. "Some Implications of Research on Language Development." In *Early Education,* edited by R. D. Hess and R. M. Bear. Chicago: Aldine Publishing Co., 1966.

*Day Care: Serving Children with Special Needs.* Washington, D.C.: U.S. Department of Health, Education, and Welfare, Office of Child Development, 1972.

Evans, E. B.; Shub, G.; and Weinstein, M. *Day Care: How to Plan, Develop, and Operate a Day Care Center.* Boston: Beacon Press, 1971.

Frank, L. K. "Introduction." In *The Complete Book of Children's Play,* edited by R. E. Hartley and R. M. Goldenson. New York: Thomas Y. Crowell, 1957.

Galambos, J. W. *Discipline and Self-Control.* Washington, D.C.: U.S. Department of Health, Education, and Welfare, Office of Child Development, no date.

Gewirtz, H. B. "Child Care Facilities and the Israeli Experience." In *Day Care: Resources for Decisions,* edited by E. H. Grotberg. Washington, D.C.: Office of Economic Opportunity, 1971.

Hymes, J. *Teaching the Child under Six.* Columbus, Oh.: Charles E. Merrill Publishing Co., 1974.

Matterson, E. M. *Play and Playthings for the Preschool Child.* Baltimore: Penguin Books, 1968.

Piaget, J. *Play, Dreams and Imitation in Childhood.* New York: W. W. Norton & Co., 1962.

Prescott, E., and Jones, E. *Day Care as a Child Rearing Environment.* Washington, D.C.: The National Association for the Education of Young Children, 1971.

Read, K. H. *The Nursery School.* Philadelphia: W. B. Saunders Co., 1966.

Ritchie, O. W., and Marvin, R. K. *Sociology of Childhood.* New York: Appleton-Century-Crofts, 1954.

Russell, D. H. *Children's Thinking.* Waltham, Mass.: Blaisdell Publishing Co., 1956.

Smilansky, S. *The Effects of Sociodramatic Play on Disadvantaged Preschool Children.* New York: John Wiley & Sons, 1968.

Stechler, G. "Newborn Attention as Affected by Medication during Labor." *Science.* 144 (1964): 315–17.

Sutton-Smith, B. "The Role of Play in Cognitive Development." *Young Children.* 22 (1967): 360–70.

## RESOURCES

*Play: The Child Strives toward Self-Realization.* Washington, D.C.: The National Association for the Education of Young Children, 1971.

Baker, K. R. *Ideas That Work with Young Children.* Washington, D.C.: The National Association for the Education of Young Children, 1972.

Bjorklund, G. *Planning for Play.* Columbus, Oh.: Charles E. Merrill Publishing Co., 1978.

Butler, A. L.; Gotts, E.; Quisenberry, N. *Play as Development.* Columbus, Oh.: Charles E. Merrill Publishing Co., 1978.

Hirsch, E. S., ed. *The Block Book.* Washington, D.C.: The National Association for the Education of Young Children, 1974.

Sponseller, D., ed. *Play as a Learning Medium.* Washington, D.C.: The National Association for the Education of Young Children, 1974.

Sunderlin, S., and Gray, N. *Bits and Pieces: Imaginative Uses for Children's Learning.* Washington, D.C.: Association for Childhood Education International, 1967.

## PROJECTS

1. Design a playroom for infants, toddlers, and preschool age children. Each room is rectangular, has windows along one wall, and has its own water source. Bathrooms are found in the toddlers' and preschoolers' rooms. What equipment will you include and where will you place it?

2. Observe a group of children playing indoors. Record the language usage of the children in the housekeeping, art, manipulative, and science areas of the room. In which area does the most verbalization occur?

3. Observe a teacher working with children indoors. Note and record how the teacher a) fosters language usage, b) extends and clarifies children's concepts, c) sets limits and controls, and d) structures the playroom environment.

4. You have a limited budget for equipment and supplies. List the types of equipment you will attempt to obtain from industries, stores, and community agencies without cost to you. Think of the different types of boxes available from the various stores. What other materials can you think of?

# OUTDOOR PLAY

*Hills and valleys*
*Fields and woodlands,*
*rocks and pebbles,*
*Sound and water.*
*Sunshine, wind and*
*secret places.* (Outdoor Play, p. 1)

All children, especially those in a group, need the exhilaration, challenge, and freedom inherent in outdoor play. Outdoor play allows each child to develop feelings of trust in herself and in others, and in her natural environment. Many experiences can be planned outdoors to foster the child's initiative, develop her autonomy, and increase her diligence.

## PHYSICAL ACTIVITY

When children are in a group situation, no matter how free, many restrictions based on space, noise level, and concern for others are necessary indoors. Outdoors, however, open spaces allow children to become as boisterous and physically active as they wish. Large muscles can be freely exercised, and tensions and strong feelings can be released in appropriate ways. Young children, whose large-muscle growth is rapidly developing, need access to space and equipment that fosters highly active, physical responses.

## SENSORY EXPERIENCES

Being outdoors offers new and varied sensory experiences. Different weather conditions must be experienced by children before they can be understood. Textures explored by children outdoors—rough barks of trees, prickly pine needles, grainy sand, rugged cement—all strengthen concept formation. The touch of dewy grass, squishy mud, and flowing water expand and extend the young child's knowledge of the world around her.

## NATURAL SCIENCE

Outdoors, the child can actually experience nature. Changing seasons are observed, seeds planted, and acorns harvested. Insects, plants, animals, and birds are available for study. Direct experience with trees, plants, rocks, clouds, sun, and sky is now possible.

## COOPERATIVE PLAY

Of course, children play cooperatively indoors; yet the feeling of open space and the large play yard equipment somehow foster cooperative play that is more complex. Informal groups develop as some children become cattle and others cowboys. Children on wheel toys become firemen with a team of trucks, delivery men, or policemen complete with safety rules. Complex schemes for rearranging equipment, digging gardens, or making cities in the sand develop as children play together outdoors.

## CONSTRUCTION

The wide-open space outdoors allows children to work together in constructing large buildings. Boxes and boards are combined to represent houses, trains, or forts. Using hammers, nails, and large pieces of lumber, children often build huge, complete structures.

QUIET SPACES   All children need quiet places in which to think, dream, and plan. The bushes, trees, boxes—little corners of space found outdoors—can give the young child the feeling of being by herself.

_____ ## ESSENTIALS OF OUTDOOR PLAY

Outdoor play is rich with activity, sensory exploration, encounters with nature, cooperative experiences, and construction. It is in no way secondary in value to indoor play. However, for outdoor play to fulfill its potential, the following factors must be present. Outdoor play must

1. Be adequately supervised by competent, trained adults.
2. Take place in an environment large enough to support individual needs.
3. Provide many learning experiences.
4. Continue throughout the year, with special preparations to meet the needs of the season.

SUPERVISION   "The key to any playground that is going to come to life is the presence of a mature, adult leader who exercises the minimum of authority and the maximum of understanding and guidance" (Hurtwood, 1965, p. 4). Creative supervision for outdoor play is essential. When you are supervising on the play yard, you should be aware of all of the possibilities for learning, creating, and knowing that are found outdoors. Adequate numbers of adults (the same ratio of adults per child established for indoor activities) must be found outdoors. Playing outdoors is a relaxing, freeing experience for the young child; it is a time of thoughtful planning, implementation, and teaching for the adult.

When supervising outdoors, you serve to facilitate play. Before the children arrive, conduct a safety check of the play yard. Broken equipment should be removed, water standing in tires or boxes emptied, and wheel toys oiled if necessary. Equipment may be rearranged to offer the children unique, challenging possibilities. You can facilitate children's play by adding new equipment or props to the yard and storing other pieces that are no longer appealing to the children.

As the children play, observe them. You may be given specific responsibility for one, two, or a small group of children outdoors. Learn to observe the play of your specific children while watching the entire group. Observing is by no means a passive activity. You must tune in on the children's play, offering help, providing additional equipment, or spontaneously entering into the play. Through observation, note the growth and development of individual children, the choices they make, and any areas of difficulty. You will remain in control of the play yard at all times. Safety measures such as removing a box from the path

*Playing outdoors is a freeing experience for the child.*

of a toddler, supporting the child having trouble climbing, or picking up broken equipment are your responsibilities. Safety rules are likewise unobtrusively enforced as you say to the child, "Ride your bike over here," "Let me hold your doll while you climb the tree; remember, we don't climb with a toy in our hands," or "Put the block down before you argue."

One student teacher, overwhelmed with the active responses of young children outdoors, found it difficult to keep track of her charges and still become involved with specific children. This student developed the habit of periodically talking an eye count of her children. This exercise sharpened her observing skills and increased her awareness of all of the children and their activities.

Facilitating, observing adults are also encouraging adults. At times, you may work alongside children, talking to them, introducing new words and ideas, taking care not to interrupt the children's thoughts and ideas. Encourage a child to make his own decisions by clarifying the choices available or by helping the child to work through the problem himself. Praise is also important. Children need the approving smile, nod, or pat on the shoulder when they have successfully completed a task. Verbal praise is also an excellent way to reinforce and encourage appropriate behavior.

SPACE    Space, space, and more space is required for a successful play yard
for children in preschool. The amount of space required varies with
state and local licensing regulations. The Child Welfare League of America
suggests that, in order to permit active play, 200 square feet of outdoor space
per child is desirable. They indicate that an area of 3,000 square feet for 15
children is optimum (*Child Welfare League of America: Standards for Day Care,*
1969). The more space available for the play yard, the greater the possibilities
for variation in learning experiences.

Actually, preschool centers are often located in church buildings, store-
fronts, private homes, or abandoned school buildings where both indoor and
outdoor space is greatly limited. In such cases, more creative, careful planning
is required to provide for the fullest possible use of existing space. Exciting
spaces for play have been developed on rooftops, on vest-pocket parks in the
inner city, or even on church driveways.

A balance between quiet and active areas is important in a play yard.
There should be areas set aside for active, boisterous running, jumping, and
climbing as well as for quiet, small-muscle manipulative play with dolls, sand,
or water. Boxes, plants, hills, or pieces of equipment can serve as barriers to
clarify areas, set limits, and suggest activities.

Various levels of tree trunks, cable tables (the large wooden center from
rolls of telephone or construction wire), boxes, or climbing bars offer a balance
between high places and low ones. The addition of a hill bulldozed or shoveled
onto a flat play area precipitates a variety of play. On a hill children can
become captains of ships, mountain climbers, or space men. The muscular
activities involved in climbing the hill and the fun of rolling down again make
even a small hill a most valuable piece of playground "equipment."

Play areas should also have a balance between sunny and shady areas. In
some play yards, the side of a building, trees, or natural terrain may provide
some shade. Other retreats from the sun can be created with beach umbrellas,
awnings, or chikechees, the thatched, open-sided hut adapted after the
Seminole Indian's home, where stories or housekeeping play can be enjoyed.

Young children need experience with a variety of textures. Some spaces
should be covered with hard material such as cement, hardtop, or asphalt.
These areas are useful for wheel toys, basketball, or other organized games for
the older children. Other areas should be open for digging, gardening, and
sand and water play. A grassy plot should be planted and reserved for special
activities. Preschool teachers have found that the use of pine bark, cedar chips,
or pine needles adds yet another texture to the play yard while keeping dust to a
minimum where grass refuses to grow.


SEASONS    Every day, regardless of the climate and the season, children in
a preschool center should spend time outdoors, both in the
morning and the afternoon. There are days when snow, sleet, heavy rain, or
intense heat make it impossible and hazardous to spend much time outside;
however, these days are relatively rare. With adequate clothing, both for adults
and children, there are few days during the year that are completely inappro-

priate for outdoor activity of any kind. The time spent outdoors during inclement weather is not extensive, so additional planning on your part may be required. Equipment and activities, varied to meet the demands of the season, keep the play yard an exciting, challenging place throughout the year.

## Spring

April showers shouldn't keep children indoors. With boots, umbrellas, and raincoats, young children can safely enjoy a walk in the soft, spring rain. After a heavier shower, children enjoy splashing and jumping in every puddle they can find. Puddles are also handy for experimenting with floating things and for making mud.

The force of spring wind is exciting. How does it feel to walk with your back to the wind? Have you tried to walk against the wind? When the wind blows, kites can fly, pinwheels turn, and bubbles float away in the air. Spring is also the time to plant gardens and watch many living things as they sprout and grow.

## Summer

Hot summer days require plenty of water play. Sprinklers, hoses, and pans of water keep children actively involved on even the hottest days of the year. When the heat is intense, however, it is unrealistic to expect young children to run, jump, or climb for long periods of time. Some large-muscle equipment could be stored, and room made for quiet activities. Special games, housekeeping equipment, or art materials are useful outdoors during summer. When it is hot inside as well as outside, many activities can be transferred outdoors. Stories can be read under a tree, cots taken out for rest time. or snacks and meals eaten outside.

## Fall

This is the time to collect seed pods, acorns, and leaves. Bulbs can be planted in anticipation of spring. It is a time of fascinating changes, during which adjustments to the cooler weather must be made. Fall is an active outdoor season, with children fully utilizing large-muscle equipment and space for running.

## Winter

With its exciting ice and snow, winter can be a most satisfactory time for outdoor play; however, both children and adults should be appropriately dressed for winter weather. This is a time for snow pants, hats, boots, scarves, and mittens. If you are not prepared for the cold, you will find yourself uncomfortable outdoors and unable to share in the children's excitement. Children can be helped with dressing a few at a time. Encourage the children to help themselves, yet be ready to assist each child.

Some equipment, perhaps metal bars, can be placed in storage during the winter. When snow falls, special equipment can be brought out. Child-sized shovels, sleds, even pot lids to slide on are all popular with the children. The older children can show the younger ones how to roll a body for the snowman or how to construct a snow fort. Snow can be packed, measured, and stored in various containers. Pictures can be drawn in the snow, or by stretching out in the snow, an angel can be made.

# PLANNING FOR INDIVIDUALS

Outdoor play spaces associated with preschool centers are often used by infants, toddlers, preschoolers, and school-age children alike. Specific planning for each age group is necessary. Some preschool centers have separate outdoor spaces adjoining playrooms that are designated for the sole use of each age group. Generally, centers must arrange for maximum use of the small play space by all age children.

Scheduling time for different age groups to use the play yard may be useful. Infants, because of their sleeping and eating schedules, may be brought outdoors when the preschoolers are engaged in learning activities indoors. Likewise, the older, after-school-age children may have almost exclusive use of the yard after four o'clock when the preschoolers are busy with quiet projects that precede their going home.

However, when play spaces must be used by all age groups simultaneously, they must be large enough for each group to have its own appropriate equipment and ongoing activities. Specific areas may be set up for use by different age groups. A basketball or volleyball court, or perhaps a badminton net, may be provided for the after-school-age children. Several sand and digging areas for older and younger children could be arranged.

Adequate storage space is almost a necessity when multiple-age grouping occurs. Aluminum or wooden storage sheds can be purchased or built. The older children's equipment can be stored during the day and brought out for the afternoon. The younger children's wheel toys and other equipment can then be placed in storage.

Each piece of permanent equipment should be flexible enough to serve different age groups. All equipment should be sturdy enough for use by young and older children alike. Boxes, hollow blocks, and cable tables are examples of equipment that can serve in many ways.

Multiple-age grouping is often advantageous. Children of different ages may wish to play together, learning from one another; cooperative play is stimulated as the older children assume a teaching role. Children often group themselves around a common interest rather than a common age.

INFANTS   Infants need their own time and space outside. Strollers, infant seats, bounce chairs, or swinging chairs can be used to take infants outdoors. These chairs can be set up where the babies can have an interesting, safe spot, either to observe the activities of the older children or the wonders of the outdoors. Under a tree, the infant may become intent in observing the patterns the leaves and sun make, or delight with the feel of soft wind on her face.

Infants can be taken outdoors singly or in groups of two or three. The crawling or walking baby also needs a protected time outdoors to practice her new locomotor skills and feel the success of mastering a difficult task. A grassy section of the yard can be reserved for these infants. Some pieces of equipment, usually something with which to pull themselves up to standing position, can be provided. A barefooted baby enjoys the sensations of grass beneath her feet. This soft, grassy section can also be used for the babies who are learning to roll over, or the beginner crawler and creeper. Cardboard boxes will keep the walking baby involved in pushing and pulling activities or in filling the boxes with leaves and pieces of grass.

Infants, developing trust in themselves and their world, must be closely supervised outdoors. The area the infant will play in should be checked for any objects that might injure her as she crawls. Babies tend to put everything they can get into their hands and mouths; therefore, you must be watchful of the baby's explorations with tasting and remove anything that is likely to be eaten.

## TODDLERS

The toddler has special needs that must be met outdoors. Once he can walk, his world and his needs expand rapidly. Large-muscle development receives much of the child's attention and energy. A variety of eye-hand-muscle coordinations are also being learned and perfected at this age.

Very small piles of sand and dirt can be specifically prepared for these toddlers. A small sand shovel, plastic cups, and other containers, plus close supervision, can provide endless hours of exploratory activity. Water play, with water provided in small dishpans, and plastic cups, pitchers, and funnels for pouring, is well liked by the toddlers. Sponges or squirt bottles can be added to the water for variety. Small spools or other floating objects also provide for fun.

Cardboard boxes foster the use of the toddler's large muscles; they are usually available from the nearest grocery store. Boxes of various sizes are good to climb in and out of, to push or pull, to stack, or to arrange in the shape of a house. Pull toys are favorites of the toddler; empty oatmeal boxes threaded together with a sturdy string are satisfactory trains for the toddler to pull behind him.

Wagons to sit in or pull are good outdoor toys. A kiddy car, without pedals, is also useful. Blocks, either large, wooden ones or unit blocks, can be taken outside. Probably the most desirable toys outdoors are kitchen pots and pans that can be filled with sand or water or banged together to make a "delightful" noise.

As the toddler learns to do things for himself outdoors, he should receive your reinforcing approval. With the ability to walk, run, and build with blocks, the child can begin to establish relationships with his peers.

## PRESCHOOLERS

Three- to five-year-old children are interested in one another. Opportunities for them to play and work to-gether should be provided. By the age of four, some children will have

*Wagons and trikes are good outdoor toys.*

developed a close relationship with another child their own age. You can facilitate these beginning relationships.

See to it that there are enough wheel toys for several children to ride at the same time. Props such as telephones, housekeeping equipment, hats, tools, and cooking utensils are useful in promoting friendships. Balls for rolling to a friend or throwing in the air to catch are needed. A variety of ropes, hoses, and tools helps to foster dramatic play for groups of children.

Water, mud, and sand are still essential materials. The preschooler will want to measure and pour water, and mold sand or mud into pies, cakes, or even mountains. Sand, mud, and water can now be used to foster cooperative play. Sometimes children together will construct entire cities, complete with bridges and rivers. Toys, cars, boats, and plastic people can be added to the sand area. The older children will continue their sand play from day to day, with the construction's becoming increasingly elaborate. Make provisions to let these preschoolers have their own sand pile, one that will not be destroyed in their absence. The pile should be large enough for a number of children to work in at the same time, and large enough for complex projects.

Sand, in order to be molded, must be damp. Therefore, water is required for sand play. Squirt bottles that are filled with water will aid each child in dampening his own area of sand. A nearby hose can be useful for dampening larger areas as children construct roads and cities.

Digging, just for the fun of it, is enjoyed by preschoolers. Some plot of ground should be available for this activity exclusively. Small, sturdy shovels, rakes, buckets, and large containers are helpful in the digging area. Larger shovels, lumber, hammer, and nails can be added to the digging area. With these materials one group of preschool children constructed a large "fort." The foundation was dug, mud was mixed with water in a attempt to make bricks, pine logs and boards were nailed together to form walls, and the roof was constructed of cardboard sheets and branches.

Woodworking is another attractive outdoor activity. Large pieces of lumber, small strips, a hammer, nails, a vise, and other woodworking equipment should be ready for children's use. Perhaps a volunteer can work with the children and supervise woodworking activities. Five year olds may actually think about plans and create diagrams before beginning to construct with wood.

Preschool children need room for active, large-muscle activity and play. A space just to run in is necessary. Plenty of equipment for climbing, jumping, and pulling oneself up on is important as the preschool child seeks to exercise large muscles. Places for children to enter into beginning team sports and games, for example, circle games or even ball games, are also necessary.

## CHILDREN WITH SPECIAL NEEDS

All children are individuals, and all must find their specific needs met outdoors. Outdoor play spaces, however, need to be carefully planned to meet the needs of children with handicaps. An interview with parents of a child with special needs, or a meeting with the parents, medical personnel, and therapists can help you determine any arrangements that should be made to accommodate the child's needs outdoors. Sometimes special areas of the play yard can be set aside for specific children.

Often children with special needs will find the same type of equipment used by all of the children suitable. When sand, mud, water, blocks, and wood are available, nearly all children will be able to use these. A different type of supervision, however, may be necessary when working with children with special needs. You might have to teach one child how to use a specific piece of equipment, telling her to put her foot on the pedals and showing her how to push, or giving explicit directions on how to climb the jungle gym. "Put one foot here; now hold on and put the other foot here." Children, especially those with special needs, may find more active encouragement and supervision helpful. Others need modification of equipment, as well as supervision.

For instance, children with poor muscle control or motor problems, as well as children who are blind, can ride tricycles. Taping the child's feet to the pedals with masking tape or a large, loose rubber band helps the child keep his feet on the pedals. Blind children, who cannot see how to pedal a bike are helped to learn how to pedal. These children can learn to ride the tricycle in safe areas, and soon gain a sense of the play yard.

Children with large-muscle problems might find the following pieces of equipment useful:

1. Irish mail—a ride-on toy operated with arm levers.
2. Platforms on wheels to balance, lie on, and scoot around.
3. Scooter cars that are good for scooting, using legs and feet.
4. Rocking horses and boats to gain balance, push.
5. Chair swings which provide more control than a regular swing.
6. Large cardboard boxes and wooden blocks to push, pull, and stack.

Children with fine motor or perceptual motor problems might find the following pieces of equipment suitable for them:

1. Large plastic nuts and screws to take apart and put together.
2. Stacking toys.
3. Clothespins and boxes and cans, so the children can place the pins along the edge or from can to can.
4. Large beads and strings to practice eye, hand, muscle coordination.
5. Things to push, such as sandbags in carriages or wagons, that help children with balance problems.

Children with visual problems may need toys that have sounding devices attached. For example:

1. Balls with bells inside or other items that make sounds let the visually impaired child learn how to bounce, catch, and throw a ball.
2. Toys to push, such as toy lawn mowers and carpet sweepers that make sounds, are useful.

# ———————————————————— SITUATIONS FOR LEARNING

The outdoor play yard is merely an extension of the stimulating, well-arranged indoor environment. The added richness of the natural surroundings and open spaces enhances possibilities for learning. Centers of interest that are fully established indoors can be arranged in varying forms outdoors.

HOUSEKEEPING    Dramatic play continues outdoors when there is some provision for a housekeeping center. Any type of structure or corner of the play yard having an element of privacy is suitable. One center constructed a teepee of bamboo stalks, attracting children to dramatic play. A wooden platform, with one or two boxes along one edge, can suggest a kitchen to some children. Bushes, screens, moveable wooden partitions, or even a different textured surface on the play yard can help children establish housekeeping play.

Props such as muffin tins, wooden spoons, and coffee pots, when combined with acorns, seeds, grass, and leaves (or sand, mud, and water), add a realism to "cooking" activities that is not entirely feasible indoors. Wheel toys near the housekeeping center add to the complexity of dramatic play, with fathers' and mothers' leaving for work on bikes or in wagons, and firemen or delivery men coming and going. Tool kits, metal lunch boxes, packing boxes, or briefcases attract children to the housekeeping area. Old vacuum cleaners, hoses, flashlights, cameras, and discarded instrument panels foster mechanical play. Some costumes are enjoyed by children outdoors. These, as all other props, should be added when appropriate and removed as the children's interests dissipate. Hats, rubber boots, handbags, wallets, and even paper shopping bags are all useful additions to the outdoor housekeeping area.

OUTDOOR ART    Actually, any art activity conducted inside can be taken outside; plan to conduct at least one art activity outdoors daily. You may find that the freedom of creating outdoors results in more imaginative art.

All types of painting are appropriate outdoors. Painting with water colors, tempera, or with real enamel is exciting outdoors. By attaching large sheets of heavy brown paper to a fence, the side of the building, or to the play yard surface itself, children are able to use tempera paints outdoors with success. Tempera paints can be mixed in empty juice cans and placed in a six-pack container for easy transporting outdoors.

Large cardboard boxes are good to paint for the sheer enjoyment of using large brushes and bright, flowing paint. Wooden structures may be painted with house paint to offer the children an experience with a different medium.

Outdoor finger painting on an old tabletop is enjoyed by the children. Making nature prints is another art project appropriate for outdoors. Children can collect items from the yard, such as acorns, seeds, leaves, or Spanish moss, and by dipping these onto sponges dampened with tempera paints, print creative nature designs.

Chalk is another medium useful outdoors. Young children have always treasured the tiny, white stones that really mark on concrete surfaces. Having white or colored chalk handy capitalizes on the children's tendencies to draw without restriction on large surfaces. The next rain washes the play yard clean again, and the children can start all over. These creations often require group effort and, being larger than life, are often freer and more imaginative than drawings on paper.

Large sheets of newsprint and wide chunks of crayon stimulate the children to explore textures. Sides of buildings, screening on windows, hardtop surfaces, tree trunks, or rough planks are all available for "rubbing" over. The sheet of paper is placed over the textured surface, then rubbed with the side of a crayon to produce a nature design.

Modeling activities take place naturally in the sand and mud outdoors. Occasionally, you may want to add a crock of clay, a hunk of salt dough, or Play-Doh for use outdoors. Creations modeled outdoors can be decorated with flowers, stones, leaves, or grass.

Block building, either with unit blocks or with large hollow blocks, can also take place outdoors. Big boxes, planks, and lumber invite the children to build larger, more complex block structures in combination with other materials. Woodworking for all ages is another activity handled easily outdoors where noise and sawdust bother no one.

SCIENCE   With nature surrounding them, children outdoors approach science with dynamic curiosity and vivid interest. The entire world is available for learning activities. Experiences with the natural as well as the physical sciences are plentiful.

The life cycle of living things can be directly observed outdoors. Seeds and bulbs can be planted and cared for. A few butterfly nets aid in the study of insects. Insect containers may be fashioned from a piece of wire screening folded into a cylinder and placed in the bottom of a plastic bleach bottle.

*Birds and animals can be studied outdoors.*

Birds and animals, either wild or tame, can be studied outdoors. Some preschools are fortunate in that they keep pets. One center had a pony, another a sheep, and one a pond with assorted ducks. Some preschools have made arrangements with animal shelters to borrow a pen of rabbits, some chicks, or hamsters for short periods of time. The care and feeding of animals is a learning experience for the children that also encourages attitudes of responsibility. The variety of living things and the conditions necessary for life are concepts that can be delivered as children play outdoors.

Outdoor water play acquaints children with several physical phenomena. Water holds some things up and not others; water dries faster in the sun than in the shade; water reflects light; and water changes its form. The containers of different shapes and sizes used in water play are helpful in developing concepts that water flows, has weight, and takes the shape of its container.

Experiences with simple machines are also abundant outdoors. The principle of the wheel can be dealt with through wheel toys. Simple machines that are used to move heavy boxes or lift lumber, such as levers, are observed during the course of outdoor play.

The physical phenomenon of light can be introduced outdoors. A prism can be used to catch the sunlight, or the refraction of light can be observed in soap bubbles and water.

## MUSIC

When you take an autoharp or ukelele outdoors, the children can join in and sing familiar songs. Singing under the shade of a tree, or gathered around a picnic bench, adds variety to the play yard.

Observing the children running, skipping, or hopping, you may be able to pick up the children's natural rhythm on drums or other instruments. Rhythm instruments can also be taken outdoors for children to use. A marching band, with each child playing a different rhythm instrument, attracts the entire population of children.

## LANGUAGE

New words are introduced to the children through the many learning situations outdoors. The names of trees, shrubs, plants, animals, and insects can be taught. Outdoor sensory experiences add descriptive words to the child's vocabulary. When you spontaneously enter into conversations in the play yard, you can add depth and meaning to the child's language.

Directed language activities are possible outdoors. Books can be taken out, especially during warm weather; a blanket spread under the trees makes a fine library corner. You may want to read poems or stories to small groups of children. Chants made up by the children as they run or jump rope should be recorded and read back to the children. One teacher compiled an entire book of chants used by the children as they jumped rope. Functional usage of the written language can be demonstrated outdoors. Signs can be written to identify sandbox cities, or to name the children's forts. Labels identifying things planted in the garden, when they were planted, and when they began to grow, can be written.

## MATH

Many opportunities to present mathematical concepts are present outdoors. The smooth stones a child gathers, the acorns she collects, the sticks or cups in the sandbox, the number of children waiting to ride the new bike—all offer meaningful experiences with counting.

Classification, basic to future mathematical concepts, is possible outdoors. Lids from baby food jars, or plastic jars, can be used as sorting trays when children begin to group their collections of seeds, acorns, or stones. After the children have had many experiences in classifying objects on their own, you can steer them to more adroit classificatory approaches, always encouraging them to name the objects and the characteristics used in classifying them.

PHYSICAL ACTIVITY Provisions for physical activities are found throughout the well-planned play yard; however, specific plans should be made to support physical activity and equipment chosen to exercise large muscles. Any piece of equipment chosen should be able to be used in many different ways and should require the child's imagination and involvement. Equipment that children can explore, change, and experiment with is most appropriate. Children should be able to master the equipment without adult assistance in order to increase their feelings of competence.

Expensive metal swing sets are only useful for swinging. The very young child cannot use a swing without adult assistance. Swings can also be dangerous when there are children of many ages outdoors; the young child cannot be expected to remember to keep a safe distance away. Used by children in other than the approved manner, swings can be extremely hazardous pieces of equipment.

*Play on swings exercises large muscles.*

Large stationary slides are also expensive and can be used only for sliding—a rather passive experience. Metal merry-go-rounds only go around, and at some risk to younger children when older children are in control. Such expensive equipment is not only of limited use, but is also susceptible to early damage.

One preschool program saved for two years to purchase metal swing sets, with each swing shaped as a circus pony. For four months the swing sets sat in boxes while the staff and parents attempted to assemble them. Missing parts were finally located, and sets were constructed at each center. Three months after the sets were completed, not one was in working order. Vandalism and normal usage by active three-, four-, and five-year-old children damaged this expensive equipment beyond repair. The sets became a safety problem, with exposed metal screw ends and sharp, protruding metal pieces.

On the other hand, another preschool center purchased sturdy ropes, gathered discarded tires, and suspended inexpensive rope and tire swings on wooden frames and from tree limbs. Placed at various levels in different parts of the play yard, they provided many hours of enjoyment for infants, toddlers, and school-age children alike.

## Climbing

Each play space should have several pieces of climbing equipment. Some commercial companies manufacture such equipment that comes in several moveable sections; it is an excellent investment for a center. Children of all ages can change the equipment as they change their play interests. Moving the equipment to meet various needs often requires group cooperation, plans, and effort. Sturdy climbing equipment can also be constructed. Trestle units, a climbing gate, or an A-frame are easily assembled by a person experienced in simple carpentry.

Cable tables, available from the local telephone or electric company, can be set at different levels to provide another excellent climbing apparatus. Tree stumps can be planted firmly in the ground at different levels, or existing trees can occasionally be made safe for children's climbing. Sand or sawdust placed around the bottom of the tree, close supervision, and rules such as 1) no climbing with something in your hand, 2) only two children in a tree at a time, and 3) no climbing above this level help to make the tree climbing a safe adventure. Tree trunks or fallen trees can be hauled into the yard; when sharp branches are removed, they give the children something else to climb on.

Small ladders, with metal hooks at one end, are handy play yard items. These can be propped and hooked onto a cable table or wooden box, and used for climbing. Ladders are also good things to carry around by "firemen" or "window cleaners." Wooden crates, sturdy boxes, barrels, even old discarded furniture often provide other equipment for climbing.

## Balancing

A part of all motor activities, balancing can be fostered by the addition of specific play yard equipment. The simplest, yet most effective, piece of balance equipment is the balance beam. This can consist of an old log, several logs

*Climbing is good outdoor play.*

placed end to end, a board placed on its side, or bricks partially buried in the ground. Stepping stones, patio stones, or old tires placed in a series provide another type of balancing experience as the children jump from one to the other.

## Pushing and Pulling

Through pushing and pulling, children experience a sense of controlling their environment. Large wooden boxes and planks require team work to push or pull into the desired location. Old tires can be pushed and rolled to new locations, stacked to make a tower, or arranged to make a fort. Small cable tables, turned on end, can be pushed around the yard. Barrels are easily pushed when placed on their sides. Heavy blocks of wood, tree trunks or even blocks of salt require group discussion and cooperation to move from place to place. Large cardboard boxes allow even the youngest child the opportunity to push and pull successfully.

## Catching and Throwing

A wide assortment of various size and weight balls is a necessity. The youngest child enjoys the simple experience of dropping a small ball over and over again, laughing as you pick it up and return it to him. Around the age of two, children like to catch a ball while seated on the ground with their legs spread apart. By the age of two and a half, some children will be able to bounce a ball. To throw and catch a ball involves coordination, skill, and practice.

## Other Physical Activities

Many other physical responses are possible outdoors when imaginative, creative equipment is at hand. Seesaws, sliding planks, and rocking boats can be purchased or constructed. Slides that are moveable and small are preferred; these can be stored when older children use the play yard. Wheeled vehicles, although of limited usage, have a place outdoors with young children; wheelbarrows, tricycles, wagons, and pedal cars enhance the child's play.

Perhaps the most essential medium for outdoor play is dirt, with room for digging. No other activity offers children quite the same sensory pleasure, freedom, and physical activity as does digging in dirt.

Margaret McMillan, in 1919, wrote that every play yard should contain a "rubbish heap":

> Our green plots and ordered walks are good and right, but who does not remember that he once liked to play in a big place, where there were no walks at all and no rules? Therefore, a play yard must have a free and rich play, a great rubbish heap, stones, flints, bags of cans, and old iron and pots. Here every healthy child will want to go, taking out things of his own choosing to build with. (McMillan, 1919, p. 47)

Surely, our modern play yards can include such a rubbish heap! Perhaps even an old toy box or storage shed can be filled with carefully selected junk. Bits of pipes, broken tools, pots, pans, interesting mechanical parts, old clocks, motors, engines, or discarded parts from anything add interest and excitement to outdoor play.

# ORGANIZED GAMES

Once in a while, organized games that begin and end spontaneously are appreciated variations during outdoor play. Children under the age of four are not terribly interested in or capable of participating in organized games. Some simple games, generally circle or singing games, can be comfortably introduced to four- and five-year-old children.

The values of playing organized games are many. The repetition involved in most singing games gives children an experience with structured language. Learning and remembering what to do next is a valuable sequencing skill. One of the most important functions of organized games is to help children develop social interaction and learn about others. When children play together, they learn to cooperate. They also have the opportunity to practice decentration. They must learn to see the game as a whole and the relationship of all its actions to the goal (Bogdanoff & Dolch, 1979, p. 38).

Organized games help children to "learn to generalize from past mistakes and choose successful game actions and to lose some of their egocentrism" (Bogdanoff & Dolch, 1979, p. 38). When children play games, they accept the roles and the ideas of others, and learn to think of the role of others in a game. Table 2 presents a description of children's thought processes and organized games that are suited to children's levels of thinking.

Table 2 ————————————————————————————————————

| Level | Child's Thought Development | Game Requirements | Suggested Games |
|---|---|---|---|
| I | Preoperational | Pattern or sequence game<br>Two-step sequence | Ring around the Rosy<br>Roll the Ball (small group)<br>Hokey Pokey (modified)<br>Humpty Dumpty and other nursery rhymes<br>This Is the Way the _____ Walks (tune of Mulberry Bush) |
|  | Very limited verbal understanding | No verbal instruction necessary to teach game |  |
|  | Strong egocentrism | Continuous participation by all<br>No waiting necessary<br>Two to four children |  |
|  | Little group awareness, child involved primarily with adults | Game depends on adult action<br>No role alternation required |  |
| II | Preoperational | Basic pattern game<br>Not more than three steps in sequence | Punchinello (circle style)<br>Did You Ever See a Lassie?<br>Hide the Clock<br>Little Sally Walker<br>Paw Paw Patch<br>Variation of Mulberry Bush (with child's choice of action) |
|  | Verbal understanding not dependable | No verbal instruction required |  |
|  | Egocentrism still strong | Continuous participation<br>Five to eight children |  |
|  | Awareness of other children's presence but most interest in adult's expectation of child's behavior | Role alternation with help of the leader only |  |
| III | Preoperational | Basic pattern game<br>Four to five steps in sequence<br>Limited choice of action within framework of game | Looby Loo<br>Doggie, Doggie, Where's Your Bone?<br>Musical Chairs (modified)<br>Are You My Kitten?<br>Duck, Duck, Goose (modified)<br>Mulberry Bush |
|  | Coordination of language with action nearly complete | Some verbal instruction supported by demonstration |  |
|  | Egocentrism less strong in game situation<br>Good awareness of all players but limited understanding of their roles in game | Wait short periods for turn with group action interspersed<br>Six to ten players<br>One-to-one interaction possible |  |
|  | Primary interest in own role | Role alternation between players may now be part of game |  |

*Table 2 (cont.)* _____

| Level | Child's Thought Development | Game Requirements | Suggested Games |
|---|---|---|---|
| IV | Late preoperational | | A Tisket-a-Tasket |
| | More objective understanding of role in action of game | Players required to make some choices of action | Squirrel in the Trees |
| | Good verbal understanding | May use verbal cues as well as action | Charlie Over the Water |
| | | | Find My Child |
| | Egocentrism diminishing | Turn taking can be part of game | London Bridge |
| | | | Knock, Knock |
| | Enjoys coordination with group<br>Will subject own interests to group effort | Understands and enjoys role alternation and some role reversal<br>Eight to twelve children | |
| V | Concrete operational | | Word games (G-H-O-S-T) |
| | Reversible thought and lessened egocentrism<br>Understands rules as objective framework for action | Decisions of strategy determine outcome of game | Tag (modified)<br>Hide and Seek<br>Kick the Can |
| | New interest in competition within coordinated effort | Competition may be used<br>Team action may substitute for personal involvement | Competitive races and relays<br>Follow the Leader |
| | Uses language easily for thought | Verbal element can be definitive part of game | Darts<br>Horseshoes |

*DEVELOPMENTAL GUIDELINES FOR CHOOSING GAMES*

NOTE: Reprinted, by permission, from R. T. Bogdanoff and E. T. Dolch, "Old Games for Young Children: A Link to Our Heritage," *Young Children* 34, No. 2 (Jan. 1979), 42-43. Copyright © 1979, National Association for the Education of Young Children, 1834 Connecticut Avenue, N.W., Washington, D.C. 20009.

Some games young children enjoy have rich cultural heritages and are a part of tradition. Games, originating in Africa, Europe, South America, and other countries, have found their way to America and reflect the lifestyles and cultural backgrounds of the children. Playing some games lets children feel their heritage is respected and teaches other children about the ethnic heritages of many.

Games should be chosen that actively involve all children who wish to play. When young children are asked to wait for their turn, they usually wander off to some more interesting activity. Games requiring no specific number of children, and those that can be played with only four or five children, should be selected. Any game that is chosen must have uncomplicated rules that are subject to change as the children wish. Teams are a meaningless concept for young children, and games requiring sides should be avoided. Introducing competition through organized games is not appropriate for children; everyone in the preschool should be a winner.

Seasoned nursery school teachers first introduce games to small groups of children indoors. Voices carry better indoors, and directions and words can be heard and understood. Later, the children who have been taught the game indoors will begin to play it outdoors, often teaching it to other children as they play.

Generally, you should begin to play the game as you teach it to the children. You may say, "Take my hands and I'll show you how to play 'frog in the middle.'" Then, beginning to walk in a circle, say, "Joe, you go into the middle and be the frog. Now we sing, 'Frog in the middle and he can't get out . . .'" and continue to demonstrate the game as it is being played.

Children generally want to play the same game two or three times in succession. Some children will leave the circle and others come in and take their place. They have difficulty, however, when more than two or three games are being played at a time. Children who show no interest in the games may be given a special invitation to "come and play with us" or asked to "hold my hand as we play this game."

Organized games add fun to holiday parties. The very familiar games that are played throughout the year take on a holiday spirit when some of the words are changed. "Frog in the middle" could become "valentine," "Easter bunny," "Santa," or "witch in the middle," depending on the occasion.

The very youngest children can play such simple games as "ring around the rosy," or "frog in the middle." The older children can play such games as "here we go looby loo," "in a spider's web," "skip tag," "did you ever see a lassie," "Punchinello," and "Charlie over the water."

# _____ GAMES FOR TWO YEAR OLDS

*Ring Around the Rosy*

Ring around the rosy
A pocket full of posies
Ashes, ashes
We all fall down.

*Swing Song*

Swinging, swinging now we go up,
Now we do down,
Swinging, swinging, Jim go up,
Jim go down.

*Running*

Running up and running down
We're running up and running down
We're running up and running down
We're running, running all around.

*Hop Up*

Hop up, hop down,
Up and down
Hop up, hop down,
Hip hip hopping down.

## GAMES FOR THREE YEAR OLDS _____

*Frog in the Middle*

Frog in the middle and he can't get out,
He can't get out, he can't get out,
Frog in the middle and he can't get out,
Watch him hop and jump about.

*Children form a circle holding hands, with one child becoming a frog in the middle. Frog tries to leave the circle and the children raise and lower their arms, preventing him from leaving.*

*Did You Ever See a Lassie?*

Did you ever see a lassie, a lassie, a lassie
Did you ever see a lassie do this way and that?
Do this way and that, do this way and that way
Did you ever see a lassie do this way or that?

*Children form a circle. One person is the lassie or laddie and demonstrates some movement. The other children copy the movement, and a new leader is chosen. Use children's names instead of "lassie" and "laddie" to vary the game.*

*Punchinello*

Oh what can you do Punchinello funny fellow,
Oh what can you do Punchinello funny you,
Oh we can do it to Punchinello funny fellow,
Oh we can do it to Punchinello funny you!

*One child is Punchinello and demonstrates a movement to the other children. They copy the action, and a new Punchinello is chosen.*

*Toodala*

Everybody move around too da la, too da la
Everybody move around too da la, la, la dy.
Make some motions, toodala, toodala toodala,
Make some motions, toodala-la-lady.

*All of the children move around, swinging and dancing. Children can stop and copy the motions of one child. New verses can be made up that describe what the children can do: "I can fly like a bird, too da la," "I can walk like a giant, too da la."*

# ———————— GAMES FOR FOUR AND FIVE YEAR OLDS

*Looby Loo*

Here we dance Looby Loo
Here we dance Looby Light
Here we dance Looby Loo
All on a Saturday night.

verse:

I put my right hand in
I take my right hand out
I give my right hand a shake, shake, shake
And turn myself about.

*Verses follow in order: left hand, right foot, left foot, my round head, my whole self. Children are in a circle. On the chorus they join hands and go around and around. On each verse they do the appropriate action.*

*Skip Tag*

*One child skips around a circle and tags some other child's outstretched hands. The tagged child skips in the opposite direction. When they meet, they shake hands. The first child goes to his place and the second child proceeds as did the first. Suitable music may be played as children skip or march.*

*Round and Round the Village*

*Children stand in a circle, hands joined. One or more children walk around the circle as the group sings or chants:*

Go round and round the village,
Go round and round the village,
Go round and round the village,
As we have done before.

*At the next verse, the children raise their arms and "It" goes in and out under their arms as they sing:*

Go in and out the window,
Go in and out the window,
Go in and out the window,
As we have done before.

*On the last verse, "It" chooses another child to take his place by standing in front of him.*

Now stand before your partner,
Now stand before your partner,
Now stand before your partner,
As we have done before.

*Basketball*

*Children stand in a circle and take turns trying to throw a ball into a basket placed in the center of the circle.*

*Charlie Over the Water*

*The children form a ring and sing or chant as they dance with clasped hands. "Charlie" stands in the center.*

Charlie over the water
Charlie over the sea
Charlie catch a blackbird
Can't catch me.

*At the word "me," everybody stoops. If the child in the center can catch someone before he stoops, that child must take the place of "Charlie." Use the children's names to vary the game.*

*In a Spider's Web*

In a spider's web, one elephant was hung,
He was lonely there, so he called another one.

*Children hold hands in a circle with one child the lonely elephant. He chooses another child, and then the children chant:*

In a spider's web, two elephants were hung,
They were lonely there, so they called another one.

*The song is repeated until the line of elephants is too long, and everyone is an elephant.*

*Toss Ball*

*Children stand in a circle. The leader calls the name of a child and immediately throws the ball into air. The child hurries to catch the ball before it bounces once, or on the first or second bounce (whatever the children are capable of).*

*Wrapping Paper Walk*

*Each child is given two pieces of wrapping paper, one for each foot. He proceeds to a goal and back by moving the paper for each foot forward* at each step. He must step on the paper at each step. Children can form two lines for turns, two trying the stunt at the same time. The next in line starts as soon as the first returns.

### Skip and Stoop

Music is played as the children skip or march about. When the music stops suddenly, the children are to stoop down immediately.

### Birds Fly

Each child places his arms at his sides, but he may wave them when the leader calls out "birds fly." When the leader names creatures without wings (pigs, cows), the children must keep their hands still.

### Do As I Say, Not As I Do

The leader instructs the group to do what she says, but to listen carefully because sometimes she will try to fool them by doing something different. She gives such directions as "Put your hands in the air" (she does so), "Bend over" (she does so), "Put your hands on your toes" (but instead she puts her hands on her head). The children attempt to copy the leader, doing only what she says. Children who miss are not eliminated; the game goes on with all included.

### Jump the Brook

Two ropes are stretched on the ground or the floor to represent the sides of a brook. The game starts with the two ropes fairly close together. The children follow a leader, jumping the brook. When all of the children have jumped, the ropes are spread a little farther apart, until the brook is too wide to cross. Using chalk lines, rather than a rope, prevents children from tripping. No children are eliminated.

### Forty Ways to Get There

Each child is given a chance to go across the room in any manner he wishes, as long as no one else has crossed the same way. He may hop, walk, skip, jump on one foot, and so forth.

### Simon Says

A leader stands in front of the children and gives them commands. The leader obeys all of the commands, but the other children are expected to obey them only when they are preceded by the words "Simon says." The leader calls, "Simon says hands on hips," and everyone puts hands on hips. But if the leader says, "Run in place," and begins running in place, the others should remain motionless.

*Duck, Duck, Duck, Goose*

*All the players but one stoop or sit in a circle. The odd player walks around the outside of the circle, touching each player lightly on the head and repeating the word "duck." This continues until the "it" player touches a head and says the word "goose." The child who has been called "goose" jumps up from the circle and chases the "it" person. If the chaser succeeds in catching the "it" person before "it" reaches the vacant space in the circle, he may then be the one to be the next "it." If he fails to tag the "it" person, he returns to the space in the circle and "it" continues the game.*

# IT'S UP TO YOU! ——————————————————————————————

Play outdoors is every bit as valuable for young children as play indoors. Children have the same opportunities outside that they have when they play indoors for learning about their world and how to relate with others. But outdoors children have added opportunities to exercise muscles, develop physical skills, and release excess energy.

Because outdoor play is so valuable for children, you, as the teacher, have a critical role. It takes a lot of careful, thoughtful planning on your part to make outdoor play valuable and safe. Perhaps your first responsibility centers on considering the needs of all the children. Spaces and equipment must be appropriate and safe for the youngest as well as the oldest children, and provisions must be made so that children with specific handicaps may take part in the activities outside.

You must also plan for children to come in contact with all of the curriculum content areas as they play outside. Some days you may plan a specific art project for outdoor play; another day you might plan an organized game or a music activity. At other times, you may be able to introduce children to concepts from science or math. Remember, all parts of the curriculum—social studies, art, music, science, and mathematics—can be experienced by children as they play outside.

You also have an important role in planning for children's safety as they play outside. Each day you must check the yard and equipment for safety and ascertain that all equipment is in good repair. It's also wise to check the ground under stationary items in the play yard, such as swings, slides, and climbing equipment. It's important that the ground under these items be continually covered with something resilient—wood chips, sand, pine bark, or anything that will provide a protective cushion should children fall from the equipment.

When planning for safety, you will also want to be sure that you can observe all areas of the yard and that you can reach any one place readily in case of an emergency. You will also need to consider safety when arranging the yard, taking care that spaces for bike riding and active running are out of the way of younger children or those children playing quietly.

Your role, however, does not end with planning for activities and safety outside, but continues as children play. You must be a teacher who is active in supervision as well as in teaching. Constant supervision of children is required; and because it is, some preschools designate one teacher as a spotter each day. This teacher is responsible for observing the yard or a given portion of the playground, and although she may enter into play with the children, she recognizes that her major role is observing children and stepping in to prevent hazards. In this way one person is constantly on guard for potential problems and is not distracted by other teachers and children.

Teaching occurs outdoors, too. As children play, you can enter into their activities. You might give them different ideas to act out or provide them with verbal labels for the things they're doing. Sometimes a well-phrased question can extend children's thinking. At other times you can add props or different toys to extend children's play.

Play outdoors takes place all year round. Each season brings different opportunities for learning, exploring, and fun. Take advantage of whatever the season brings to foster children's learning and pleasure as they play outdoo.s.

## REFERENCES

Bogdanoff, R. T., and Dolch, E. T. "Old Games for Young Children: A Link to Our Heritage." *Young Children* 34 (1979): 37–45.

*Child Welfare League of America Standards for Day Care Service.* New York: Child Welfare League of America, 1969.

*Day Care: 8 Serving Children with Special Needs.* Washington, D.C.: U.S. Department of Health, Education, and Welfare, 1972.

Hurtwood, L.A. *Playgrounds.* New York: Guggenheim Museum, 1965.

McMillan, M. *The Nursery School.* London: J. M. Dent & Sons, 1919.

*Outdoor Play.* Project 3.: U.S. National Committee for Early Childhood Education, n.d.

## RESOURCES

*Designing the Child Development Center.* Washington, D.C.: Office of Economic Opportunity, 1968.

*Found Spaces and Equipment for Children's Centers.* New York: Educational Facilities Laboratories, 1972.

Friedberg, P. M. *Playgrounds for City Children.* Washington, D.C.: Association for Childhood Education International, 1969.

Frost, J. L., and Klein, B. *Children's Play and Playgrounds.* Boston: Allyn & Bacon, 1979.

Stone, J. G. *Play and Playgrounds.* Washington, D.C.: National Association for the Education of Young Children, 1968.

Sunderline, S. G. *Housing for Early Childhood Education.* Washington, D.C.: National Association for the Education of Young Children, 1968.

## PROJECTS

1. Design a play yard for a multiple-age-group preschool center. You have a square-shaped area to work with that is adjacent to the building. Water is available from faucets on one side of the building. There are two large trees in the left-hand corner of the yard. Your budget for equipment is $100.

2. List the equipment you would provide for a) manipulative play, b) imaginative play, c) physical play, and d) dramatic play.

3. Observe a group of children playing outdoors. Record the language of the two-, three-, and four-year-old children. In which area of the play yard (housekeeping, climbing bar, sand, block, etc.) do the children seem to verbalize most?

4. Observe a teacher working with children outdoors. Note and record how the teacher a) encourages safety measures, b) uses an experience to foster language development, c) reinforces children, d) arranges equipment to obtain more complex responses, and e) actively observes the children.

# THE CURRICULUM IN A PRESCHOOL PROGRAM

## PART FOUR

A preschool center is neither a place where formal education takes place in rigidly separated segments of teaching, nor a place where learning is an accident—something that may or may not happen. Rather, the preschool provides a homelike atmosphere of informality, security, and planned experiences in which children can learn and grow. There is no formal subject matter in the preschool. You should structure experiences that will contribute to each child's understanding of himself and his world.

Each child must learn for himself, at his own level and rate of speed. Although some group experiences—stories, singing, discussions, field trips—do take place in the center, they are only supplements for individual learning. Each child must form for himself his own understanding of the world. Learning must be an individual matter, for the interests and abilities of young children vary greatly. Some children will be able to listen to long, involved stories; others may not be able to attend to a short story, even when cuddled on the lap of a teacher. Some children will want to plant seeds over and over again; others would rather build in the sand.

Curriculum in a preschool does include content from every possible field. The language arts, science, math, art, music, and social studies are included in the daily program of activities. These, however, are not introduced to children as rigid, separate, or isolated subjects, but rather are interwoven through all of the experiences and activities of the day. One is not separated from another.

Language cannot be separated from any activity in the preschool. As children play, they talk. A field trip taken to foster the children's knowledge of their neighborhood is rich with language. In art activities designed to foster creativity, the children verbalize their ideas as well as expressing them through the media.

Young children naturally express themselves with their emotions that are close to the surface and hard to control. The curriculum in the center provides for the child's expression through music, language, and art. Providing the child with the raw materials to create with, surrounding him with beauty and the artwork of others, fosters development of esthetic appreciation.

By acquiring knowledge and skills, becoming familiar with the world, and being able to apply their knowledge and skills to new situations, children in the center develop intellectual competence. Children who can deal with their environment effectively and intellectually feel better about themselves and see themselves as competent, able people, in control of themselves and their world.

# THE YOUNG CHILD AND LANGUAGE

*Speech is the best show man puts on* (Whorf, 1956, p. 249)

8

The baby coos and gurgles back to her mother, the toddler chatters to himself as he plays, the four year old makes up jingling nonsense words for the sheer fun of it, and the five year old dictates a complete story to her teacher, who records it. Each of these children, at her own level, is demonstrating the power unique to human beings—the power of language. According to Green,

> Of all the skills the child masters during the preschool years, learning to talk is by far the most difficult and most marvelous. Unlike learning to sit, to crawl, and to walk, which baby will do when he has sufficient motor control of his body and with very little if any outside help, baby will not learn to talk without much patient teaching from the adults who surround him. (Green, 1960, p. 14)

Human language is learned. How children the world over learn language, how they manage to match the sounds they make with those of the speakers around them, is a topic of extensive research and discussion. Why the baby coos, how the child learns the meaning of words, and how he incorporates the rules of grammer into his language are still questions without absolute answers.

Carroll (1965) believes that the ability to learn and to use language stems from at least three interrelated sequences of development: 1) cognitive development—the child's capacity to recognize, identify, discriminate, and manipulate the features of the world around him; 2) development of the capacity to discriminate and comprehend the speech he hears from others in his environment; and 3) development of the ability to produce speech sounds and sequences of sounds, based on the physiological makeup of the child.

## PHYSICAL FACTORS

Humans can speak because of their unique physiological makeup. Language, in this respect, is clearly organically based. In order for the child to speak, she must have functioning speech organs, auditory apparatus, and neurological organs. Children with certain physical impairments have delayed, inhibited, or no speech. Defects in the tongue, palate, lips, nose, ears, as well as in the other physical parts of the body used in speaking can cause defects in children's speech.

## SOCIAL FACTORS

In order to learn to speak, a child must develop the capacity to discriminate and comprehend the speech she hears from people in her environment. It is apparent that children imitate the speech they hear from others; however, imitation is not the entire answer to how language is learned. Even with direct teaching, the child still confuses rules from the language she hears. Dramatic evidence of how resistant to external correction the child's rule system can be is reported in this conversation by Gleason (1967, p. 441).

> *Child:* My teacher holded the baby rabbits and we patted them.
>
> *Adult:* Did you say your teacher held the baby rabbits?
>
> *Child:* Yes.
>
> *Adult:* What did you say she did?
>
> *Child:* She holded the baby rabbits and we patted them.
>
> *Adult:* Did you say she held them tightly?
>
> *Child:* No, she holded them loosely.

Children do learn to speak the language of their parents and home community, and they do so with ease and speed; however, imitation is influenced by other factors. Children pick the model they wish to imitate. They hear speech from other children, from television, sales people, teachers, parents, and others; however, the more closely they identify with a model, the more they will imitate the speech of that model. This may account for the close relationship between the mother's speech and vocabulary level and that of the child, for the child probably identifies more closely with her mother than with others in her environment (Stodolsky, 1965).

The reinforcement the child receives from people in the environment also appears to influence her learning of the language. A concerned, interested adult who reinforces the child's beginning attempts at communication seems to foster the child's language acquisition.

—————————————————————————— COGNITIVE FACTORS

The ability to understand that a word stands for, or represents, something is essential for language acquisition. Once children's cognitive development allows them to represent things in their world by naming them, they can begin to conceptualize and categorize. Children's ability to recognize, identify, discriminate, and manipulate the features of the world around them influences their attainment of language.

While authorities disagree on exactly how language is learned and what factors influence language attainment, they do seem to agree that, at least in our society, language is the key to success at every level of life. Children entering a grade school with a normal vocabulary, the ability to listen, and to express themselves through words will no doubt experience success in the highly verbal atmosphere of the school. All school activities require language competency on the part of children in order for them to succeed in any way.

The relationship between language and cognition is very apparent on standardized measures of achievement and intelligence tests. Such tests, for all of their weaknesses, inappropriateness, and misuse, are still widely used today. They are heavily based on the individual's ability to manipulate and apply abstract verbal concepts; and they do seem to be valid predictors of a child's success in school and in later life.

Children who have limited opportunities to share ideas through language, and few experiences to have ideas about, are those who demontrate deficits in their language development. Research conducted on children reared in unstimulating environments, having few experiences, little opportunity to share ideas through language, and poor language models, has shown that they will have deficient language skills.

As children interact with the environment, those mental processes which make it possible for humans to acquire, store, and arrange information develop. Language provides labels for concept formation and allows humans to communicate what they know. Thus, cognition and language development are closely related.

## LANGUAGE DIFFERENCES _____

At one time it was felt that disadvantaged children had no language; hence, they were unable to express themselves. Now educators have become aware of the fact that all children do have a language with which they can make themselves fully understood, but only to those others who speak the same language.

*Many children speak several languages.*

According to Birren and Hess,

> Recent studies of peer groups in spontaneous interaction in northern ghetto areas show that there is a rich verbal culture in constant use. Negro children in the vernacular culture cannot be considered "verbally deprived" if one observes them in a favorable environment—on the contrary, their daily life is a pattern of continual verbal stimulation, contest, and imitation. . . . There are many other speech events associated with the vernacular culture of the ghetto: jokes, songs, narratives, and of course the hip vocabulary itself. All of these reflect the value system of the vernacular, and because it is opposed in many ways to the standard culture of the school, it does not appear in school contexts. (Birren & Hess, 1968, p. 95)

Many children are not always familiar with the language of the preschool. Children coming from homes or communities in which two languages are spoken may actually learn to communicate in two or even more languages. Many of the children who speak two languages are from Latino backgrounds. The number of Latinos living in the United States is believed to be well over 11 million (Valverde, 1978).

Children who speak a language other than English must find a bilingual, bicultural experience in the preschool. Bilingual-bicultural education has been defined as "a program of instruction which uses two languages for instruction, one of which is English. The program also pays particular attention to the heritage and cultural back ground of the students it serves" (Valverde, 1978, p. 5).

Language patterns also differ from region to region in the United States. The speech patterns of a child from the northeast coast of the country differ from those of a child from the southeast tip of Georgia; the speech of a Texan child differs from that of a child from Harlem. A child who has moved to Florida after having lived in Milwaukee gets confused when he hears his neighbor ask, "Is your mother going to carry you to school?" And the child moving from Florida to Milwaukee fails to understand when the Milwaukee children offer him a drink from the "bubbler."

No one language pattern is considered superior to another. Each one is complex, expressive, and has rules of syntax and grammar. And each one communicates. Reminding us that different regional speech patterns have been accepted in our nation, Strickland (1967) recalls the speech of the presidents of the United States. Roosevelt's speech was that of the aristocrat from suburban New York, complete with a Harvard accent; Truman's rich Missouri speech was often coarse and raw; Eisenhower's speech was typically midwestern; and Kennedy's accent—his "idears about Cuber"—was very pronounced. These patterns were all accepted by the nation at large. If Americans can accept speech differences in the presidents of their country, then it seems logical to accept and respect the speech of the child, whatever dialect he may use in order to communicate and express himself. When working with children in a preschool center, you must learn to recognize and respect the validity of dialects or language differences among the children, recognizing that these differences do not mean retarded or deficient language development.

## LANGUAGE IN THE PRESCHOOL CENTER _____

Children usually come to a group setting with established language patterns; however, in the case of a preschool center, children may experience the language environment of the center as one of their first language contacts. Thus, the preschool center must take responsibility, along with the child's parents, for developing the child's language. The center, rich with trained, nurturing adults, other children, and things to manipulate and to think and talk about, is a naturally ideal environment in which to foster language growth.

Language is a part of every action and function in the center; each experience with speaking and listening has an effect on the child's later development and success in life. The language the child hears and responds to as an infant and toddler sets the stage for nearly all of her later development and growth. If a center is language-poor, with unresponsive adults present as model figures, with few opportunities for children to talk, with nothing to listen to, and with little to see or do, children's language will be inadequate, and they will be unprepared to take their places in our verbal society.

## INFANTS _____

Infancy has been called that period of life without speech (McCarthy, 1946, p. 10). Actually it is full of speech and language, and is critical to future language development. Babies do communicate. They cry (even their cries can be differentiated), mew, gurgle, chuckle, and grin. By the age of six months, the baby's cooing changes to a kind of babbling—an experimentation with the production of a variety of sounds. Squeals, vowels, consonants, and a variety of tones and reflections are present.

Babies are very responsive to the human voices they hear. A two- or three-month-old baby can be quieted, soothed, or distracted by the sound of your voice. In the second half of the first year of life, that baby may recognize his name and the names for many of the things in his environment. He actually responds to your commands and verbalizations.

No planned program of language development can be prescribed for all of the babies within a preschool center. Each child is individualistic; each will respond differently to the language he hears. Research does indicate, however, that all babies need a single mother figure or single adult to care for them in a personal manner, interacting with them warmly and responsively, for normal language and speech to develop.

Realizing that the infant must hear language in order to reproduce it, several commercial toy companies have developed mechanical devices that will "talk" to the baby. The baby pulls a cord or bumps the device which activates a recording of a voice. These devices, although they may attract the baby's attention for a moment or two, soon lose their attractiveness. A device simply cannot offer the child the stimulation that human interactions can give. It cannot produce the surprising responses of a person who can laugh when the baby laughs, or coo and squeal and make different sounds. A person can surprise the baby with a laugh, or be surprised by the baby's squeal—all in a warm, loving, and personal manner.

To the very young infant it really doesn't matter what is being said, just as long as the person talking is responsive. Physical contact is essential: you can hold the baby, look directly at him, touch his arm or leg, stroke his body, or even tickle him gently. If the infant babbles a sound, you should repeat the same sound back to the infant. The infant, having been reinforced in these initial attempts at babbling, babbles again. If you vary the sound, a circular type of babbling results, with your imitating the infant and the infant's imitating you.

Some adults laugh at the idea of cooing and gurgling back to an infant, and others are fearful of fostering baby talk. Green states,

> some parents tell me that they would not dream of cooing or gurgling at their baby in the nonsensical way recommended. But how lovely it is to see a mother cradling her baby in her arms and crooning to him, or to see a father tickling Johnnie's tummy and babbling, "booboo boo to you young man," while Johnnie chortles and chuckles, "talking back." In such intimate scenes of loving sympathy and understanding, the child grows up with a sense of security and learns to delight in his own "talking," which brings such approval and enjoyment (Green, 1960, p. 21).

As the infant grows, warm emotional ties continue to be important; however, the things you say to the baby become increasingly important. Although the infant will not understand exactly what you are saying, he will absorb the rhythm and the emotional content of the speech. The repetition of small sentences and describing things while doing them foster the child's understanding of words.

You, as well as the child's mother, should utilize each and every contact with the baby to communicate through language. Hum, chat, sing, and talk to the baby during each routine care-giving experience. In talking to the baby there is no need to speak baby talk, but you may want to revise your speech, using short, simple sentences, speaking slowly, repeating phrases, and stressing nouns and verbs. Always using the child's name, talk to the child while he's being dressed: "Now let's put your arm in here," or "John's leg goes right here," and "Now for your shoes—here's one and there's the other." Name the parts of the body during bath or changing, or name the things around the child while completing the routines. Feeding is an excellent time to talk to the baby. A breast- or bottle-feeding baby is usually absorbed in the task of eating, but the baby sitting in a highchair, beginning to eat solid foods, enjoys conversation during his mealtime. You can talk about the food the child is eating: "Look how Jim eats his ham," "Now how about a drink of milk from the cup?" "Those peas are green," or "Do you like the sweet apple?"

It's hard to determine exactly how much a baby understands; however, at around eight months of age, the baby may extend his arm as you say, "Put your arm through here and your sweater will be on," or he may wave to someone who says "Bye-bye," or respond when told "Daddy is coming."

Mother Goose rhymes and action songs and games are appropriate at this age. "Pat-a-Cake" may be old and tired for an adult, but to the eight-month-old baby it's stimulating and delightful. Such nursery games as "so big," "this little piggy," "dance Thumbkin dance," and "Bo Peeper" enthrall children as young as six months of age. The rhythm, sound, and pattern of language in these rhymes, plus the personal response the adult and child bring to them, has great appeal to the baby.

Read to a baby? Why of course! Just as soon as the baby is able to enjoy it, you should read to him daily. Hold the baby on your lap, or if he's still tiny, in your arm, and begin to show him simple picture books. Point to an object in the book, name the picture, and tell the child something about it. The baby may pat the picture, gurgle over it, or even squeal. Pictures of animals delight the baby, who may even try to make the sound the animal makes if you provide a model. Sometimes baby may try to pick the picture off the page or even, if food is pictured, try to eat it. By six months of age or so, the baby will begin to point to objects as you ask him, "Show me the rabbit," "Where's the doggie?" or "Where's the baby?" Surely, the year-old baby should be familiar with several books and able to "read" some to himself, looking at them and turning the pages.

*Infants communicate too.*

Many commercial books are available for babies. Simple, sturdy books with large pictures of single objects are satisfactory for the very young child. These are often constructed of laminated cardboard or heavy paper and have brightly colored photographs or simple illustrations. Usually the books deal with everyday objects, people, or animals. Illustrations with many fine details that incorporate a large number of objects are less appealing to the very young baby than less complex drawings or illustrations.

Although simple illustrations are most successful with the young child, one teacher found that she could skim through a popular magazine while holding the baby on her lap. Although the baby was not able to handle the magazine, he enjoyed looking at the pictures of food, flowers, and people. Books can also be constructed from magazine pictures that are mounted on heavy cardboard or between plastic sheets.

Cloth books, with shoddy pictures printed on flimsy materials are often sold as appropriate books for babies; however, they are a poor investment. The cloth pictures are rarely of a quality that is appealing to the adult or the infant, and the material soon frays, or if washed, disintegrates. Furthermore, the flimsy pages cannot be grasped by the infant to turn them; he cannot even pat and stroke the pictures without eventually wadding the cloth book into an unmanageable mess.

Other children are always present at the preschool center, and babies are extremely responsive to them. During the waking time of the baby, he may be carried to other parts of the center where older children can talk to him, read books to him, sing their songs, recite poems, or otherwise verbally delight the baby.

# TODDLERS

A baby says a word and the entire world listens. The parents record the word in the baby book and the preschool staff spreads the word: "Carmen said 'up' today!" Everyone seems to realize the importance and meaning of the child's very first spoken word. It is soon followed by many other words, and by the time the toddler is two years of age, she is adding words to her vocabulary daily.

Each toddler shows individual language development. Some jabber incessantly, imitating the sounds and intonations of the adults around them. They may use few distinguishable words, but they make themselves clearly understood. Some children seldom speak, but then one day begin using complete sentences as if they had just learned to talk overnight. Others who have seemed to enjoy learning to talk suddenly stop talking, concentrating entirely on perfecting their walking and running skills instead.

Usually, toddlers use one or two words in combination to mean many things. "Mommy up" can mean anything from "Mother is going up the stairs" to "Mother, please pick me up." Somewhere around two years of age, the child begins to incorporate "me," "I," and "you" into her vocabulary. She can now listen to simple stories and follow simple directions.

The toddler's developing concepts are apparent through her language. As Green puts it, "Birdie may apply to everything that flies—an airplane, a butterfly or a leaf blown by the wind. Moon may be anything round—a penny, a biscuit, a plate, or a saucer. Until he has sorted the problem out and discovered that everything has its own name, he naturally remains very much restricted in vocabulary" (Green, 1960, p. 40).

The toddler's favorite phrase is "What's that?" She will spend hours running around asking adults to name everything she touches. Her vocabulary rapidly increases; some estimate that the toddler around three years of age possesses over one thousand words. She does have a fairly standard grammar construction, and she can use such abstract words as "up," "down," "now," "soon," and "sometime" with accuracy. Children under three gain satisfaction from the power language gives them as they express their thoughts in words and make others understand.

Toddlers in a preschool center need opportunities to find out about their world, and they need the labels to go with the experiences they have. Language programs for toddlers in a center should be planned to meet individual needs, giving each child many shared experiences to talk about with concerned adults and other children. A young child in the center needs someone to talk to—a person who enjoys listening to her sometimes imperfect speech and responding clearly, slowly, and with patience and affection.

## LISTENING

Listening begins early in life. The young child, under the age of three, requires many opportunities to listen to herself speak, and to listen to other children and adults. Listening need not be a passive experience for the toddler. All young children must move, and even their movements provide opportunities for listening: "Listen! How do your feet sound running on the ground?" "Listen! How do your hands sound when you clap them together? "Listen! Who is playing outdoors?" Children enjoy listening to adults sing, talk, and read to them, and they enjoy the sounds of music and nature around them.

## Music

Music provides very definite listening experiences for toddlers. They move their bodies, swaying to music with a beat, or they jump, bounce, and hop to a lively tune. Even soft, soothing music is enjoyed by the very young child. She may even begin to recognize favorite songs and request them over and over again. Folk tunes, marches, and nursery rhymes are popular with toddlers.

During singing time, you may sit on the floor with an autoharp, guitar, or such a simple musical instrument as a string of bells, tone blocks, or a triangle, and begin to sing with one or two children. Other children may come over and join in the fun; others will leave the activity and go on to something else that has caught their eye.

Twos and threes will not necessarily sing. They may pick out phrases of songs, humming them or saying them in a sing-song fashion. Select songs for toddlers that have simple, repeated word phrases and melody sections that allow them to give a rhythmic response—bending knees, bouncing, hopping, jumping, walking to the music. Such songs as "Hey Betty Martin" and "Skip to

My Lou" have repeated phrases and melody and allow the toddler to tiptoe or skip while the teacher sings the song. Later, you can substitute the child's name for "Betty" or "Lou."

Young children enjoy making their own music. Drums, bells, or cymbals can be used by the toddler who shakes, waves, or rattles the instrument in response (but not in time) to other sounds and rhythm patterns. Pots and pans or blocks pounded together, pieces of sandpaper rubbed together, or pebbles rattled in a taped box allow the child to explore the possibilities of sounds and encourage her to try to reproduce sounds herself.

## Stories

Simple, well-chosen, and well-read stories become favorites of young children; they will want certain stories read again and again. Children under two still require simple picture books, but rather than having you point to and describe the pictures, they may want to "read" the book to you and do the pointing and describing. Reading to only one or two children at a time, encourage the personal involvement of the child, stopping to answer her questions and responding to her comments and explanations. Listening to stories at this age is often a conversation time, with questions, answers, comments, and discussions flowing from the pictures or story.

Books about the child's life, about animals in their natural settings, about families, or about machines and the world around her are most appropriate for children under the age of three or four. Children are especially responsive to stories that they can relate to. *Saturday Walk, Just like Me,* and the *Bundle Book* are deeply satisfying and emotionally relevant to the young child. Each will hear her own personal story and will pay attention to the ideas that are important to her.

The Angus books by Marjorie Flack present factual information about animals and life in an exciting manner appropriate for toddlers. Her other books, *Wait for William* and *The Story about Ping,* are equally excellent. Lois Lenski's books, *The Little Auto, Airplane,* and *Papa Small*, although outdated in many respects, are still useful to the toddler who is in the process of understanding everyday life. Ruth Krauss has written a number of books that appeal to toddlers and are especially suited to their needs and interests. *The Carrot Seed, The Growing Story,* and *The Bundle Book* are all delightful. The stories of Ezra Jack Keats, *The Snowy Day, Whistle for Willie,* and *Peter's Chair*, are beautifully written and deal with events that toddlers are personally interested in. Several of the Little Owl and Kinder Owl books published by Holt, Rinehart & Winston quickly become favorites of children as young as thirteen months of age. *Good Night Mr. Beetle, Good Night, Good Night,* and *Daddy Is Home* are beautiful in their simple, rhythmic passages with phrases that can be repeated by even the youngest child.

It is often suggested that stories read to the toddler should be true to reality. The child under four often humanizes the objects in her environment and does not need to be further confused by books about animals that talk, think, and feel like humans. The folk tales of *Little Red Riding Hood, The Three Pigs,* and *The Three Bears* might also be better reserved until the child is older and has the ability to separate fact from fiction. The real world, just as it is, is exciting, bright, and full of magic and mystery for the toddler.

Toddlers want to have their favorite books read repeatedly, getting to know them as friends. These books provide them with emotional support in their lives. Books about the toddlers, themselves, always have great appeal for them. You should compose simple books about the children in the center; they are of the highest personal value and interest. Cut pictures from magazines or use photos of the children to write "Jose's Day," "A Day at Head Start," or "A Day at Mulberry Center." The story, a very simple account of what happens during the day, may read, "Jose gets up and washes his face. Then he gets dressed to go to the center. At the center he plays and eats lunch. He likes to play with blocks and paint." Other books could be written about mother or father going to work, or brother and sister going to their school.

## Poems

Long before children are able to sit and listen to a complete story, they should have been read some poetry. Mother Goose, with its repetitive humor, rhythm, and possibilities for personal responses on the part of a child, should be familiar to all children in the center. The baby has played "pat-a-cake" and "Bo Peeper," and now she can become acquainted with "Jack Be Nimble," "Mary Had a Little Lamb," "Jack and Jill," and all of the other Mother Goose songs that deal with children or animals in realistic settings. Mother Goose verses that offer

*Children talk to one another.*

children realistic, childlike experiences are compiled in *The Family Book of Nursery Rhymes* by Iona and Peter Opie and in Leslie Brooke's *Ring o' Roses.*

Never ignoring Mother Goose, you may want to introduce other poems to the children. Two and three year olds may be interested in a few of the Dorothy Aldis poems as they apply to their personal experiences. They will enjoy listening and singing to "Here We Go Round the Mulberry Bush," "The Bear Hunt," or simple made-up poems. You may be able to sing spontaneous poems to the children as they play. For example, children on a seesaw enjoy having you sing, "Seesaw up, seesaw down, Jim goes up, Tom goes down." Neverthe-less, Mother Goose, with its richness of language, rhythmic pattern of sounds, humor, and surprises remains the primary poetry experience for toddlers.

SPEAKING   Listening and speaking are, of course, interrelated. During the toddler years, a period of extremely rapid language growth and development, many opportunities for speaking should be provided by the center. The importance of staff members who understand the value of adult-child verbal interaction cannot be overestimated.

The quality of the adult-child interaction seems to be as important as the amount. Research conducted in centers revealed that adults frequently use language to give commands or to stop or prohibit some behavior or action. When children are spoken to in this way, they answer only infrequently (Tizard, 1970). Cazden (1966) suggested that adult language in a preschool center be as precise as possible, using many concept words, descriptions, and abstractions that relate to the experience of the child. She believes that adults should act as resources for children's language: rather than asking questions that can be answered with a "yes" or "no," or those for which the answer is clearly obvious to all, ask questions that foster children's thinking, making them relate one experience to another (Cazden, 1971, p. 153).

You can use any number of situations to stimulate conversation with the child. You can talk about the child's body parts and what they do, or talk about the activities the child is involved in: "Mona is building in the sand," "Hank is painting with red," or "My, you surely do know how to ride the bike!" Engaging the child in a discussion of how she feels is helpful for children just learning words and giving labels to feelings. You may say "Are you unhappy? I haven't seen you smile today," or "You must be very angry to knock down the building you were making. Can you tell me about how you feel?"

Talking with the toddler about the objects or toys that surround her is also of value. According to Hawkins, "Something which is of interest to the child, and to the adult, creates a bond of communication of shared interest." (Haw-kins, 1967). You should use descriptive words when conversing with children about objects. It is also important to supply the child with the names of the things she is playing, working, or merely coming in contact with.

In talking with young children, remember the importance of expanding and elaborating on what the child says. In response to "Me want," you could say, "Yes, you would like the cookies, but we will save them for our party later on today," or if the child says, "Dog bark," you may respond, "Yes, but he won't bite; he's barking at the kitten, or he wants to eat" (Cazden, 1966, p. 134).

You should continually be aware of opportunities to encourage the children to use language to help them solve problems. When children spill paints, help them to work it out in words: "What should we do? You take this sponge, and I'll move this paper. Now you wipe here . . . ," or, when the child gets her pants caught in a bike wheel, "Let's move the wheel backwards and see if that will free your pants."

Not all talk in a preschool is adult-child interaction. Children talk to one another, they chatter to themselves, and they eventually learn to use language to get along with one another and to plan with others.

Toddler play is characterized as being of a parallel nature. Two or more children may play side by side with the same materials. Seemingly, they are playing with one another; actually, each is carrying out her own play activities. The language interaction of toddlers is often similar to their play. A child says something and waits for another child to respond; but the two children are discussing different topics that bear no relation to one another.

Though this speech is not true conversation, Cazden reported that young children, toddlers, and preschoolers alike use all their grammatical skills when talking to other children. She made the following suggestions to maximize the benefits of child speech within a center program (Cazden, 1971, p. 165).

1. Mixed age grouping is of value. Children speak more when there is no one present of a superior status—when nothing the child says can be held against her. It may be helpful to have younger children present so that the older children can explain things to them. The younger children are not degraded for not knowing everything.

2. Provide objects and things for the children to do and to talk about. A piece of complicated machinery leads the children to discuss how it might work, what might happen if . . . , and how can they take it apart. Animals and insects to talk about are equally important. "How can a bunny rabbit talk to you? He don't even talk to no one."

3. Provide opportunities to speak for aesthetic pleasure. Children play with syntax and sound and demonstrate skills which go beyond any formal program. Songs, poems, and literature allow children to play with their language. Jotting down the interesting ways children state things and the poems and songs they make up reinforces their use of speech and language for pleasure.

You can also structure some situations to stimulate children's speech. Cutting pictures from magazines or catalogs and mounting them on durable pieces of cardboard serves many purposes. A group of action pictures can be mounted on cardboards of the same size to encourage the children's use of verbs. You may ask, "What is the boy doing?" "How is he running?" "Can you run like that?" A child can carry the set of cards around with her, sometimes using them as a set of playing cards, or spreading them out on the floor to discuss them, or hiding them in a pocket to look over in a secret, quiet place.

Another set of cards might include everyday things found in the center. The children can match the picture to the object, talk about what it does, or name the object. Still another set of cards might contain story pictures that stimulate the child to tell the story about the picture. In storytelling from pictures, toddlers may first merely name the objects in the picture. You can, if desired, help the child talk about what is happening, what will happen, or what happened before.

A combined program of speaking, listening, and reading from pictures and books leads the toddler to develop and enjoy his language skills and prepares him to develop additional skills.

# PRESCHOOLERS

The preschooler is "flowering with language" (Gesell, 1940, p. 46). Fours and fives talk, talk, talk. Fours will ramble on about anything and everything, jumping from one subject to another with abandon. They make up words, and laugh with enjoyment at their cleverness. They chatter nonsense verses and jingles. They verbalize during all activities—while painting, drawing, riding a bike, climbing a tree, or sitting and reading a book. Their pronunciation is usually correct, and their grammar is generally standard. The four uses language as a tool to express himself fully and to communicate clearly with others.

Fours do experience a stage of experimenting with language and often shock unsuspecting adults with their use of "bathroom" words. You should take this language experimentation in stride, as you do the young child's giggling over nonsense words. The interest in bathroom language diminishes as the child approaches the age of five and learns how to say things, when (and when not) to say them, when to listen, and when and how to enter into a serious conversation.

Fives, with a wide vocabulary, display maturity and poise in talking to adults and children alike. For all practical purposes, the normal five-year-old child has mastered language. He is ready for new, stimulating experiences in listening, speaking, reading, and writing.

LISTENING    The general atmosphere of the preschool and organization of the playrooms contribute to the development of listening skills in preschool children. Good listening on your part as children talk with you, responding to their statements, engaging in serious conversation with them, and allowing them to speak more than you do, helps to establish the attitudes necessary for facilitating listening behavior on the part of the children.

Listening, not just hearing, is a major means of learning. Through listening, children increase their vocabulary, learn the structure of language, and add concepts and ideas. The National Council of Teachers of English has identified four types of listening (NCTE, 1954, p. 80-81):

1. Passive or marginal listening is prevalent in nursery school or kindergarten as children are engrossed in one activity but listen just enough to be aware of what is being said. Listening is not the focus; it is marginal.

2. Appreciative listening is involved when the child enjoys a story, a poem, or a recording.

3. Attentive listening is involved in situations when the child listens to directions or announcements.

4. Analytical listening occurs when the child analyzes what he hears in terms of his own experience. One may hear the child as he ponders, "I wonder why."

The listening experiences of the children throughout the day possess some of the elements of the four types of listening. Group discussions take place, directions are given, visitors share with children, children listen to other children and to themselves.

## Story Time

Perhaps the most enjoyable and valuable listening activity is story time. You, too, will probably enjoy the relaxation, the sharing of feelings, and escape or humor that story time brings. Through stories, children come to appreciate the sounds and patterns of language and share vicariously in experiences they may never be able to have.

Thousands of children's books are published each year, but few are suitable for reading to preschool children. You must be able to analyze the books available and, based on your knowledge of children's interests and needs, select only the finest to share with them.

*Story times are special.*

Fours and fives still enjoy many types of stories about themselves; but they also enjoy stories about places, people, and times far away from them. Preschoolers like action stories; stories about things that go—engines, planes, and machines; stories about children, animals, and places; and humorous stories. Nonsense folk tales and fantasy tales are now appropriate. Preschoolers, still working through the differences between fantasy and fact, now understand when you tell them that a story is "just pretend." A factual story, such as McCloskey's *One Morning in Maine* should be introduced as a story that really happened, and the house that Sal and Jane actually did live in can be shown to the children. Other stories, such as *Little Red Riding Hood,* or *The Tale of Peter Rabbit,* should be introduced as fiction. Preschoolers can be overheard to say, as if reassuring themselves, "The wolf really didn't eat Little Red Riding Hood; it's only a story," or "Peter Rabbit really didn't talk; it's just a story for fun."

With so many different children's books available, you may be tempted to read a different story every day. But most children enjoy really getting to know a story and will request their favorites with frequency. Remember that it is only through frequent readings and contacts with a story that a child can incorporate it into his repertory of knowledge.

Also remember to choose books portraying a variety of children and people. Books about black, chicano, Indian, and Asian children in their natural settings—unstereotyped and proud—are now available. Books portraying women and girls as hopelessly stupid, unimaginative, and completely dependent upon men and boys to solve their problems can be replaced by books illustrating females as useful human beings, with interests and minds that reach out into the world. Books portraying older persons in a variety of roles can also be selected.

You should take personal likes and dislikes into account in selecting stories for children. If you do not like a story, are ill at ease with the content, or object to the style of writing or to the illustrations, you will probably communicate these feelings to the children, perhaps causing them, in turn, to dislike the story.

A list of stories enjoyed by children and appropriate for preschoolers could never be completed. Some sources for annotated bibliographies for children are:

1. Louise Griffin, *Multi Ethnic Books for Young Children,* National Association for the Education of Young Children/ERIC Clearinghouse on Early Childhood Education, Urbana, Illinois.

2. *Children's Books for $1.25 or Less, The World of Children's Picture Books, Books in the Preschool,* and *Bibliography of Books for Children,* which are all available from the Association for Childhood Education International, Washington, D.C.

After selecting a story to read, practice reading it before a mirror or reading it into a tape recorder. Some teachers practice the story on their husbands or children before they tell it to children in the center.

Usually, the entire group of fours or fives wants to listen to the story; however, all of the children should not be required to participate in the group activity. Provisions should be made for children to play quietly if they desire to leave the group.

Some special place, either inside or outside, can be established as the story place. It should be as isolated as possible from the other activities in the center to allow the children to practice appreciative, attentive, and analytical listening skills. One teacher of young children swore that none of her classes over the years liked to listen to stories, and that they were unable to get involved in them. Her problem turned out to be the location of the story place. She read to the children with her back to a large bin of blocks and large, wooden wheel toys, so that the children were constantly looking at the toys. Merely by turning herself and the children around, placing the children with their backs to the blocks, she was able to capture and hold their attention throughout a story.

To attract children to story time, you could establish a kind of tradition that sets a special spell:

1. Using a magic stick or wand, draw a circle around the story place, asking everyone to sit in the magic ring.
2. Use a long ribbon and have each child hold on to it. "Today the magic ribbon will take us to China where a little duck named Ping lives."
3. Wear a story hat or party crown when it's time for story hour. It may be a witch hat for Halloween, a crown for a story about a king, a cap for *Caps for Sale,* or a party hat for a fantasy tale.
4. Use a hand puppet or finger puppet to gain the children's attention and to introduce the story to them.

After the story has been read, allow some time for discussion. The children may want to see certain pictures again, or hear parts of the story repeated. The children can discuss which parts of the story they liked the best or the things that made them feel sad, frightened, or happy. You may ask, "How would you feel if you were the girl?" "How do you think George felt when . . . ?" or "What do you think would happen if . . . ?" to stimulate more conversation about the story and to encourage the children's thinking.

Children should be allowed to bring their own personal response to the story. The book should be available to them in the library area following the reading. Puppets, flannel boards, and props encourage children to act out stories, retelling them with the aid of a prop in their own way. Records, film strips, or tape recordings of the stories may be available to give the children still more experience with them.

## Poetry

You can keep a stock of poetry in readiness to share with the children. Love of poetry begins, however, as you spontaneously recite poems to fit the experiences and activities of the children. It doesn't work to say to a child who has just seen a dragonfly, "Just a minute, I'll go find a poem about a dragonfly." It does work when you are able to say, the moment the dragonfly lifts his wings and flies off, "A dragonfly upon my knee is sitting looking up at me." (Aldis, 1952, p.

35). Children are brought to poetry through their ears, in very spontaneous, personal ways.

Children, whose own speech is so rhythmic and repetitive, find the alliteration, repetition, and rhythm of poetry naturally appealing. Mother Goose should not be abandoned because the children are turning three, four, and five years of age. New and varied verses from Mother Goose can be selected to share with them. Children march to some verses and dance and act out others. Different versions of Mother Goose can be chosen to read. Arbuthnot cautioned against moving to other poetry before the child has internalized the rhythm, sound, and richness of Mother Goose. (Arbuthnot, 1969, p. 58).

The poetry of E. Lear, written so long ago, is still fascinating to children. "The Owl and the Pussy Cat" is just as nonsensical and purely silly as the speech of the four year old. The melody and rhythm of Lear's poetry continues to impress preschoolers.

Children are also delighted by the poems of A. A. Milne. His egocentric king and children hold appeal for the young, egocentric child. In "The King's Breakfast," the king cannot even control himself as well as the four- and five-year-old children, and Christopher Robin, after all, is just like them.

Dorothy Aldis wrote poems especially appealing to the three, four, and five year olds. Her poems, short, catchy, and often humorous, are all about young children and the things they do and feel.

Contemporary poetry can also be introduced to the children. The poetry of Nikki Giovanni, although possessing some sophisticated concepts, can still be enjoyed by children for the power and beauty of the words and the feeling and mood they bring.

Such valuable anthologies of poetry as *Time for Poetry*, M. H. Arbuthnot; *Sung under the Silver Umbrella,* Association for Childhood Education International; *The Golden Journey*, Louise Bogan; *The Birds and the Beasts Were There*, William Cole; *Reflections on a Gift of Watermelon Pickle*, S. Dunning; *All Together*, Dorothy Aldis; and *All the Silver Pennies,* Blanche J. Thompson could be obtained for use by the entire center.

You should develop an individual poetry file or best-loved poem collection. Many of these poems can be memorized for incidental use with the children. Parents will appreciate receiving copies of poems the children have especially enjoyed hearing at the center. Booklets entitled "Circus Poems," "Christmas Poems," or "Halloween Poems" can be compiled and forwarded to the parents for use at home.

Children enjoy poetry as long as it is read to them by someone who likes it and reads it well. (Arbuthnot, 1969). But one reading is not enough. The same poem must be repeatedly read to the children, first for them to enjoy the pure sound of the words, and then over and over for them gradually to begin to understand the meaning of the words. Poetry, enjoyed by children with their daily experiencing, becomes a part of their lives forever.

## Finger Plays

Originating many years ago and often used in Froebelian kindergartens, finger plays have always been enjoyed by both children and adults. "The Bear Hunt," whether it's told as the "Lion," "Elephant" or "Seal Hunt," is still popular in many nations, and "Pat-a-Cake" and "All for Baby" have survived many generations of children.

You will find a knowledge of several catchy finger plays valuable in capturing the children's attention before reading a story, in introducing some important announcement, or during group activities. Children do become involved in attempting to make their fingers and hands act out the story, and the structured language of the finger play promotes language patterns. Finger plays are useful when the bus hasn't come, when the children are waiting for a treat, when the promised visitor has not arrived, or anytime when children must be kept waiting.

*Finger plays are attention-getting.*

On the other hand, finger plays are usually of very poor quality from a poetic standpoint. Very often they are of the cute, trite variety that some adults seem to think children like. If you use a finger play to give exercise to restless children, you'll find them rather limiting in that they are, as the terminology implies, only for fingers. Rather than waste time on substandard poetry for finger plays, many teachers instead select poems that children can move to more fully and freely.

Many Mother Goose verses can be used as finger plays. "Humpty Dumpty," "Jack and Jill," "Little Miss Muffett," "Jack Be Nimble," and others are excellent finger plays or verses to act out with entire bodies. Other, more traditional finger plays are:

*Pound, Pound, Pound*

Now we're pounding with one hammer,
With one hammer, with one hammer,
Now we're pounding with one hammer,
Now we'll pound with two.

*Children make a fist and use it as a hammer. Then they use both fists. As the play continues, the feet and head are also used as hammers.*

*Five Little Chickadees*

Five little chickadees peeping at the door,
One flew away and then there were four.
Four little chickadees sitting in a tree,
One flew away and then there were three.
Three little chickadees looking at you,
One flew away and then there were two.
Two little chickadees sitting in the sun,
One flew away and then there was one.
One little chickadee sitting all alone,
He flew away and then there were none.
Chickadee, chickadee, happy and gay,
Chickadee, chickadee, fly away.

*The Wiggle Song*

My fingers are starting to wiggle,
My fingers are starting to wiggle,
My fingers are starting to wiggle,
Tra la, tra la, tra la.

*Play continues with "fists," "hands," "arms," "feet," "toes," "legs," "head," and "all of me" starting to wiggle.*

*Where is Thumbkin?*

Where is Thumbkin? Where is Thumbkin? Here I am,
Here I am.
How are you this morning? Very well, I thank you.
Run away, run away.

*Play continues with "pointer," "tall man," "ring man," "pinky," and "all men."*

## Music

Increasingly social, cooperative, and interested in group activities, preschoolers not only enjoy music time, but they learn complete songs that they are able to sing by themselves or with the group. Listening to music and making music continue to give the child valuable language experiences.

Preschoolers find songs with strong rhythm, simple words, and simple melody appealing. Music that the children can move to, either with their entire bodies or just with their hands, is enjoyed. Preschoolers are able to keep time to music with their hands or with simple rhythm instruments.

Although preschoolers can participate in a group music time, music should not be limited to this experience. During an indoor activity time or outdoor play, you may begin to sing a song the children like, and the children may join in. Or the children, themselves, may begin to sing a song and you can pick it up, encouraging others to sing along.

Children should be able to listen to a song many times before attempting to sing it. Introduce a song to the children by singing it informally as they dress to go home, wake up from naps, or during play. Later, at the piano or during music time, the same song can be sung again. Some children will chime in after having heard the song many times. Children should be introduced to the song as a whole in order to appreciate its mood and content. Later, the refrain or repeated phrases can be taught separately for the children to "join in." Songs can be taught from records which should be played several times for listening. After the children know the song, they can sing a familiar refrain as it is repeated on the record.

Preschoolers can respond to music with instruments, exploring the different qualities of sounds instruments make. Percussion instruments— triangles, cymbals, rhythm sticks, blocks, coconut shells, bells—can be purchased or made by the children. Children can easily make rattles, placing any rattle material—rice, pebbles, beads—inside empty cans and sealing the cans with strong tape. Children can create their own rhythm sticks with sticks they find on the play yard. Melody instruments, such as marimbas, melody bells, xylophones, and resonator bells are usually purchased to obtain high quality of sound; however, children may be interested in experimenting with water glasses filled to different levels to make their own melody bells, or with flower pots of different sizes hung with ropes onto a broomstick. Harmony instruments, such as the autoharp and piano, must be purchased, but the children should be free to experiment with the sounds that these instruments make.

Often parents, neighbors, or volunteers will be delighted to bring their violins, banjos, guitars, or horns into the center to play for the children. To increase the value of these visits, familiarize the children with the instruments and the compositions to be played before the actual experience.

Musical experiences that are kept informal and incorporated into many other activities foster children's awareness of music and sound around them. Children should have time to experiment and explore musical instruments, opportunities to play their favorite record or the piano by themselves, and time to sing by themselves or with others. If you are flexible, accepting and appreciating each child's efforts to participate in the group, you allow children to grow in their listening abilities and in their creative responses to music.

## Television

There are several excellent television programs for children. "Mister Rogers' Neighborhood" and "Captain Kangaroo" are shows of high quality, appropriate for young children's viewing. However, in a preschool center, the use of television should be limited to special, rare occasions.

Many of the excellent children's television shows are designed to supplement the child's experiences and serve those children who do not have the opportunity to participate in a rich, exciting, stimulating preschool program. Children in a center, who have opportunities to sing, dance, listen to music, records, stories, and poetry, paint and draw, and play in the sand and mud, have little need for the vicarious experiences television offers. Furthermore, even the very best of television shows does not allow the children to experience truly for themselves; they are only passive observers of the experiences of others. Television can never act as a substitute for the personal give-and-take of relationships with adults and children in the center.

## Planned Listening Experiences

As the ability to listen is crucial to all language development and, later, to the development of the child's reading ability, you will want to devise planned listening experiences to foster the child's awareness of listening, his ability to discriminate between sounds, and his comprehension of what he has heard.

## Pill Bottles

Montessori designed a series of wooden cylinders, all of the same size, with various materials enclosed in each cylinder. Two of the cylinders held sand, two salt, two pebbles, two peas, two metal pins. Her children developed the ability, by listening to the sounds the cylinders made when shaken, to match the two containers holding the same material. You, too, can use plastic pill bottles that are partially filled with bits of material and securely taped shut. The children can then shake these bottles, attempting to find the two that make the same sound. Sugar, salt, sand, rice, paper clips, or anything that will rattle can be enclosed in the bottle. Once the object of the game is demonstrated to a small number of children, they can experiment with the bottles independently, either during play or activity time.

## Picture Sounds

From the large collection of pictures in the preschool center, a group can be selected to illustrate different sounds. These should be mounted on heavy cardboard. Picture sounds is played with a small group of children and a leader. The leader places the cards face down and asks a child to select one. The child, without letting anyone see his picture, tries to imitate the sound the picture suggests. The other children or adults try to guess what picture the child is holding from the sound he has made. The game should start with human or animal pictures. The complexity of the activity may then be increased by adding machine sounds or other sounds more difficult to guess, such as the click of a camera, soda being poured into a glass, or the ticking of a clock or a watch.

## Silly Game

This game is patterned almost exactly after a test item on the Stanford-Binet IQ test. The leader or adult gives the child two, three, or four directions to follow in sequence; for example, 1) pick up a red crayon, 2) put it on the desk, 3) touch Pam. The child listens to the directions, recalls them in sequence, and implements them. He then selects another child to be "it."

## Drum Patterns

Drums can be used in many ways to increase children's listening skills. You can beat a pattern of sounds on the drum, or tap them out with rhythm sticks, and then ask the children to repeat the sound pattern by clapping their hands, hopping, or using the rhythm sticks. The pattern should be very simple at first and gradually increase in complexity.

Children's names can also be "played" on the drum. Each syllable in the name is given a beat. Bobby would be two equal drumbeats; Timothy would be three. The accent in José can be copied with an accented drumbeat. Children, listening to the drum and the name at the same time, may walk, hop, or jump to the beat of the drum.

## Tape Recorders

Tape recorders fascinate children and adults alike. Children want their voices recorded and enjoy listening to themselves and their friends. Discussions, stories, or individual reports by the children can be recorded. If the tape recorder is left on during play or activity time, the children can later identify their voices, the time the blocks fell, and the other sounds of play.

You can take the recorder around the room and yard, taping the sounds of the kitchen, office, nursery, or play yard for the children to listen to later and attempt to identify. The tape recorder may be used to capture the sounds of home, the sounds of the street, the sounds of night, the store, post office, or farm for children's listening analysis.

## Records

A collection of records should be available for children's listening experiences. It can include folk songs, classical and popular songs, opera, blues, and jazz—whatever the children enjoy. The Young People's Record Guild and the Children's Record Guild are examples of companies that offer a wide variety of quality records that can give children the opportunity to listen to stories and songs and participate in activities without the direct contact of an adult.

**SPEAKING**  Children must have the opportunity to speak constantly if they are to learn. All activities in the center should be thought of as language activities, and the children should be encouraged to talk, talk, talk. The preschool should provide informal opportunities for children to talk to adults and to one another, and structure more formal situations that allow children to speak in front of a small group of their peers, the total group, or even a group of adults. "Show and tell," a large-group activity in which children must sit and wait their turn, is somehow inappropriate in a preschool. While allowing the child to speak before his peers, it does not stimulate sufficient discussion on the part of all of the children and offers only a limited opportunity for any one child to speak. Furthermore, it is nearly impossible for young children to sit attentively for long periods of time or to be responsive to the limited language power of another small child.

Situations can be devised, however, to offer children the opportunity to speak before the group. Children can be asked to explain how they made a particular wood structure or how they finally managed to get the block tower to balance. Small groups of children, returning from an individual field trip, can describe the trip to the other children. The very special events of a new baby in the family, grandmother coming to visit, or the mouse that got into the house still demand telling to the entire group.

Four-, five-, and even some three-year-old children do participate in group discussions when they are personally involved in the topic. Children might discuss the problem of paper towels in the toilet and reach a quick, satisfactory conclusion, or they may decide how they will share the new red fire engine at play time, or discuss why the hamster died and the procedures for the funeral. Older children should also be able to participate fully in planning activities for their day. Being aware of the children's limited abilities to anticipate the future, you should structure the discussion, setting up guideposts for their planning. In these group planning times, children can decide what the menu will be for the party, how to arrange for a visitor, or what they will want to ask on a field trip.

## Creative Dramatics

This activity begins simply, perhaps even when the infant first shows his mother "so big." Children respond to stories and poems, acting them out for themselves or for an audience of other children or adults. Unlike formal dramatics, creative dramatics is a spontaneous expression of the children's understanding of some story, poem, or event. It is free from outside directions, memorized lines, formal stage directions, and costumes; at times, it is even free from an audience.

Creative dramatics focuses on a simple plot with dialogue that is short and concise. The importance of creative dramatics is in the opportunity it gives children to interpret a story through actions and words.

With three-, four-, and five-year-old children, creative dramatics may begin with asking, "Show us something you do at home. Do not tell us, but just show us with your body, and we'll guess what it is you're doing." Young children can also be requested to move their bodies to poetry or to express themselves to music, moving as the raindrops, falling leaves, or wind. From these beginnings, you may lead the children to dramatizing a walk in the rain or a trip to the beach. You may say, "Let's pretend we're going for a walk in the rain. What should we put on? Show us how you would put your boots on. What color are they? Now let's go outside. Open up your umbrella and we'll take a walk." The children pretend to jump over puddles and dodge raindrops. When the spontaneity of the moment has passed, the imaginary walk is ended.

Following the reading of a poem or Mother Goose verse, such as "Hippety Hop to the Barber Shop," the children may spontaneously get up and pretend to go to a barber shop. Or everyone could be Jack and Jill and pretend to go up a hill. The entire group can act out "Humpty Dumpty," with children deciding ahead of the play to be either the king's horses or the king's men.

These simple beginnings set the foundation for more structured dramatics. Stories selected for dramatic play should be very familiar to the children and should involve as many of them as possible. Stories with simple plots, repetitive phrases, and action offer good beginnings. *Caps for Sale, Ask Mr. Bear,* and the favorite folk tales of *Three Billy Goats Gruff, The Three Little Pigs,* and *The Three Bears* are examples of stories fours and fives can act out. Some of the children can participate and others watch, with new actors being chosen for the next performance.

Costumes are not necessary in creative dramatics, and props should be limited in order for the children to draw on all of their powers of imagery. Young children do, however, insist on some "pretend" props. A few blocks in the center of the room can represent a campfire, a scarf can become a ball gown or witch hat, two chairs can suggest Billy Goat's bridge and a carpet scrap become the ocean.

Children should not be asked to memorize lines when acting out stories. You can help the action along by providing some of the background description and some of the lines to help the children remember the sequence.

Savoring the accomplishment of the familiar, the children will want to act out a favorite story again and again, changing it a little each time, adding to it, and leaving some things out. Following the story, some evaluation of the activity can take place. The children might be asked to describe the parts they liked the best or to think of some improvements for the next version. Children should be given specific praise for well-executed parts. The child who spoke in a low, gruff voice can be told, "You really made us feel frightened," and the child who moved in a special way told, "Your moving in that special way made us feel that we were watching the brownies."

As creative dramatics is unrehearsed, spontaneous, and involves all of the children, it can be used to present programs to other children and, on occasion, adults. However, the children should be under no pressure in performing for an audience. They merely act out a story, as they have done so many times before, for their enjoyment and the pleasure of others.

## Puppets

Another form of creative dramatics, puppets promote verbalization on the part of the child. A simple puppet on his hand seems to enable the child to speak about things he wouldn't be able to without the puppet. Puppets are used by individual children independently or by small groups of children working together to portray a story.

Commercial puppets are available, but for maximum involvement and pleasure on the part of the child, puppets should be made by the children themselves. Tongue depressors can be used to support cutout figures for stick puppets, paper plates that are stapled to popsicle sticks become face puppets, and finger puppets can be made from a paper ring with figures pasted to it. Old socks, with the help of staples, strong white glue, buttons, and magic markers, can be turned into sock puppets. You can help the child position the sock on one hand and determine the place for the eyes, ears, and mouth.

A puppet stage can be a table turned on one end, a discarded cardboard box, or the back of a chair. Children in one center set up a puppet stage in an open, low window and played to the children in the play yard. The children, running in and out of the center, took turns as audience and puppeteers.

You can use puppets to assist specific children in their language development. You and the children, one or two at a time, can carry on a conversation with puppets on your hands. You may ask, "What did you do today? How did you ride your bike? What did you see on the field trip?" and other questions to help stimulate conversations.

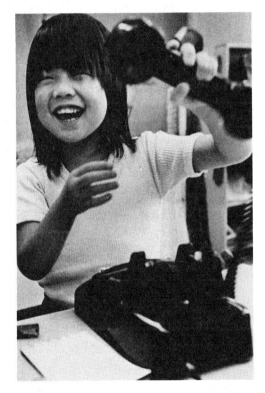

*Telephones stimulate oral language.*

## Telephones

Real telephones that are no longer operative can be obtained from the public relations office of the local telephone company to stimulate the children's conversations. With a real phone in their hands, the need to communicate without using gestures becomes very evident. Telephone companies will also, on a short loan basis, provide telephones that actually can be hooked up to work in the playroom, allowing the children to converse with someone across the room.

## Audio-Visual Aids

Filmstrips, slides, movies, and snapshots foster much vocalization on the part of children. Films of favorite stories are useful in promoting children's speech when used without sound, letting the children relate the story as the film is viewed. Films, slides, and movies of the children in the center are most valuable. When they see themselves, children explain to one another what they were wearing, doing, or saying when the picture was taken, and how they feel seeing themselves. These pictures need to be shown several times, once just for fun, again to allow the marvelous feeling of watching themselves "sink in," and perhaps one more time for the children to take turns telling about the pictures.

**READING** "Will he be ready to read?" "Will the experiences at the center prepare my child for reading?" "Why don't the teachers use readiness workbooks or some other prescribed readiness kit?" According to Martin,

> Learning to read is not something that happens after a stereotyped readiness period in the first grade or kindergarten. Learning to read is the job of a lifetime. Two- and three-year-old children who are read to a lot begin their reading careers early. The day a child gets hold of a sentence pattern that works for him, and reads it into the telephone directory or the Montgomery Ward catalog or his daddy's newspaper at night, he is launching himself on his reading career. He is role playing himself as a successful reader. The day a child reads a book from memory, he is furthering his reading career.
>
> He is in truth finding joy and power in the pages of a book, a psychological posture that every successful reader continuously brings to each reading encounter, knowing, subconsciously if not consciously, that he can make a go of print. This is the first and foremost reading skill (Martin, 1972, p. 10).

The preschool center, offering many experiences with the sounds of language and exposure to printed words, begins the "job of a lifetime"—that of teaching the child to read. Each experience in the preschool, every activity, teaches the child that he is successful; and each encounter with books, poetry, magazines, and newspapers teaches him that the printed word holds personal excitement and meaning for him. Reading, actually an extension of the listening and speaking activities that permeate the center, is a result of the child's successful and enjoyable experiences with language.

In order to promote each child's success with reading, you should carefully define the skills and competencies a child must have before being able to read. You should work to strengthen your program to include those activities that not only help each child to live more fully each day of his life, but also foster his readiness for reading.

According to Carpenter, "Readiness for anything is a state of being. It is a composite of many factors and must be measured in many ways. It is not a thing to be taught. It can neither be purchased in a box nor developed on paper. It is an individual state unresponsive to mass production. It is a part of life." (Carpenter, 1961, p. 1). Wilson and Hall, reinforcing the idea that readiness for anything involves individual differences, stated that the concept of readiness in learning assumes acceptance of the significance of individual differences, for it acknowledges that readiness for a particular learning is not obtained by all children at the same time. (Wilson & Hall, 1972, p. 90). They have identified the following reading readiness components: physical readiness—general health, sex, hearing, vision, and age; perceptual readiness—auditory, visual, and directional; cognitive readiness—the child's mental age; linguistic—oral language facility, speaking, and listening; psychological—the child's attitude toward himself and others, school, and the process of reading; environmental—the child's home and experiential background.

## Physical Readiness

A program that is geared to the total development of a child must concern itself with the child's physical growth and development and general health. If children are to be able to read, they will require nutritious food, adequate rest, and physical safety. Vision and hearing may be checked and monitored to insure that no abnormalities are present. Regular physical exams may be conducted in the center, and appropriate assistance provided for those children with special physical needs. Hearing aids, glasses, and other corrective devices may be supplied.

## Environmental Readiness

Children with a poor experiential background have difficulty bringing meaning to the printed word. Before a child can read, he must have had exposure to ideas and concepts represented by the printed word. Children who have never seen a zoo, ocean, river, or skyscraper cannot easily bring meaning to the printed symbol.

The preschool should provide children with many varied experiences in order to build a foundation for reading. Children should take trips, cook and eat new and interesting foods, care for and raise animals and insects, meet other people, and learn about the broader world through stories, pictures, and slides.

## Psychological Readiness

The child's psychological health and development warrants as much concern as does his physical health and well-being. Each child, as a result of individualized care and education, must see himself in the school, family, and community as a successful human being—a learner and a doer.

Psychological readiness includes the child's ability to relate to a group of children, to wait his turn, and to be responsive to other's needs. The desire to read (fostered in the center by experiences with books and poetry) and the desire to learn and to find out for oneself must also be present in order for a child to be able to read.

## Cognitive Readiness

As reading is essentially a cognitive activity, the child's mental age has traditionally been thought of as the best indicator of his reading success. Concept formation, abstract reasoning, and the ability to gain meaning from symbols are related to the child's intelligence and cognitive functioning. Nevertheless, according to Wilson and Hall, "[Studies] have shown that mental age is not as significant in determining reading success as is the type of instruction offered, and that there is no single criterion for children's readiness to read" (Wilson & Hall, 1972, p. 97).

## Linguistic Readiness

Listening and speaking skills provide the base for bringing meaning to the printed symbol. The child with a limited vocabulary who has had few opportunities to speak with adults and peers, or the child with limited listening skills who has not had the experience of comprehending the speech of others, will most likely have difficulty in learning to read.

## Perceptual Readiness

Learning to read requires "perception of printed word forms." (Wilson & Hall, 1972, p. 98.). Children need to recognize printed words and letter sounds in spoken words. The two major means of perception employed by reading children who possess adequate sensory functioning are visual and auditory. Visual and auditory perception, plus the ability to perceive the connection between the printed word and the spoken word, are essential to learning to read.

**Visual Perception**  Young children with adequate vision may need additional practice in visual discrimination and in sharpening their observatory skills in general.

*Sorting Activities*

Button boxes, a box of leftover earrings, or material scraps, when used with sorting trays, give the children practice in classifying objects and also in seeing likenesses and differences.

*"What Has Changed?"*

A more structured game than sorting, yet one of high interest and appeal to children because it involves them directly, is "What has changed?" Several children are selected to stand in a row before a group of other children. You or the child leader changes something about the children in the row while the other children are hiding their eyes. When the leader says, "Open your eyes," the children in the group try to find the thing that has changed in the row. Sometimes the row of children has turned around, or one child has changed positions with another child. Later, a child's glasses, belt, or scarf can be put on another child. You can promote the use of complete sentences and expression of thought. The children may say, "She's changed!" and you can say, "Yes, but tell us the name of the one who has changed and how." Another variation of the game is to add a child to the line, ask one to sit down, or to add a hat, book, or other object.

*Bingo Games*

Many commercial bingo games are available for children to match pictures of objects that are alike and different. You can make additional bingo games by using the children's snapshots. These can be mounted on heavy cardboard squares, with two pictures of each child included. Children play the game by matching the two snapshots that are alike. The children's names may be written in manuscript under the pictures, and children can match these to a set of cards that contains the names only. Later, the names can be cut off the pictures, and children can match picture cards with name cards. Children can also sort these cards according to sex, age, or friends.

*Pegboards*

Pegboards and pegs should always be available to the children. Occasionally, you can sit with the children and introduce a game to them as they manipulate the pegs. You can make a pattern with the pegs and ask the children to copy it with their pegboards. Designs should be simple at first and gradually increase in complexity. The same game may be played with stringing beads, parquet blocks, or other small objects. A set of cards, each depicting a peg pattern, can be left with the pegs for the children to play the game independently.

*"What's Missing?"*

In this game, children are presented with a tray of varied objects and told to look at the tray very carefully. While they hide their eyes, remove one of the objects. The children tell what is missing.

**Perceiving Meaning from Symbols** The language experience approach to reading, as described by Roach Van Allen, begins with the child's experiences, is built on the language arts of listening and speaking, and relates the printed word with the spoken. (Allen & Allen, 1966).

*Children see the spoken word being transcribed into symbols.*

### What a Child Thinks About He Can Tell About

The language experience approach is based on the idea that anything the child thinks about he can tell about. Children should be given many opportunities, not just during a structured discussion time, to talk with others and describe their thoughts, ideas, and experiences. "Tell us about your vacation," "Tell us how you felt when the dentist looked in your mouth," "Tell us how you built the castle," "Tell us what book you like best," "Tell us why you picked orange," "Tell us what you think." And when the child shares his ideas, you should listen appreciatively and attentively, expanding on the child's comments, perhaps adding a new thought or enriching experience. As a child paints a picture or creates a collage, you may ask him to talk about it and write his words under the picture.

### What a Child Tells About Can Be Written

When a child tells you about an idea or experience, or when he shares something in an especially interesting way, you can say, "I'm going to write that down; you said it so well." Then the child can watch his spoken words being transcribed into written words.

You should, according to advocates of the language experience approach, act more like a secretary than a teacher, recording as much of the child's speech as possible. When you record children's ideas, experiences, and stories, children will often ask "Do you have time to take dictation now? I have a story that needs writing."

Group dictation is also valuable in demonstrating the connection between the spoken and printed word. A group of children may want to cooperate in dictating a letter, invitation, or thank-you note. After a discussion of what should be included in the letter, you can write the children's words down with a dark marking pen on large chart paper.

Observing their spoken words being written, children begin to perceive the relationship between the spoken word and the symbol. An initial awareness of the letters of the alphabet and the uses of capital and lower-case letters, periods, commas, question marks, and quotation marks develops. Children see that each word is separated from the other by a space and that writing goes from left to right across the paper, just as individual words are formed from the left to the right.

### *What Has Been Written Can Be Read by Others*

After children have dictated their ideas, you or another adult can read the words back to them and to others. When reading back the dictated story, letter, or poem, you may run your hand from left to right under the words as you read them, further promoting the understanding that what has been spoken can be written and what has been written can be read by others. Stories, poems, and letters written by others can be read to the children, increasing their awareness that the written word can be read, and that they can read what others have written.

### *Using the Language Experience Approach in a Preschool*

Individual children, small groups of children, or the total group may be involved in dictating stories or messages to you, so that you can record them and later read them back to the children. Language during play may be recorded as children request signs to go with their block buildings that might read, "Do Not Walk Here," "Airport," or "Store." Signs that are used outside might say, "Ride Slow," "Stop," or "Go." The functional use of the written language can be illustrated as you write messages on the board. One day a group of children in one preschool requested a marching band. The teacher, realizing that a marching band would disturb the children who were at rest in the next room, suggested that they wait until the next morning to have the band. The children responded by saying, "Yes, but you'll forget, and we won't have a marching band again." With that the teacher said, "I'll write 'Marching Band' on the board to remind all of us of the promise for tomorrow." The next morning each child who came into the playroom ran up to the board and pointed to the words. "Don't forget," they said, "the note says 'Marching Band,' and today we'll march."

Recording information in the center is a continual process. Charts such as the following may be constructed as the children dictate their ideas and experiences:

| *What We Saw in the Park* | | *The Bubbles Are* | |
|---|---|---|---|
| Robin | bird | Susan | shiny |
| Mark | grass | Robert | pretty |
| José | squirrel | Ann | sparkly |
| David | swan | Carmen | slippery |

*What We Will Ask the Fireman*

Can you slide down a pole?
Where do you sleep?
How do you know where the fire is?
What do you eat?
How do you ring the bell?

News stories can also be written as messages on the board or on chart paper and read to the children. You can use these messages to capture the children's attention and to increase the use of the written language. It is very special for children to have their news shared in this adult way. Some ideas for news stories are:

| *New Shoes* | *Rain* |
|---|---|
| Carmen has new shoes. | Rain, rain, go away. |
| They are red. | We want to play. |

| *A New Baby* | *Today* |
|---|---|
| John has a new baby. | Today a friend will come. |
| It is a boy. | She lives in China. |
| What will the baby be named? | She lives far away. |

A child may want to dictate his own news story to you so that you will write it on the board and, at an appropriate time, read it to the children. Children soon begin to know when they have an item that deserves to be shared in this unique manner.

Ultimately, you will have the children dictate their own complete stories of a creative nature. Interesting pictures or picture books without words can stimulate the children to dictate stories of their own. Complete stories can also be dictated around such themes as "All about Me," "What I Want to Be When I Grow Up," "How I Go to Sleep," or "Things That Frighten Me."

Some children's stories seem to demand a personal response and can be used to stimulate creative dictation from the children. Each of the Holt, Rinehart & Winston Kinder Owls and Little Owls seem to end with an inherent suggestion that the children dictate their own story. *What Is Big?* ends with the statement, "A dinosaur is the biggest thing I know," and leads the children into a discussion about the biggest things they know. You can record their ideas and the children draw pictures. The pages can later be compiled into a book for the library table. *Round Is a Pancake* by Joan Sullivan ends by stating, "Look all around, in the sky and on the ground, you will find round things everywhere."

This naturally stimulates the children to look around and find some, and you can record their observations in a booklet.

*And To Think That I Saw It On Mulberry Street* by Dr. Seuss can lead the children to dictate stories entitled, "To Think I Saw It On Ridgedale Road," or on whatever street the center is located. Some of Seuss's other books, *If I Ran the Zoo,* or McEillecot's *Pool* can encourage children to tell how they would run the zoo or what they might find in the pool.

WRITING     Young children do not write, and should not be expected to write; they do not yet have the muscular development required. However, the preschool should foster the children's interest in writing and promote their desire to write.

The child's manipulation of art materials—his control with crayons, scissors, paintbrushes—exercises the same muscles he will later use in writing. Many four- and five-year-old children actually incorporate in their paintings and drawings the slanted and straight lines and the circles and dots used in manuscript writing. The manipulation of toys, beads, pegs, puzzles, snap beads, and woodworking tools also strengthens the child's muscular control.

Children gain appreciation of the written symbol as they see their words being written by you, or as they see their names written on their artwork and belongings. Other messages are written in the center: You write to the director,

*Children stamp their names with a printing set.*

to the cook, to the child's parents, to the storekeeper, and to the policeman. Invitations to visitors, thank-you notes to volunteers, and other communications are sent and received. At every opportunity, the children should observe you writing.

Manuscript writing is recommended for young children for two major reasons. First, children who have had a lot of experience drawing and painting have already mastered the basic strokes required in manuscript writing—the line and the circle; and second, manuscript writing more nearly resembles the print that children will encounter in their initial reading (Leeper, 1979).

You should use capitals only at the beginning of sentences or to begin proper names in order to facilitate the child's adjustment to the use of capitals in the grade school. Parents can be informed about the use and purpose of manuscript writing. Perhaps you can forward a copy of manuscript letters to the parents to illustrate what you mean by manuscript writing. If a child asks why his mother writes his name differently from the way you do, you might answer, "There are many different ways to write. In the center we write this way; your mother writes your name another way."

Some children will demonstrate a desire to begin writing by attempting to write their names or to form specific letters. For these children, large pencils, marking pens, crayons, and large sheets of unlined paper can be provided. At first, the child will write letters all over the page; later, a sheet of paper can be folded, and he can be helped to write on the folded line if he is ready and desires this challenge.

A card on which the child's name is printed in manuscript can be prepared to serve as a model for the child interested in writing. Large plastic letters can be purchased for children to form their names, or a printing set may be used. Children can also trace their names in sand trays with their fingers. Children will differ in their readiness for each of these activities. Individual guidance should be given when a child asks and is ready for it.

## IT'S UP TO YOU _____

Language is a part of all of the activities of the preschool. At no time, except perhaps when the child is sleeping, is she without language. Not only does language permeate the entire school day, but it may be the most important part of the school's curriculum.

Without language facility, both speaking and listening, children will be limited. Ability to use and understand language is necessary for later school success and absolutely essential for success in later life.

You, as a teacher, have a large responsibility in providing opportunities for children to develop power with language. It's not enough to say that all of the activities of the day revolve around the use of language. Special attention must be given to see that each individual child is developing skills in listening and speaking, and building a foundation for later reading and writing.

An understanding of the theories of how language develops and of the developmental stages children pass through as they learn language provides you with a foundation for planning language activities. But the most important factor in promoting language is you, the teacher. For it's you who builds the atmosphere of acceptance in the preschool. It's you who takes time to listen as children haltingly try to explain their block building. It's you who plans some special game for a particular child in order to build better listening skills. And it's you who will be able to take pride in the children's increasing skills with language.

## REFERENCES

Aldis, D. *All Together.* New York: G. P. Putnam's Sons, 1952.

Allen, R. V., and Allen, C. *An Introduction to a Language Experience Program.* Chicago: Encyclopaedia Britannica Press, 1966.

Arbuthnot, M. *Children's Reading in the Home.* Glenview, Ill.: Scott, Foresman & Co., 1969.

Birren, J. E., and Hess, R. D., *Influences of Biological, Psychological, and Social Deprivation upon Learning and Performance.* Washington, D.C.: U.S. Department of Health, Education, and Welfare, 1968.

Carpenter, E. *Readiness Is Being.* Washington, D.C.: Association for Childhood Education International, 1961.

Carroll, J. B. *Language and Thought.* Englewood Cliffs, N. J.: Prentice-Hall, 1965.

Cazden, C. B. "Some Implications of Research on Language Development in Pre-school Education." In *Early Education,* edited by R. D. Hess and R. M. Bear. Chicago: Aldine Publishing Co., 1966.

⎯⎯⎯⎯ "Language Development in Day Care Programs." In *Day Care: Resources for Decisions,* edited by E. Grotberg. Washington, D.C.: Office of Economic Opportunity, 1971.

Gesell, A. *The First Five Years of Life.* New York: Harper & Row, Publishers, 1940.

Gleason, J. B. "Do Children Imitate?" *Proceedings of the International Conference on Oral Education of the Deaf,* June 17–24, 1967. Washington, D.C.

Green, M.C.L. *Learning to Talk: A Parent's Guide to the First Five Years.* New York: Harper & Row, Publishers, 1960.

Hawkins, D. I. "Thou, It." (Paper presented at Primary Teacher's Residential Course, Leicestershire, England, April 3, 1967. Reprinted by Educational Development Center, Newton, Mass.

Leeper, S. H.; Skipper, D.; and Witherspoon, R. *Good Schools for Young Children.* 4th. New York: Macmillan Publishing Co., 1979.

Martin, B. *Sounds I Remember.* New York: Holt, Rinehart & Winston, 1972.

McCarthy, D. "Language Development." In *Manual of Child Psychology,* edited by L. Carmichael. New York: John Wiley & Sons, 1946.

National Council of Teachers of English. *Language Arts for Today's Children.* New York: Appleton-Century-Crofts, 1954.

Stodolsky, S. S. *Maternal Behavior and Language and Concept Formation in Negro preschool Children: An Inquiry into Process.* Doctoral dissertation, University of Chicago, 1965.

Strickland, R. G. "Needed Research in Oral Language." *Elementary English* (1967): 257.

Tizard, J. *Child Welfare Research Group: Report on Work Carried Out 1967–1969.* London: University of London, Institute of Education, Department of Child Development, 1970.

Valverde, L. A. *Bilingual Education for Latinos.* Washington, D.C.: Association for Supervision and Curriculum Development, 1978.

Whorf, B. L. *Language, Thought, and Reality.* Cambridge and New York: Massachusetts Institute of Technology and John Wiley & Sons, 1956.

Wilson, R., and Hall, M. A. *Reading and the Elementary School Child: Theory and Practice for Teachers.* New York: Van Nostrand Reinhold Co., 1972.

## RESOURCES

Cohen, D. *Literature with Children.* Washington, D.C.: Association for Childhood Education, International, 1972.

Fisher, C., and Terry, C. *Children's Language and the Language Arts.* New York: McGraw-Hill Book Co., 1977.

Hall, M. *Teaching Reading as a Language Experience.* Columbus, Oh.: Charles E. Merrill Publishing Co., 1970.

Herrick, V., and Nervobig, M. *Using Experience Charts with Children.* Columbus, Oh.: Charles E. Merrill Publishing Co., 1964.

Sadker, M. and D. *Now upon a time: A Contemporary View of Children's Literature.* New York: Harper & Row, Publishers, 1977.

Siks, G. *Drama with Children.* New York: Harper & Row, Publishers, 1977.

## PROJECTS

1. Record the speech of a two-, three-, four-, and five-year-old child during a fifteen-minute period. Record each child's use of verbs, descriptive adjectives, and spontaneous expressions. How does the speech of the two year old compare with that of the three year old? How does the speech of the three-year-old child compare with that of the four, and how does the speech of the four year old compare with that of the five year old?

2. Record six questions a child under the age of four asks. Does the child wait for an answer? How do you answer? Record the questions of a four and a five year old. Do their questions differ in any way?

3. Record stories dictated by two children of differing ages. How do these stories differ?

4. Observe a class or group of four- or five-year-old children in a preschool for a morning. Give your reaction to the children's speech and language as concerns the entire group. Record original or unusually interesting remarks, remarks displaying a sense of humor, language used as a tool for thinking or solving problems, and language used as a social tool. Make note of children's pleasure and interest in new words.

5. Observe a baby between the ages of nine and eighteen months during the waking hours. Record, as well as you can, the sounds the baby makes and when they are made. What can you do to encourage this vocalization? What can you do in response to this vocalization?

6. Read a story to a fifteen month old, a two year old, a group of threes, and a group of four or five year olds. Record the story you selected for use with each age child. Record the responses of the children.

7. Compile a poetry file for use with young children. Include poems that children can become personally involved with through movement or dance.

8. Compile a list of games that could be used with young children to foster listening skills and visual discrimination.

# ARTISTIC EXPERIENCES FOR YOUNG CHILDREN

*Each child is unique in what he brings to the activity—his complex understandings, his purpose, his reactions in the process of self-expression.*
(Brittain, 1979, p. 21)

*Art is emotionally satisfying.*

Smearing a handful of applesauce across the tray of his highchair, the nine-month-old baby experiences his first attempts at scribbling. The pleasure of feeling the cool, smooth applesauce squish between his fingers and the surprise of seeing designs on the tray as his hands move back and forth give him a rewarding sensory experience. This might be thought of as the beginnings of the child's artistic awareness and expression.

All young children draw, scribble, and experiment with materials. Whatever they use—a stick in the sand, applesauce, crayons, paints, paper—children the world over scribble. To many adults, these first scribblings of the young child seem an unimportant mess—merely the result of undirected muscular activity. These adults fail to appreciate, understand, or value the beginning artistic expression of the young child. Experiences in scribbling and drawing freely are essential to the child's total development. Harris and Goodenough believe that scribbling and drawing experiences are essentially cognitive experiences in the child. They cite evidence indicating that the drawings of a young child are an expression of his mental maturity, and that the child draws only what he knows cognitively (Harris & Goodenough, 1963).

By just playing around with crayons and paper, paints, clay, or wood, the young child is giving expression to his ideas; he is representing his concepts in a concrete, yet creative manner. Artistic development is closely tied to other development in the child. Working with materials assists developing muscular control, giving the child opportunities to practice eye-hand-muscle coordination. Children grow socially as they work together, chatting with one another over their paintings, sharing materials, and finding an outlet for their emotions through artwork.

## ART IS EMOTIONALLY SATISFYING

Just as adults find emotional release and satisfaction in working and producing with their hands, children also find art activities deeply satisfying. The sensory pleasures of the materials, the physical acts of marking on paper or pounding clay, and the knowledge that they have the power to bring something into being produce feelings of competency, pride, and accomplishment in young children.

Feelings that children can neither name nor identify can be released and expressed through their artwork. Anger and frustration can be taken out on clay or wood in a manner acceptable to all involved; joy and happiness can be expressed through bright, fluid, shiny paints. The very personal involvement of the child with the materials makes her artwork so emotionally satisfying.

## ART IS SOCIAL

Sitting around a table covered with bright bits of paper, paste, and scissors, the four year olds laugh together, enjoying one another's company as they form a bright collage. Doing something together, with opportunities to communicate and freedom to do as they wish, fosters children's interpersonal relationships and builds social skills.

Responsibilities are shared during art activities—brushes need to be washed and returned to the easel after use, tables need to be cleaned, toys must be put away. Materials are shared and cared for by all children. Knowing that there is enough time and material for all, children learn to take turns at the woodworking bench, with the blocks, or at the finger-painting table.

Recognition of the ideas of others evolves from experiences with art. Each child's product is different and is valued as a unique contribution. There is no one right way to use the materials; each child's way is right for him. Everyone has different ideas and all the ideas are valid. Through experiences with art, children can learn to value differences among people, to accept uniqueness and nonconformity rather than distrust it.

## ART IS COGNITIVE

The stage at which children draw, paint, and use other art materials is indicative of their mental development. The Lantz Easel Age Scale, a measure of intelligence obtained by examining children's easel paintings and the Goodenough-Harris Draw-a-Man test, which uses drawings of a man to determine the child's mental maturity, are two examples of intelligence tests based on evaluation of children's art products. Both tests demonstrate the close relationship between art and cognitive development.

Through art, especially the activities of drawing and painting, children are able to represent their thoughts and ideas, giving them order and structure. As they draw, paint, construct, or model with clay, they clarify their concepts

*Drawing requires concentration.*

about the things they have experienced. Through art, children sharpen their awareness of their world.

Perceptual skills, closely related to the growth of concepts, develop as children explore various materials and become more sensitive to the stimuli around them. They experience different shapes, sizes, textures, and colors. All of their senses are strengthened as they perceive their environment with heightened awareness.

Problem-solving skills, involving children's reasoning powers, develop through art activities. Children must decide, for themselves, how to fit the wood together, how to join the two boxes together when making a box sculpture. No one will tell them what to make or how to make it; they must invent for themselves, think for themselves, solve problems for themselves and utilize all of their cognitive powers.

Language, closely related to the thought of the child, abounds during art activities. Children talk to themselves and to others as they paint, draw, model, or construct. "See, I'm making my house. Now it gets to be night," they say as they paint, or "piddely, and squiggly, hit, hit, hit," they sing as they work with clay. When their work is completed, they describe to others how it was made: "I punched a hole here, and put the string through, and then I tied it together here." New concept words are frequently used during art activities, and you might even introduce some: "The paint is smooth and shiny and the sandpaper is rough." "This paper is bumpy." "The wood is hard and the nails are sharp and pointed." "Some brushes are big and others are small."

## ART FOSTERS PHYSICAL DEVELOPMENT    You need only observe young children at work

during art time to realize just how physical art experiences really are. The young child scribbling uses her whole body as she moves her crayon over the paper or as she pounds the clay. Pushing boxes to construct a building, pounding nails into wood, or lifting and moving blocks to complete a structure are all very physical acts.

Small muscles are exercised and strengthened as children attempt to control and manipulate small crayons and bits of material, string beads, thread needles, or cut with scissors. Each of these activities helps to prepare the child for writing later on.

## ART IS CREATIVE    As an outlet for creative thought, art gives children the opportunity to respond to materials in an individual

way. Each child brings his own ideas, feelings, and interpretations to the art experience; each child is thinking for himself. Maslow believes that creative people who have confidence in themselves, their ideas, and who can meet change with creative responses are necessary to the future continuation of society (Maslow, 1959). By encouraging children to respond in unique ways and to create new products, you are fostering creativity in children that will help them live more fully now and in the future.

*Children create.*

To be creative is to take a risk. Will the new creative response be accepted? Will the child be ridiculed for doing something in a different way? Creativity must be fostered and nurtured in an environment that supports divergent thinking—an environment in which different ideas are not only accepted, but are highly valued. The staff must demonstrate, subtly and openly, respect for themselves and each other, respect for the children and their parents, and respect for visitors and volunteers from the community. Children, secure in a climate of respect for others, feel free to create, knowing that any mistakes they might make will be accepted without ridicule or condemnation.

You must also respect children's efforts in their artwork; their scribblings, their immature attempts to pound a nail into wood, their primitive explorations of clay and other material must all be treasured. Children who are expected to conform to an imposed standard in their artwork cannot be creative.

Follow-the-dots patterns, coloring books, and the like have proved to hinder creativity and artistic expression in the young child. Materials such as these teach the child that there is only one correct response—only one right way to do it. No unique product results from coloring in the lines of a coloring-book picture; there is no room for the child to think for himself. According to Lowenfeld:

> It has been proved beyond any doubt that such imitative procedures as found in coloring and workbooks make the child dependent in his thinking; they make the child inflexible, because he has to follow what he has been given. They do not provide emotional relief because they give the child no opportunity to press his own experience and thus acquire a release for his emotions; they do not even promote skills and discipline, because the child's urge for perfection grows out of his desire for expression; and finally they condition the child to adult concepts which he cannot produce alone, and which therefore frustrate his own creative ambitions." (Lowenfeld, 1957, p. 18)

The physical conditions of the school play an important part in the development of creative expression in young children. If children do not have sufficient space in which to work, their creativity will be hampered. A lack of adequate materials forces the rationing of supplies. Spilled paint, when it's the last paint available until next ordering day four weeks away, becomes a tragedy instead of a learning experience. If materials are stored where children can neither see them nor obtain them without help, their responses become limited to what you choose for them.

A drab, disorderly room, with bare walls and monotonous arrangements, depresses children and adults alike and does little to stimulate children's artistic awareness or expression. On the other hand, a room that is overly filled with stimulating items, too much equipment, too many choices, and too much excitement confuses children, negating their ability to make creative selections. Surrounding the children with beauty, however, stimulates them to interpret and incorporate this beauty in their art products. You can work with the children to keep their playroom attractive and orderly. Children's paintings, drawings, and other art products, as well as the artwork of others, should be displayed. Wild flowers, dried seed pods, and other beautiful touches can be added to the room. Returning from a nature walk, children can be given vases and jars in which to arrange their collection of dried flowers, weeds, or seed pods. Some centers ask children to decide on centerpieces for lunch tables. One day a group of children built a block structure for their centerpiece while another selected a potted plant for their table. A three-dimensional collage was utilized as a centerpiece—an arrangement of fruit, the leaves from vegetables, or even a shiny, purple eggplant, surrounded with frilly green carrot leaves.

A beauty corner was established in one center. The teacher would bring some lovely, artistic object to the center—a glass figurine, a vase, a delicate wood carving, or piece of jewelry—and display it in the beauty corner. The fragility of the objects was explained to the children: "You can't touch this because it breaks very easily, but you can enjoy it by looking at it with your eyes." In this way, this teacher fostered the concept that sharing and knowing can result from looking.

Artistic books can be placed in the library corner, and prints of famous paintings shared with the children. They may enjoy many different types of artwork—sculpture, metal work, paintings—and especially seem to enjoy work that portrays other children. Changing the prints frequently and mounting some on cardboard for the children to handle and discuss, promotes the beginnings of artistic appreciation and encourages children in their own creativity. Prints of paintings can be found in magazines or Sunday newspaper supplements; they can also be borrowed from the local library or art museum.

A rich experiential base is requisite to creative development. What can a child paint if he has no ideas to express or happenings to interpret? Many sensory experiences should be given the children to increase their capacity to take in information about the world around them. Adults can direct them to observe the beauty found in a perfect spider web wet from the morning dew, in the pattern of the sun streaming through the leaves of a tree, or in the effect of the shadows on the sidewalk. Children can be directed to listen to the sounds of the birds, to the mellow sounds of sleigh bells, or to the clanking of cowbells. They can be asked to feel the smoothness of the plastic or shiny metal, or to touch the sticky tape. They can smell the pine needles, hay, clover, or cloves, and they can taste the different spices. Linderman states that "It is important to lead the child into these experiences, but to let him discover things for himself. He must perceive his environment in his own way. He should not be told how a thing smells. Rather, encourage him to explain what the smell is like or what it means to him. Do not hurry the child to answer because this forces him to a premature focus." (Linderman & Herberholz, 1969, p. 19) To be aware of the beauty in the environment, and to perceive the environment in great detail from many points of view is vital to the child's developing artistic expression.

──────────────────────────────────────────── **INFANTS**

The early sensory experiences of infants build their foundation for later artistic expression. Seeing, feeling, and acting on the environment through muscular responses, the baby receives stimulation from the adults who care for her and from the objects she is provided with. "In caring for and holding the baby, the adult provides the warmth and rhythmic stimulation the baby needs to feel comforted. This physical contact reduces tensions in the baby, and allows him to become aware of, and to respond to, other stimuli in his environment (Dittmann, 1968, p. 20).

Babies need visual stimulation—things to watch and objects to reach for. Until the middle of the first year of life, babies do not realize that an object is still there when out of their sight. The development of object permanence—the ability of the baby to recall an object even when it is not visible to him—means the development of imagery and use of symbols. Now, the baby evokes an image of something she no longer sees in order to think about it. This ability requires her to use symbols to represent the object, and may be thought of as the beginnings of expression—the baby's very first attempt to create a picture in her mind.

For art experiences, infants need many things to see and to feel, and the freedom to explore materials. They need to act on their environment by splashing soapsuds, smearing oatmeal on their tray, playing in sand and mud, and dropping objects. Each of these experiences provides the sensory stimulation necessary for later artistic expression.

## TODDLERS

Before the age of two, children's artistic expression is an extension of their sensorimotor development and activities. Children's first experiences with art are usually exploratory—they scribble, make marks, or punch clay without attempting to represent anything. At this stage, you should provide materials for the children to explore through sensorimotor activity.

Scribbling, the major artistic activity of the child under the age of two, is at this stage merely a result of muscular activity and exploration. The child has little interest in his scribbles, either while making them or after he has finished. Every part of the child moves—his hands, arms, and legs all seem to be working to move the crayon over the paper. The scribbling, so muscular, so uncontrolled, doesn't stop at the edge of the paper; it continues over the tabletop. Once the young child begins to mark, he cannot stop his movement.

Large sheets of paper and large crayons that will not break under the pressure of a two-year-old's hand are appropriate for the toddler. He should not be interrupted during scribbling; you should not ask him to name his scribble or attempt to label it for him. As the child is really not interested in the completed scribble, there is really no need to mark it with his name, and if a scribble is to be saved for a record of the child's development, it may even be wise to place his name on it *after* he has finished working. At this stage, interrupting to write his name on the paper may cause the child to attempt to copy your tight little markings rather than continuing to scribble freely.

Children may produce dozens of scribbles at one time. You may want to save some of these to give to the child's parents or to keep as a record. Others may be displayed around the room, although children will not identify their own work.

It is not necessary to hurry the children on to other art media. To two year olds, the crayons, by themselves, are a satisfying experience. They spend hours putting the crayons back in the box, dumping them out again, peeling the paper off them, chewing them, rubbing them on their faces, shoes, or legs or rolling them off the table (Biber, 1962).

A painting easel may be introduced, with one color of paint, if the twos seem ready for the experience. Smocks should be provided for the children and the floor under the easel should be washable. Two year olds will paint over the entire paper, the easel, and whatever else is near—hands, arms, shoes, and floor.

Blocks should be available for the toddler to explore with. He may line them up in a row or sometimes stack one on top of the other. The toddler should not be urged to "build something"; he merely explores the properties of the blocks.

Some modeling materials can be made available to children under the age of two. Soft clay or Play-Doh can be punched, poked, or squished by the young child without any attempt on his part to represent something or to control the medium.

At about two years of age, the child begins to gain significant control over his muscles and over art materials. Now, he begins to notice when he's made a mark and confines his scribbling efforts to the paper. Forms and shapes begin to appear. The child can now execute a circular and oval shape, and his scribble lines meet one another.

Certain patterns, lines, and shapes can be repeated by three-year-old children. When the child begins to draw shapes, he also begins to demonstrate an interest in his scribbles. He may say, "Look what I made," or talk as he scribbles, saying, "Here's my house. Now here's daddy, and the sun, and this is me." According to Lowenfeld (1957), this naming of scribbling is highly significant as it indicates that the child's thinking has changed. He now is thinking in terms of images, not merely engaging in muscular activity as he did before the age of two.

The two- and three-year-old children still produce stacks and stacks of scribbles at one sitting. A plentiful supply of large sheets of paper and large crayons that do not break easily are still the basic art tools. Three year olds, however, may enjoy seeing their names put on the scribbles and having them displayed in the room. Those scribbles that are sent home can be displayed on the refrigerator door or in the child's room. The three-year-old's interest in his scribbling may even lead him to ask you to write down the story of the scribble.

Felt-tip marking pens, with their vibrant colors, are well liked by toddlers and produce exciting designs. These pens, along with shiny paper, tinfoil, or wax paper, give the toddler an interesting change from the usual crayons and paper. Chalk, and a place to use it freely—either on the sidewalk, on a chalkboard, or on a large sheet of colored paper—is enjoyed by the older toddler. Pencils break too quickly under the uncontrolled pressure three year olds exert; they are not appropriate drawing materials at this stage.

Although they still exercise little control over paint, three year olds enjoy sloshing bright, fluid colors over a large sheet of paper. Only one or two colors are necessary for these children, with plenty of provisions for spilled paint. Children this age often paint over and over a paper, until the paper is completely disintegrated.

Clay, salt dough, and other modeling materials become increasingly interesting to three year olds. Soft, pliable clay can be balled into child-sized pieces and made available daily. Exploration of the clay is still the primary focus of the child. Cookie cutters, clay tools, or rolling pins should be reserved for older children.

Threes may begin to learn to paste. Various bits of material, pictures, ribbons, and dried flowers should be provided for the children to paste onto sheets of heavy paper. Cutting has not yet been mastered by many of the children, so materials to be used with paste should not require cutting. Sometimes the child explores the paste, finger painting with it, piling it high on the paper, smearing it around. Often things stick, not as a result of the paste being placed on the right side of the paper in the right amount, but as a result of the child's random explorations. These explorations should be permitted and valued as a learning experience. To show children exactly how they should use paste would limit opportunities for them to learn for themselves.

Given a dish of Cheerios and pipe cleaners, three year olds will enjoy stringing the Cheerios onto the pipe cleaners, eating them, and chatting with one another. Stringing macaroni on shoestrings, soda straws that have been cut into bits, or beads is another social art activity enjoyed by toddlers while serving to develop their small-muscle control.

The toddler enjoys finger-painting experiences. Finger paints can be purchased or made and, for the child under the age of four, should be used directly on the tabletop. Paper cannot hold up under the repeated scrubbings the young child executes with finger paints; besides, his interest is in manipulating the slippery, gushy paint over the surface, not in creating a product. Lowenfeld cautions not to overuse finger paints, believing that the activity does not allow the child to express himself or to represent his ideas (Lowenfeld, 1957, p. 91). However, when children have had ample opportunity to draw and scribble, an occasional finger-painting session may be appropriate. Read, on the other hand, believes that finger painting may be of high value for the young child, as it provides an acceptable outlet for sensory expression and messiness (Read, 1966).

A rather unusual activity that the toddler enjoys, and that does help him develop muscular control, is punching holes in paper with a hole punch. There is no real goal to this activity, but punching, talking, and gathering up the "holes" can be a satisfying experience for these children. Older toddlers enjoy building with blocks, and they may even create some structures. Woodworking, with very soft wood, a hammer, and nails can be introduced. The children will merely hammer the nails into a piece of wood, with no attempt to build anything or create a design. The pounding itself, mastering the nails and wood, satisfies. Rarely does the child hurt himself, for he cannot really pound hard enough to injure a finger if hit.

# PRESCHOOLERS

The preschooler enters into the symbolic stage of artistic expression. Four- and five-year-old children gradually begin to recognize shapes and figures that seem to represent things in their scribbles. Often these children, after finishing a scribble, look it over and say, "Oh, now I see; it's a truck," and they point to some circles or shapes that make them think of a truck and name the wheels or windshield. If preschoolers are asked what they are drawing, they may respond, "I don't know yet; I'm not finished."

The preschooler is able to reproduce shapes, and may select a certain shape to represent or symbolize something. A human figure is often one of the first representations. A circle or oval becomes a head, with eyes, and sometimes a nose and mouth. Legs and arms are attached directly to the head, and the resultant shape is called "a man," "me," or "mother."

Gradually, the child's symbols become highly differentiated, complex, and comprehensible; however, the work of a four- or five-year-old child in no way resembles that of an adult. Children's artwork represents their ideas and concepts, not those of an older person. The child's product becomes very important to her, and she demands that her name be written on it. Often, she desires to take it home with her or to have it displayed in the playroom.

## MATERIALS FOR PRESCHOOLERS

All of the materials utilized by the toddler are still important to the preschool child. Many teachers limit the child's time with the basic materials by introducing new ones too quickly. The preschool child, after a period of exploration and experimentation with materials, now needs the opportunity to use these same materials to represent her ideas, to create products, and to gain skill and control over the media. Of course, adding new materials and challenging the child with new and different ways of using them is motivating and stimulating; however, you should introduce new materials and ideas slowly, giving the children ample opportunity to explore and master each new material, and remembering that all children need the opportunity to draw, paint, model, construct, and build with blocks on a continual basis (Brittain, 1979).

### Crayons

Children never outgrow their need to represent their ideas and feelings through drawing. Crayons and paper should be available to the children at all times. Large crayons are appropriate for preschool children; however, the fives, and some fours, enjoy working with the thinner crayons. All colors can be provided. Some sets of crayons may be stored in their original boxes for individual children to take to draw with in some corner of the room. Crayons may also be stored in color-coded tins or boxes, with red crayons in one box, and blue, green, yellow, and so forth in their own individual boxes. Another box of crayon scraps, with broken crayons and stubby crayons, is useful for outdoor drawing or group work.

Large sheets of paper, of many different textures, shapes, and sizes, should be available for the children. If interest in drawing lags, you can add pieces of sandpaper, thin sheets of wood, cardboard, boxtops or Styrofoam meat trays. Colored construction paper, wax paper, and tinfoil are all exciting to try to draw on and can be used to add variety to the crayon table.

Crayons may be used in combination with other materials. Children may draw a figure or shape on one kind of paper, then cut it out and mount it on a contrasting sheet; or crayon drawings can be combined with material scraps. One group of children, having drawn their families, found scraps of material in the collage box, and pasted these on their figures to represent clothing.

Paint and crayons can be used in combination with one another. A crayon picture or drawing can be washed over with some type of fluid paint. The wax of the crayon resists the paint, which covers the background. Drawings of Halloween or night pictures, for example, are enhanced when washed over with blue, black, or purple paint. Water colors or thinly mixed tempera paints that are nearly transparent are suggested for washes, as children's crayon drawings are not heavy enough to resist very thick or opaque paints.

Texture can be explored with crayons. Using the box of crayon scraps, the children can rub over a piece of paper that is covering some textured material. Children can carry their paper around the room, placing it over various textured surfaces—the floor, the plaster walls, a rough door, a screen—whatever is available. If the young child cannot control the paper, crayon, and textured object at the same time, you can tape the object to the tabletop, have the child place her paper over the taped object, and then rub with the crayon. Cardboard sheets, with various objects glued to them, can also be used as texture boards for children's rubbings.

Children in a center should be free to draw whatever they wish; however, you may occasionally introduce a theme, or suggest a subject to them. No child should be required to draw what you have indicated or identified as a theme; the theme should serve only to stimulate thought. Near Mother's Day, you might suggest that the children make portraits of their mothers, themselves, or of their families for mother. Or you may suggest illustrating a story the children have written, or drawing the things they like to do best, or the animals they wish they had, or the things they saw on the trip.

You can mount drawings on colored construction paper or in paper frames made by folding the edges of a sheet of paper down one inch all around, and pinching the corners into a frame. Children usually want to take their drawings home with them, but some will allow the center to display their work. As these drawings represent the child's ideas, concepts, and feelings, they can provide a valuable record of her growth and development in a preschool program.

## Paints

Some form of painting activity should be continually available to children. Many of them will paint picture after picture, repeating the same theme, using the same scheme and colors. Easels, paints, brushes, paper, and smocks should be easily accessible to the children and arranged in such a way that the children will need little assistance in order to paint. Paper can be stored near the easel, and the easel itself equipped with clips, clip clothespins, or large thumbtacks. A variety of brushes, including small, narrow ones, should be placed point up in a can or container in the easel tray or stored next to the easel in some container.

Children should also be able to clean up after their painting without your direct assistance. A can of water at the easel may be used for soaking and washing brushes, or brushes can be carried to a sink and washed out there. Wet paintings can be clipped to a clothesline to dry or taken by the children to a hallway or some out-of-the-way area for floor drying. The children are actually learning through clean-up activities. Watching the paints run together from the brushes or being responsible for preparing the easel for the next artist are valuable experiences for a young child.

Simple smocks and some protection for the floor if it is unwashable are still in order for preschool painters. They become involved in watching the paint drip off the brushes and the fluid action of the paint running on (and off) the paper. Old shirts with the sleeves cut off or plastic sheeting attached to a plastic headband can be effective protection for the children. Whatever type smock is chosen, children should be able to put it on, take it off, and hang it up without your help. Smocks with elaborate bow ties, or smocks that must be pulled over the head, are much too difficultfor these children to handle successfully.

Preschool children usually paint in the same manner in which they draw. They use the same symbolic representation in their easel paintings as appears in their crayon drawings. Details may be omitted in the paintings, as the children do not yet have the control to execute them. People, animals, mechanical things, houses, boats, and trucks frequently appear in children's artwork.

Paints can either be mixed from dry tempera or purchased in liquid form. The colors should be bright and strong and the mixture thick. Watery paints with weak colors hold little attraction for these children. Mixing small amounts of paint daily insures freshness and limits the amount of waste due to drying or molding paints. Children should be taught how to mix their own dry tempera paints to foster their feelings of competence and independence. The primary colors of red, yellow, and blue can be toned by adding black or white paint to them. Other colors, such as avocado green, turquoise, lavender, beige, and gray are appealing to children and serve to stimulate new interest in painting. When a variety of colors is introduced, the end products of the children are often suitable for framing.

Some teachers have found that paint washes from clothing and hands more quickly if a bit of soap powder or liquid detergent is added to it. Detergent also allows tempera paint to adhere to waxy surfaces. Liquid starch added to tempera seems to stretch the paint, while retaining the thick, desirable texture. A drop of oil of cloves or peppermint can be added to retard spoiling or molding.

After the children have had many experiences with easel painting, some variations can be introduced. When they paint on a flat surface, either on the floor or on a tabletop, children can wet their paper with a sponge and water and sprinkle dry tempera from a large flour shaker onto the wet paper. Colors will blend into one another and new colors will result. Or children can wet the paper and paint over it with a brushful of wet paint, producing rainbow effects. Another variation children enjoy is to dip a dry brush into a pan of dry tempera and paint over a paper that has been completely moistened with a sponge and water. The experimentation involved in these activities is interesting and valuable to the children. Later, they may begin to incorporate these techniques into their paintings to produce specific effects.

Q-tip painting is also popular with children. Liquid paint is prepared and placed in muffin tins, and shiny shelf paper and Q tips are provided. The child dips a Q tip into one of the colors and uses it as a brush over the shiny paper. The fine Q tip permits the children to incorporate details into their paintings; and it is a lovely sensory experience for them to guide the soft cotton tip over the shiny, silky paper. Some teachers find this activity suitable for days when the weather is bad and tempers have flared because of the extended time indoors.

Water colors, especially the ones that come in small tin boxes, are inadequate for young children; however, if water colors are of good quality and purchased with each color in a separate tin or cake, they can produce colors strong enough for young children to enjoy. Textured water-color paper and large water-color brushes should be used.

Mural painting as a group activity is not usually of interest to preschool children. They are still highly egocentric and see little point in making a group picture. Furthermore, they do not have the ability to cooperate on something as individualistic as a painting. The very largeness of a sheet of mural paper may be enough to negate the young child's interest in the project. Nevertheless, the beginnings of a type of mural painting may be possible. By dividing a large sheet of brown kraft paper into sections and giving each child her own individual space to paint in, the child's individuality is protected while a type of group activity is fostered. The paper can be divided into squares, with children working around the paper, or you can draw a large scribble design on the paper and designate a section for each child to paint in. The mural can be cut apart after the group has enjoyed it, and each child can take her own painting home.

## Chalk

The bright colors, softness, and ease of application make chalk a favorite of preschool children. In addition to white chalk, brightly colored chalk, both in large chunky sticks and in regular-sized pieces, should be provided. The white chalk works best on colored construction paper or other dark surfaces, and the colored chalk on light-colored paper or surfaces. Chalkboards should also be available for the children's use.

Children's chalk drawings can be preserved by spraying them either with hair spray, a special fixative that can be purchased from school supply stores, or a solution of liquid starch and water in a squirt bottle. In experimenting with chalk, small dishes of liquid starch, sugar water, or buttermilk can be placed on the chalk table. Children dip their chalk into the liquid and then paint with the chalk on dry paper. Sometimes this almost becomes a finger painting experience. Sponges and water may be provided with the chalk on another occasion.

Children dampen their entire paper with the sponge and water and then draw with the dry chalk.

## Needles and Thread

Requiring an amazing degree of small-muscle coordination, stitchery is enjoyed by young children. Each playroom should have its own sewing box, equipped with large-eyed needles, embroidery thread, sewing thread, scissors, material scraps, and buttons. Children can use such a kit to make clothing for dolls, puppets, and for other sewing projects.

Young children's beginning efforts at stitchery can be successful when they are provided with large darning needles, yarn, and a sewing base that allows the large needle and heavy thread to slip through easily. Plastic screening, cut into 5-by-7 or 8-by-10 inch pieces, with the edges bound with masking tape to form a frame, is an appropriate first sewing material for children. The needle and thread are easily pushed through the pliable plastic screening holes, and interesting patterns of thread and screening appear. Children can be taught to thread their own needles and knot the thread. Usually, one or two children master the technique quickly and assist in teaching the others the skill.

Burlap is another material that is easily handled by young children. It can be placed in a sewing frame or stapled onto a sheet of construction paper to enable children to work with it. Onion and potato sacks with their large net holes, if well supported in sewing frames or with masking-tape borders, can also be used for initial sewing experiences. Few children will attempt specific designs or representations in their sewing, yet the designs that result from random stitching are pleasing and of interest to the children and their families.

Sewing, an adult activity, is very appealing to children; boys, especially, seem to be drawn to it. It may be that they seldom have the opportunity to participate in something thought of as feminine at home. Children of both sexes should be encouraged in their sewing efforts; the activity can be of great benefit to their development.

## Paste and Paper

In learning to use scissors, three- and four-year-old children will cut fringes on paper, cut pieces of paper, cut their hair, their clothing—anything they can find. The first experiences the child has with cutting are random explorations. She cuts just because she can, piling up great heaps of scraps, covering an entire table and floor with them. The thrill is in cutting; no product is necessary to satisfy the child.

After the task of mastering the scissors is accomplished, cutting takes on new purposes. Pictures can be cut from pages of magazines or from greeting cards. Figures can be cut from the children's drawings and mounted on other paper, or paper can be folded and designs cut into it.

Young children should be supplied with scissors that actually do cut. Pointed scissors are appropriate for young children if they have adequate control and are able to understand potential dangers. Left-handed scissors, with identifying colored handles, should be provided in the playroom.

A variety of materials should be provided for children's cutting experiences. Cloth is usually very difficult for children to cut, but newspapers, magazines, textured paper, tagboard, construction paper, tissue paper, ribbons, thin Styrofoam, and plastic can all be used by the children in their cutting activities.

Pasting requires knowledge and skill. The very young child is interested only in the paste itself, experimenting with it as if it were paint. Children's first attempts to paste things together often result in failure. They paste the wrong side of the paper or, with the idea that a lot of paste will make something stick better, pile mountains of paste onto the paper only to have the object fall off as the paste dries. However, children soon learn through trial and error, without your help, the proper amount of paste to use.

Several kinds of paste should be provided for use with different media. White library paste can be smeared onto things with a popsicle stick or, better still, fingers. It can be stored in either plastic containers or tins, or in glass jars with screw tops. Small containers can be carried anywhere in the room and are handy when individual children desire to paste. Mucilage, in bottles with rubber tops, is useful for some projects, and the strong white glue in squirt bottles, although expensive, does form a strong bond with a wide variety of materials. Make sure all bottles or containers are kept clean.

## Collage

With its immediate product and textured, three-dimensional effect, collage is a favorite of preschool children. It is a form of art in which bits of flat objects are pasted onto a surface.

Anything can be used to make a collage. A box of scrap materials, kept freshened by removing unusable items and adding new interesting ones, results in many exciting products. Additional collage materials should be organized in shoeboxes, plastic containers, or cookie tins, with each container holding a different type of material. Cloth and material scraps, carpet scraps, buttons and beads, plastic objects, wooden pieces, dried flowers and seeds, shiny papers, feathers, straws, toothpicks, and shells are some of the materials that can be used. Categorizing these materials gives children yet another experience in ordering their world and facilitates finding the desired material easily. Furthermore, when materials are sorted and stored by categories, children can select a specific box to portray a topic or theme. Following a trip to the zoo, rough and bumpy carpet scraps were used by one boy to represent an alligator; the straw box was selected by a girl to help her portray a bridge that had fascinated her on the trip.

Children are most interested in collage if they themselves have gathered the materials. Going for a walk with the object of collecting materials to make a nature collage, or going through the center in search of scraps for a center collage involves children fully. A workbench collage can be made from scraps of wood, sawdust shavings, and bits of metal pieces found at the workbench; a playroom or yard collage can be made from findings in a room or yard.

*Working with wood is satisfying.*

Food is *not* appropriate for use in collages. Using macaroni, peas, corn, rice, beans, or popcorn in this way is not only wasteful, but also confuses the young children as to the distinction between edible and nonedible items. Certainly, you should exercise discretion before using edible items in any type of children's artwork.

Mosaic, in which small bits of material are used to form designs, is another type of collage. Young children cannot handle small bits of paper to form a mosaic; however, if paper is prepared in strips about an inch wide and eight inches long, children can snip pieces of paper from the strip and paste them onto another sheet of paper to form designs without too much difficulty. Eggshells, dried and crumbled, can be used to create a textured mosaic. Sometimes construction companies will donate small, leftover bathroom or kitchen tiles that can be fixed to heavy cardboard with strong white glue.

Rock salt, the type used to sprinkle over icy sidewalks or to freeze ice cream in homemade freezers, is another interesting mosaic material. This salt, like eggshells or sawdust, can be dyed by shaking a small amount of it in a screw-top jar that has been coated on the inside with a little bit of tempera paint mixed with a little alcohol. The alcohol keeps the salt from becoming too wet, quickening the drying process. Only a small amount of paint is necessary: just enough to coat the sides of the jar. The material is shaken in the jar until all of it is covered with paint. Rock salt, sawdust, and eggshells can be fixed with strong white glue to nearly any background.

Brightly colored tissue paper can be used to make other mosaics. You can cut the tissue paper into small pieces. The children then dip the pieces into liquid starch, sugar water, or diluted mucilage and arrange them on their paper in pleasing designs. A light-colored background, white or some pastel, is essential for the tissue to retain its transparency. When the tissues are pasted one on top of the other, new colors result, adding to the attractiveness of the design.

## Wood

What could be more satisfying than creating with wood! Joining two pieces of wood, hammering a nail into a board, or sanding a rough piece of wood gives children a sense of real accomplishment. The products, though not representational, are highly valued: they have weight, they take up space, they are solid! Just the sensory experience of working with wood, smelling its sweet smell, feeling its heaviness and roughness or smoothness, gives children satisfaction. Woodworking calls for responsibility on the part of the children. It makes them feel grown up, capable of exercising control over their environment.

Soft wood and high-quality, actual tools are required. The tools chosen need not be large, but they must actually be able to saw, hammer, or screw. Steel tools, well cared for, will last for years. Young children need 16-inch to 20-inch saws, medium hammers, sandpaper, assorted nails, and C-clamps or vises to hold work steady. A coping saw with a supply of blades may be provided for older children, along with planes, hand drills, chisels, and pliers. Such tools are not necessary at the preschool level. Tools should be kept in good working order. Saws that are sharpened and oiled are safer than dull saws.

Wood can be obtained from lumberyards or carpentry shops. Woodworking shops at high schools or vocational schools may also have wood scraps that they will gladly give to the center. Home builders and parents may also have access to a supply of scraps.

Other materials can be combined with wood. Bits of metal, hooks and eyes, hinges, locks, pipes, plastic parts, carpet scraps, or bits of wire can be used to finish off wood products. White glue, wires, or nails can be used to attach these findings to the wood product. One cabinetmaker supplied a center with odd-shaped pieces of scrap wood which the children turned into furniture to which they added carpet scraps for upholstery.

The woodworking bench can be a regular, unused table equipped with a vise or several C-clamps to hold the wood. A pegboard with hooks can be mounted near the bench to hold tools. Many times children want to paint their products. Although tempera can be used, enamel or water-base house paint gives a better effect to the child's product. Furthermore, painting with paint that smells, and is sticky, and needs turpentine to clean it off is an exciting experience for the child. The fact that enamel paint stays shiny, even when dry, cannot be overestimated. The extra precautions and cleanup such paint requires are well worth the effort.

Woodworking is not a dangerous activity for young children when introduced properly and well supervised. The young child does not have sufficient strength to hammer a nail into her finger or to cut herself severely with a saw; however, you should introduce safety rules to the children. Demonstrate the power of the hammer to the group by smashing a tin can in front of them. Pass a saw around for the children to feel the sharp teeth in beginning a discussion of safety rules. Rules can be compiled from the children's suggestions and can be posted near the woodworking bench. The children cannot read these rules, but they are impressed with the importance of recorded sentences. Such simple ideas as "Keep your hand in back of the saw, not in the path of the saw," or "Never argue with a tool in your hand" can be told to the children as they begin working with the wood.

As woodworking does require special skills and supervision, it is often useful to have a parent, high school student, retired person, or other volunteer to guide this activity. Young children, as they do not create definite products, do not need a guide with sophisticated woodworking skills—only a person who can make suggestions for removing a nail or joining two pieces of wood.

## Prints

The process of stamping something on a surface to make an impression or print of it can be explored with young children. Before a printing experience, children should have some real purpose in mind for printing, such as repeating a pattern, and some familiarity with the process. Your clothing or that of the children may be printed with all-over designs, or the wallpaper in their homes or at the center may have an all-over print on it that can be pointed out to the children. Some children's books may also provide examples of designs that are repeated throughout. Gift-wrapping paper and shopping bags can provide some other examples.

Anything can be used to print with. A variety of gadgets or found objects can be placed on the printing table. Paint is mixed to a heavy consistency in a shallow tin or dish. A sponge, or folded up piece of paper toweling, is saturated with the heavy paint solution and placed in the bottom of the shallow tin, forming a printing pad. Children lightly press their object into the paint, and then stamp the object onto their paper or other surface.

Cardboard-roll printing is easily handled by four-year-old children, and even some threes. The cardboard roll found inside paper toweling or toilet paper is used to print with. The child holds the tube in her hand, dips one end into the paint, and then prints circles over her paper. Turning the roll around, she can dip the other end in a second color and make a two-color print.

Spools, cookie cutters, hair rollers, tin cans, forks, box lids—really, anything the children find—can be used to print with. Their first attempts at printing will not result in any planned patterns or designs, but will be more random in nature. Later attempts may result in designs and patterns.

Vegetable printing is also of interest to children. Cooks can be requested to save bits of vegetable scraps for children to print with. (Children and parents should be informed that it was scrap food destined, for some reason or other, to the compost heap or garbage bag.) Half an onion, with its concentric circles, leaves lovely prints. Grapefruits, oranges, or apples that are cut in half leave equally pleasing designs. You can cut a potato in half and scoop out a design with a teaspoon. Pieces of carrots, celery, and turnips are also good for printing purposes.

Pieces of sponges that are large enough for the children to handle make irregular, interesting prints; and if you're lucky enough to live where Spanish moss grows, it can be wadded into a ball and dipped in paint to leave a lovely dappled print on paper.

Roller printing results in an all-over design of a somewhat surrealistic character. A piece of string is dipped in strong glue and then wrapped securely around an empty juice can or cardboard roll. When the string has dried and is completely attached to the can, it is rolled across a piece of sponge saturated with heavy paint, and then rolled across the paper. These prints make lovely wrapping-paper, or even wallpaper designs.

Smaller designs result when children print with fingertips and thumbs. The same process is used, with children touching their finger to the paint, and then printing with it on paper.

When children first begin to print, one color of paint is sufficient. Later, several colors can be prepared for the children. The paint and the paper should be varied. Prints can be made on newspaper, tissue paper, brown wrapping paper, textured paper, Styrofoam meat trays, or box lids.

## Construction Materials

Construction with scrap materials can be thought of as three-dimensional collage. Young children who have explored many two-dimensional activities are ready to arrange materials in space.

Hundreds of boxes, paper cans, and other containers can be obtained from local factories and packaging plants. Cleanser cans or cracker and toothpaste boxes are often available as factory rejects. A large supply of masking tape, wires, and strong glue permits the children to put these boxes together to form fantastic shapes and huge, tall structures. If factory-reject boxes are not readily available, everyone can save boxes from the center or home—oatmeal, cookie, gelatin, soup, soap, pin, tape, tissue, and the like—and when this collection is large enough, the children can use them to build imaginative structures which, if desired, can be painted.

Soft wire that is coated with plastic in various colors or pipe cleaners can be used by young children to create stabiles. A stabile is a fixed mobile, with a base made of clay, wood, or Styrofoam. (The clay base is usually easiest for the children to handle.) Toothpicks, straws, wires, pipe cleaners, or even stems of weeds or twigs are stuck into the clay base and decorated with bits of multi-colored construction paper, ribbons, beads, or other such things.

After making a clay-base stabile, a wood-base one might be attempted. With a wooden base, wires are used. The wire is attached to the base with a wood staple, and then decorated with feathers, buttons, corks, straws, or anything else that can be supported by the base and wire arms.

Mobiles are more difficult for the young child to construct. Some fives, however, may be able to understand the concept of a mobile—that it should hang freely for the air to breeze through it and move its parts—and can attempt to construct one. Mobile bases are usually made from coat hangers. Strings with ribbons, paper, cutouts, beads, or other things on them are attached to the hanger. You must generally assist in the tying process. Group mobiles may be tried, with each child making some contribution to the mobile and you doing the attaching. The finished mobile can be hung from the ceiling, giving the children a feeling of accomplishment.

Children are able to execute paper constructions if they are introduced to the various techniques of paper sculpture. Strips of paper can be curled, looped, and stapled together to form circles and ovals. Paper can be folded into a fan, and strips can be made into accordion pleats. Larger pieces of paper can be rolled into cylinders or cones. These paper designs can be attached to cardboard, boxtops, or heavy construction paper with glue or staples.

## Clay

Squishing the damp clay between their fingers, pounding it, rolling it, and smashing it on the table, the children chat and laugh together, delighted to be sharing the joy of working with clay. Many types of clay can be provided: potter's clay in red, gray, or white, is purchased ready-mixed or in powdered form, and nonhardening modeling clay with a plastic or oil base and Play-Doh are readily available.

Clay should be kept moist in a container with a tight lid. Old diaper pails or clay crocks are satisfactory for this purpose. The clay should be moistened with water occasionally to keep it pliable and smooth. If potter's clay is used, the products can be fired. If, before firing, the clay becomes dry and hard, it can be rejuvenated by soaking it in water.

Children should be able to work with some type of modeling material daily. In addition to potter's clay, one of the following mixtures should be ready for the children.

*Salt Dough*

Salt
Flour
Water

*Mix equal parts salt and flour. Add enough water to moisten well. Knead until a uniform, pliable dough is formed. Add a few drops of food coloring if desired. Salt dough will harden if left in the air, resulting in lasting products for the children.*

*Baking Dough*

4 cups flour
1 cup salt
1/2 (approximately) cup water

*Mix to make a pliable mixture that does not stick to the hands. Knead for five minutes or until smooth. Make flat or standing forms and moisten slightly when sticking pieces together. Bake on baking sheet for 1 hour at 350°. Children can form interesting sculptured shapes and forms with this dough.*

*Sawdust*

Sawdust
Wallpaper paste
Water

*Mix equal parts of sawdust, wallpaper paste, and water. If mixture is sticky, add more sawdust. This material can be molded into sculpture; it will harden as it dries.*

*Cornstarch Clay*

1/2 cup cornstarch
1 cup salt
1 cup boiling water

*Mix all ingredients and boil to a soft ball stage; knead on wax paper until malleable. Use at once or wrap in a wet cloth to keep a few days. For a colored mixture, add powdered paint to the water.*

*Crepe Clay*

1 fold of crepe paper (any color)
1 cup flour
1 tablespoon salt
Water

*Cut crepe paper into pieces and place in large bowl. Add just enough water to cover pieces and soak for fifteen minutes. Pour off excess water. Mix flour and salt and add enough to make a dough. Knead well until blended.*

### Cornstarch Dough

1 cup salt
1/2 cup cornstarch
3/4 cup water

*Mix ingredients thoroughly and place in a double boiler over heat. Stir for two to three minutes until the mixture becomes a thick lump. Remove from pan and let cool on a piece of foil. When cool, knead and model into flat forms.*

As children work with clay and dough, you can demonstrate various techniques. For example, to attach parts of clay to one another, a small piece of clay can be dissolved in a small amount of water to form slip. This slip is used like glue, to attach pieces of clay together. The two edges are smoothed with fingers or tools, completing the joining procedure.

Tools to produce texture in clay can be introduced to the children. Tongue depressors, spoons, or clay tools can be added to the clay area after the children become more interested in creating products than in merely exploring the medium.

## ———————————— EVALUATION OF ART ACTIVITIES

As children grow in their ability to control and manipulate various media, they become increasingly concerned about the products that result from their efforts. They talk spontaneously about their paintings and creations to one another, discussing how they obtained a certain effect or what they like in another's work. Capitalizing on this spontaneous and natural interest of the children, you can lead them into an evaluation and analysis of their own work and the work of others.

First of all, you should show your appreciation of each child's efforts. The meaning of every painting or creation is purely personal and subjective; there is no right or wrong to any art. However, you can point out certain characteristics to help children grow in their ability to evaluate art. You may say, "I like your colors," or "This line curving upward leaves me with a happy feeling," or "You have a good idea. Your painting makes me remember when I went swimming." Children may be asked what parts of a painting they like the best, what parts they would change, how they arrived at a certain effect, or why they selected certain colors or materials. These questions lead them to clarify their thoughts and feelings, helping them to understand and enjoy their own work as well as the works of others.

Douglas and Schwartz (1969) found that very young children, four years of age, could be taught to evaluate their work and the works of others. When children were presented with artworks of others, and were led in a discussion of color, line, texture, and form, their own art products took on new dimensions and maturity.

Through questions, comments, and sharing of art products, children develop an understanding of the meaning of art, a greater awareness of the world around them, and additional skills in artistic production.

## IT'S UP TO YOU

"After spending a great deal of time watching nursery school children paint, we concluded that there is no need for any formal teaching in the procedures of painting to any nursery school children" (Brittain, 1979, p. 158). If you do not actually need to teach children to paint or draw, then what is your role in children's artistic expression?

Rather than directly teaching children to draw or paint, you should act as a guide and nurturer of children's artistic expression. In order to do this, you must first fully understand the stages of children's art. Understanding that children progress from scribbling through representational work helps you to recognize progress and to provide children with plenty of opportunities for exploration and free expression. When you understand the stages of children's art, you can readily identify the progress they are making, and it's easier to give them the time needed to draw and paint without hurrying on to adultlike products.

Arranging an attractive and orderly room environment is essential. When the art materials are arranged in order and children have free access to them, self-confidence and self-direction in their work increases, as well as their free expression.

Displaying children's work, the work of artists, or arranging flowers, plants and sculpture pieces adds beauty to the room. In England the British Infant School teachers arrange beauty corners throughout the school. At times children take part in creating these beauty spots, giving the total school the feeling of a museum full of beauty.

Children also need ideas to express through the visual arts. Providing children with actual experiences is another role you fulfill. When children have seen and heard many things, when they've experienced the cold bite of snow on their faces, the softness of a kitten, or the wonder of a moth emerging from a cocoon, they will have the ideas and emotions to express through their artistic work.

You also have a responsibility to those children in the class who have special needs. Children with special needs find artistic expression highly motivating. Gainer and Kuku suggest, however, that children with special needs may, in fact, require some demonstration of materials in order to gain control over the media. "In visual art, we teach as sequences specific techniques for making clay. . . . Each step of the sequence requires a minimum number of practice sessions" (Gainer & Kuku, 1979, p. 144).

Finally you help children develop the skills to evaluate their own work and that of others. Evaluation isn't the process of judging children's artistic products as "good" or "bad;" rather it's the process of leading children to recognize form, color, shape, line, or texture in their work and the work of others. Through discussions, either with small groups of children or individuals, children can being to recognize that their artistic expressions are valued, as is the expression of others.

## REFERENCES

Brittain, W. L. *Creativity, Art, and the Young Child*. New York: Macmillan Publishing Co., 1979.

Biber, B. *Children's Drawings from Lines to Pictures*. New York: Bank Street College, 1962.

Dittmann, L. *Early Child Care: The New Perspectives*. New York: Atherton Press, 1968.

Douglas, N. K., and Schwartz, J. B. "Increasing Awareness of Art Ideas of Young Children through Guided Experiences with Ceramics." *Studies in Art Education*. 8 (1969): 2–9.

Gainer, R. S., and Kuku, E. "Something to Sing About." *Childhood Education*. 55 (1979): 141–48.

Harris, D. B., and Goodenough, F. *Children's Drawings as Measures of Intellectual Maturity*. New York: Harcourt Brace Jovanovich, 1963.

Linderman, E. W., and Herberholz, D. W. *Developing Artistic and Perceptual Awareness: Art Practice in the Elementary School*. Dubuque, Ia.: Wm. C. Brown Company, Publishers, 1969.

Lowenfeld, V. *Creative and Mental Growth*. New York: Macmillan Publishing Co., 1957.

Maslow, A. *Motivation and Personality*. New York: Harper & Row, Publishers, 1954.

Read, K. *The Nursery School: A Human Relationships Laboratory*. Philadelphia: W. B. Saunders Co., 1966.

## RESOURCES

Cohen, E. P., and Gainer, R. S. *Art Another Language for Learning*. New York: Citation Press, 1976.

Haskell, L. L. *Art in the Early Childhood Years*. Columbus, Oh.: Charles E. Merrill Publishing Co., 1979.

Herberholz, B. *Early Childhood Art*. Dubuque, Ia.: William C. Brown Company, Publishers, 1974.

Linderman, E. W., and Herberholz, D. W. *Developing Artistic and Perceptual Awareness: Art Practice in the Elementary Classroom*. 3d ed. Dubuque, Ia.: William C. Brown Company, Publishers, 1974.

Lowenfeld, V., and Brittain, W. L. *Creative and Mental Growth.* New York: Macmillan Publishing Co., 1975.

## PROJECTS

1. Observe children scribbling. Record their verbalizations and physical movement. Keep a record of their scribbles and identify the progress they make. What changes and development in the scribbles do you note as the children grow? Collect scribbles from one child of any age over a period of a month. What changes do you note in these scribbles?

2. Observe children working with clay. What do they say as they work?

3. Ask a teacher to allow you to supervise children working at a woodworking bench. What mathematical, scientific, and social concepts do children use when working with wood?

4. Observe during an art activity period in a preschool. Note how the teacher supports each individual child's work while keeping in charge of the total class. Note the arrangements of the materials that permit children to develop independence. Note the verbal and nonverbal interactions that take place between the children and the teacher.

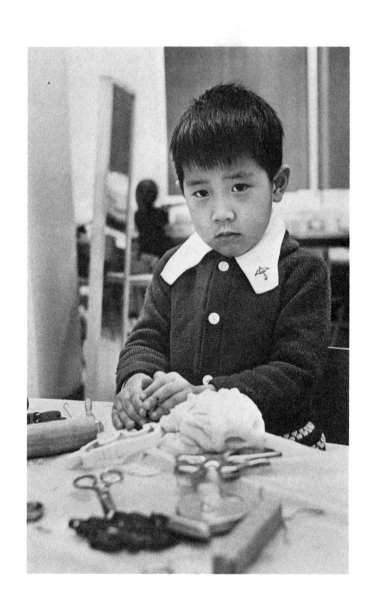

# SCIENCE FOR YOUNG CHILDREN

*Children have abundant curiosity. Most are eager to explore, discover, learn, and create anew.* (Holt, 1977, p. 3)

# 10

Children, with their abundant curiosity, are natural scientists. They are eager to discover all they can about the world in which they live. As they poke, taste, take apart, and mess around with mud and water, they're developing all of the skills of a scientist. They observe: "Hey, look at the ants; they're making a hill." They begin to classify their world: "Put all of these leaves here; they go together." They advance hypotheses: "What will happen if we put the mud in the sun? Maybe it'll turn into a brick." And children do draw conclusions from their explorations: "It doesn't work that way; you have to move the block here."

Children, like scientists, use the scientific method, solving problems as they observe, infer, classify, and reach conclusions. "These methods used unconsciously by children are the methods that a scientist uses consciously in his process of 'finding out', they are really just extensions of the abilities present in every individual which enable him to find out about his world" (Science 5/13, 1972, p. 1).

Children are so interested in finding out about their world that it might be difficult for you to try to stop them. Yet, you, as a teacher, do have a responsibility to enhance children's natural curiosity and to foster it within the safety of the preschool environment. To enhance children's scientific explorations, you should provide a rich environment.

> Providing things for small children to discover is the prime function of the nursery and infant school. A rich environment this is called. Rich it is indeed; a fantastic conglomeration of paints and brushes, Plasticine and clay, old stockings, jars and tins; cartons that have once held cereals, detergents, cigarettes, sugar, almost anything under the sun; hammers and nails, scissors and paste, berries and nuts, teasels and twigs, shells and old bird's nest, spiders in jars, live guinea pigs, wooden spoons—it would be totally impossible to list a tenth of all objects to be seen. (Science 5/13, 1972, pp. 1–2)

These things can be organized, however. One teacher collects "concept boxes." In each box she has the materials and things that could be considered to foster a given concept. In one box she keeps all of the things that could be used to foster children's understanding of air. Balloons, pinwheels, feathers, plastic straws and cups for blowing soap bubbles in the wind, a kite, silk for making parachutes, and so on are kept together. In another box magnets and things connected with the use of magnets are found (Navarra & Zafforoni, 1960).

Other boxes might contain things for floating and sinking, for playing with mirrors and light, for growing seeds, or for observing insects.

Although science activities should take place throughout the playroom and yard, special areas of interests can be set aside for specific explorations. This area may contain living animals, growing plants, or a place to experiment with sand and water. The outdoors should also be organized, at least in your mind, for children's scientific explorations.

Much outdoor play is naturally directed toward science. It's all around the children and can't be ignored; yet you can capitalize on children's interests by taking different materials outside—kites to fly, seeds to plant, animals to observe. Or you can focus children's attention to the environment around them. One day you could take magnifying glasses outside for children to observe insect or plant life more closely. Another day you might give children paper tubes to look through and focus their observations on specific parts of the environment.

*Living things are interdependent.*

Another way to organize children's environment for scientific explorations is to think in terms of all of the concepts from science that children come in contact with. Organizing the science content of a preschool program around key scientific concepts and understandings helps you to order science materials and experiences for the children. When you think in terms of key concepts for children's learning, you provide unity to the spontaneous and incidental explorations of the children. Key concepts are "door openers for thinking about a set of phenomena or a group of ideas" (Wann, 1962, p. 106). Thinking in terms of key concepts prevents presenting a series of unrelated experiences to children, and keeps their natural experiences with science from becoming random encounters. When you are aware of some general scientific understandings, you are better able to present experiences to the children, and extend and deepen these experiences, expanding on children's knowledge of their world.

Some key concepts that children experience over and over again throughout their lives are (Craig, 1947)

*Children explore space.*

1. The universe is very large—concepts of space.
2. The earth is very old—concepts of time.
3. The universe is constantly changing—concepts of change.
4. Living things are interdependent on one another—concepts of interdependence, or interrelationships.
5. There are a great many variations in the universe—concepts of variety.
6. Life is adapted to the environment—concepts of adaptation.
7. There is an interaction of forces—concepts of energy.

# CONCEPTS OF SPACE

Children become aware of space early in life. "The first break with an absolute view of the world comes in the first year of life, when the child, instead of being one with space, becomes aware of himself as an object in space. When the child searches for a hidden object, he sees himself as an object as well" (Forman & Kuschner, 1977, p. 87).

From the time children discover that they are separate from space, instead of one with it, they react to space daily. They climb in and out of boxes, on top of and under tables, through tunnels, and high into trees. They sense being in different-sized spaces as they ride in small cars, go into a large auditorium or supermarket, enter a crowded room, or walk on an empty parking lot or through an open field. Even very young children personally experience space in their immediate environment. The concept that the universe is a very large space can be developed through these personal experiences.

Astronauts blast off and take a long journey to the moon, and the children travel to Georgia to see a grandmother, or they travel from the preschool on a bus to spend a day at a lake, ocean, or park on the other side of town. Soon the children begin to develop an awareness that the world is very large.

Some children may have traveled by plane, ship, or car and can relate these experiences as you trace their journey on a map. Or perhaps parents can relate a long trip they took, tracing the route on the map, explaining to the children that the trip took a very long time because they traveled so very far.

Older children can also begin to understand the vastness of space as they observe an airplane traveling across the sky, the moon, stars, sun, and clouds. Of course, accurate concepts of the size of the universe are not developed in young children; however, the preschool can foster the development of their thought about such dimensions.

# CONCEPTS OF TIME

In the preschool, the routines of the day, the patterns of the week, and the planning you do with the children all help the children to develop concepts of time. A field trip will be taken tomorrow, the party for the two-year-old boy will be in two days, yesterday we made cookies that we will eat today in the afternoon, and in the evening it is time to go home.

Records of time passing can be kept in the center. The day the seeds were planted can be recorded, the number of days it took before the seeds began to grow can be noted, and the day the first fruit appeared, marked on the calendar. Rote marking of a calendar appears to be a useless activity for very young children; however, when you structure situations, such as the experience of seed planting, the children can increase their awareness of the passing of time. The days that pass before it is time to water the plants again, or time to feed the snake, can be recorded, and the number of days before it is time to celebrate Valentine's Day can be marked off.

You can also record how long it takes the children to walk, hop, run or skip across the play yard, or to bounce a ball across the room or clean up their block building, or how long it takes for the cookies to bake.

Experiences in which children play with and manipulate the things that are used to measure time can be provided. A stove timer can be set to tell children how long they have before clean-up time is over, and an hourglass can be used to time play activities. Stopwatches can also be used by the children, or they can set an alarm clock to go off when it's time to put the bread in the oven.

Many timekeepers should be available for children to take apart and manipulate. Moving the hands of an old alarm clock and playing with a stopwatch may teach children more about time than any teacher-directed activity. One industrious group of four-year-old boys became so astute at handling time concepts that they were able to set an old alarm clock to go off during play activities and hide the clock from the teacher. Although searching for a ringing alarm clock in the play room was somewhat trying for the teacher, she did appreciate the joke and the skill and knowledge it took for the boys to carry it off.

# CONCEPTS OF CHANGE _____

Everything changes. The children themselves change—some days they are happy, other days they are sad; some days they feel sick, other days they are well. The sweater they wore last fall doesn't fit anymore, and they need new boots again this year. Children in a center see the babies change and grow, and they try to remember back to the time when they were babies and could neither walk nor talk. They see the sun rise and set, changing the temperature and the sky.

Weather changes play an important part in the child's life. The clothing that is needed to play outdoors or the games that will be played when the child goes out are meaningfully related to changes in temperature and weather. You can help the children become aware of the changes of the seasons. Even children in Florida, California, and in other temperate climates can become aware of subtle seasonal changes—shifts in winds, differences in foliage, or temperature variations.

Shadows change. The young child may not be concerned with why they change, but experimenting with shadows at different times of the day—in the morning, at midday, and again in the late afternoon—may be the beginning of the child's understanding that time changes as the position of the earth in relation to the sun changes. The shadow of the building on the play yard can be marked as it changes during the day, or children may enjoy drawing around one another's shadows on the play yard, noticing how they change as the time passes.

Sprouting seeds and growing plants are of continual interest to children, and each playroom and yard should have a wide variety of them. Before they planted seeds for the first time, a group of three year olds was not interested in, or aware of, the parts of a plant. After several experiences with planting seeds and observing them grow, the same group developed some understanding of the nature of roots and the need plants have for water, sunshine, and soil. The children also learned some of the names for parts of plants—stem, leaf, and flower. All of the three year olds seemed to grasp the fact that the weeds grew faster than the plants in the play yard garden.

Four-year-old children are ready to be introduced to the vocabulary of plant parts—roots, leaves, stems, buds, flowers, fruits, and seeds; the fives, if they have had an extensive background with seeds and plants, may be interested in experimentation. "What will happen if we only water these seeds?" "Why did the plant die?" "What's inside a seed?" "Do seeds have tops and bottoms?" "Do roots always grow down?" Fives can benefit from planting some seeds on a wet sponge or dampened paper to observe the root pushing from the shell of the seed and the green sprout reaching for sunlight. Or they can take apart a lima bean that has been previously soaked in some water for an hour or so and, peeling away the tough skin, discover the tiny lima bean plant tucked between the two halves. They can also taste the seed.

Young children are impatient, and seeds selected for them to plant should be chosen for their ability to produce quickly with a minimum of care. Seeds that are large enough to handle and see should be chosen for the youngest children. Before attempting any planting experiences with the children, you should experiment with the seeds, determining the optimum depth, soil, drainage, and water required for success. Some seeds that sprout quickly and produce easily are radish, bean, corn, and melon. Each child can plant a number of seeds in discarded Styrofoam cups, in pint milk cartons, or in flower pots.

Planting, a messy project, is easier outdoors, but it can be done inside on newspaper-covered tables. Children should be able, perhaps with the guidance of a volunteer or older child, to fill their own containers with a layer of pebbles for drainage followed by a thick layer of dirt, and then to plant their seeds. You may wish to plant several extra cups of seeds to provide plants for those children whose seeds do not come up. This is not to hide from the children the fact that some seeds do not grow, but to dispel the bitter disappointment of children whose seeds did not successfully sprout. Later, the plants can be taken home and enjoyed by the children's families.

Slower in sprouting, but growing into beautiful, exotic, and hardy plants are avocado, orange, grapefruit, and apple seeds. The fun of feeling the smooth outside skin of an avocado, learning its name, spreading the oily fruit on a cracker, and examining the large seed is an exciting experience for young children. The avocado seed is planted by spearing it with toothpicks in the midsection and suspending it bottom down (larger, flattened end) in a glass or container of water, keeping the bottom of the seed covered with water.

Grass seeds are fun to experiment with. A dampened sponge, sprinkled with Timothy grass seeds, turns into a mass of green grass in a day or so, and a large pine cone, stuffed with a mixture of dampened sand, dirt, and seeds and kept dampened by spraying with water, turns into a stunning green tree within a week.

Seeds are not always necessary to produce plants. Some plants will grow from cuttings or parts of a plant. A carrot, radish, parsnip, or turnip can be cut about an inch from the top, the greens removed, and anchored in a dish of water and gravel. Lacy, new green plants will grow. The top of a pineapple can be planted in the same manner and, once the roots appear, transferred to a pot of soil where it will produce a full, exotic plant. The pineapple is cut with about an inch of the fruit attached to it, the green leaves intact, and placed in about an inch of water. The water may need frequent changing as the fruit molds and the water sours. Roots will develop within a month or so. (Some gardeners are successful in starting the plant in soil from the beginning. They leave about an inch of fruit attached to the top and scoop out part of the flesh leaving a "cap." After the fruit dries for about a day, the pineapple is planted with the cap submerged in the soil.)

In the four- or five-year-olds' room, each child can make her own terrarium. Large food jars that are gathered from the kitchen can be placed on their sides, or stood upright, and filled with a layer of gravel for drainage, a bit of charcoal to prevent spoilage, and planting earth. Small green plants, moss, and ferns can be gathered by the children on a nature walk, or seeds planted within the jar. The plantings need only be watered once, and then the jar lid is closed. Drops of water will collect on the sides of the jar and provide a continual environment for living plants.

Planting activities should not be limited to the indoors. A vegetable garden and a flower garden should be available for the children in some part of their play yard. Gardening is easier with the young child when a volunteer or staff person has completed the initial digging of the garden. The children may be able to observe this process and assist in smoothing the dirt with rakes and hoes. Large spaces are not necessary for outdoor gardens. A bit of land around the steps or foundation of the center can accommodate several tomato plants, and the strip of earth between the surfaced play yard and the fence is sufficient to grow many bearing plants such as beans, mustard greens, or peas.

Children's experiences with change should not be limited to observing the weather or plants. Kamii and DeVries (1978) suggest that children's observations should be focused on the way objects change. "Actions can be performed on objects to make them move . . . pulling, pushing, rolling, kicking, jumping, blowing, sucking, throwing, swinging, twirling, balancing, and dropping" (Kamii & DeVries, 1978, p. 6). In selecting objects for the development of the idea of change, they suggest that you keep at least four criteria in mind (Kamii & DeVries, 1978, pp. 8–9)

1. The child must be able to produce movement on the object by her own actions.
2. The child should be able to vary actions.
3. The reaction of the object should be observable.
4. The reaction should be immediate.

With actions on objects, the idea is that to nurture an "experimental attitude, we must encourage such children to act on the object to test their hypotheses" (Kamii & DeVries, 1978, p. 11).

# CONCEPTS OF INTERRELATIONSHIPS _____

In a preschool, the interrelatedness of life is evidenced in the diversity of people working together to create a place where they can function in harmony with one another. Caring for numerous pets and living things within a preschool fosters a deeper understanding of the interdependence of man, animals, and plants.

With pets in the center for the children to care for, the dependency of the pets on the children can be observed. The children must feed, water, and clean the pets in order for them to live. The children also become aware of the dependence of animals on one another. The snake eats small frogs, frogs eat insects, larger insects eat smaller insects, and smaller insects eat plants.

Living things in a classroom also help to foster language development. "Look what the bunny is doing!" Can you hop like a rabbit?" "What is happening to the tadpoles?" "What do you think the snake will eat?" "Why do you think the turtle has a shell?" And the graphing activities and recording of information that goes along with caring for animals provides a functional introduction to the use and purpose of the written language. Charts can be made to record the number of days it took for the eggs to hatch, to mark the day the gerbils were born, or to tell how many insects the frog has eaten. Even though you will do the reading and writing involved, the children become increasingly aware of the importance of language.

Some pets belong to the preschool as a whole, with primary responsibility for the care and feeding of them rotated among the different groups. Each playroom, however, should have its own selection of pets. Caution should be used in choosing pets for young children, and safety measures and health regulations closely followed. Children should be taught specific safety measures when handling pets, being sure to wash their hands after handling them or their cages. Adults should be responsible for any cleaning of cages that might contaminate the children. It is always wise to check with the local health department before bringing any pets into the preschool, as various communities are sometimes know to have specific outbreaks of animal diseases.

INSECTS    Young children are fascinated by insects. They carry them around in their pockets and spend hours playing with ants or observing a spider spin his web. The staff can construct insect cages from wire screening and the bottoms of plastic bleach bottles, or from large empty food jars. Insect cages are also commercially produced.

A preschool need not be in the middle of the country for the children to enjoy insects. Ants, spiders, flies, gnats, beetles, and many other insects are found in both city and country. A preschool in the middle of a large city even waged a campaign against cockroaches; the staff and children learned about them, and how they could be eliminated from the center.

## Praying Mantises

Almost surrealistic in appearance, with its hands folded as if to pray, the mantis is an excellent insect to raise and care for in a preschool. Mantises can be purchased as egg cases from a seed company or found outdoors, either before the egg case has hatched or after, when the mantises are young. Adult mantises can also be found and easily captured. The praying mantis feeds on other insects harmful to crops and vegetation, and this usefulness to man can be stressed to the children. Although the mantis does not eat vegetation, his jar home should contain growing plants for him to sit on and hide under. The mantis also drinks the water that collects on the leaves of the plants or that is

*Caterpillars are observed.*

sprinkled there for him to drink. A jar home is recommended as the mantis is long-lived and enjoys green, growing plants.

Live insects are required for the mantis to feed on—anything from roaches to mealworms or spiders will do. A piece of banana peel inside the jar attracts fruit flies for very young mantises to eat. The adult mantis, however, needs a large supply of bigger insects. If provided with adequate food, a mantis will live for many months inside a jar, and some even become tame enough to drink water from a spoon or to sit on a very still child's fingers to drink. Children accept the mantis eating other living insects without dismay, and the experience of seeing a mantis depend on other living things helps them to become aware of the interdependency of all living things.

## Ladybugs

Ladybugs, also very useful to man, are frequently found by young children and can live in a jar home. A ladybug, however, must eat aphids; if a good supply of aphids is not available to the center, the children should let the ladybug fly away. Aphids can be found indoors on house plants, or outdoors on rosebushes and geraniums, as well as on other plants. Ladybugs are used by farmers to control aphids and can be purchased from seed companies. Other than the aphids, the ladybug requires no special living conditions; it can be cared for in a jar or screen home with some twigs or green plants for it to sit on.

## Caterpillars, Cocoons, and Butterflies

In the spring the children delight in capturing and observing caterpillars, and in the fall it is common for the children to find cocoons hanging on bushes, leaves, or weed stalks. Both caterpillars and cocoons can provide still another experience for children to watch living things depend on one another. If a caterpillar is found, and the child wishes to keep it in the center, the leaves of the plant the caterpillar was found feeding on should be noted and large quantities of the same variety should be provided for it. No water is required in the jar as long as the caterpillar is still eating large quantities of leaves a day. Once the caterpillar has consumed the foliage necessary for it to spin, some sticks or branches should be added to the jar home for the caterpillar to attach itself to. Often the caterpillar spins or turns into a cocoon before the children's very eyes. After the cocoon, or chrysalis, has been formed, a few drops of water can be added to the jar to simulate the moistness of the outdoors, and the jar kept in a relatively cool place.

Children can hold a fully spun cocoon in their hands and feel the delicate life inside wiggle and move in response to the warmth. In the spring, with a little luck, a moth or butterfly will emerge, dry its wings, and be ready to be released outdoors. Both younger and older children can benefit from the experience of observing the caterpillar, even though the younger children may not fully understand the transformation to a butterfly. While the younger children may not even remember the caterpillar or relate it to the butterfly, the older children may have recorded the day they caught the caterpillar, the amount of food it ate, the day it began to spin, the day the cocoon was completed, and the number of days it took before the butterfly was ready to emerge.

## Walking Sticks

The walking stick is an insect that looks so much like a stick that it is often mistaken for one until it begins to walk away. Looking carefully among shrubs and bushes, the children may be able to spot some of these slender, green or brown insects. A walking stick eats vegetation, and the leaves it is found on should be taken for its food and sprinkled with water occasionally. Walking sticks are common on or among oak and cherry trees and can live in a jar or screen home.

## Ants

There are many hundreds of varieties of ants, and it may even be possible to collect and raise several different types. Three and four year olds merely enjoy collecting the ants and observing them make a home, while the fives become deeply interested in the diversity of jobs ants have, the different ways in which they build tunnels, and how they eat.

Ants can be found almost anywhere—in an anthill, under a stone, in a dead tree stump, or in the cracks of a city sidewalk. You can dig a shovelful of them into a glass jar and cover the outside of the jar with a sheet of dark paper to simulate the underground. A secure lid is necessary, or the jar may be placed in a pan of water, inhibiting the ants from crawling from their new home to some other place in the preschool where they may not be as welcome.

When the dark paper is removed from the outside of the jar, the children can observe the tunnels and passageways the ants have made. Ants will keep aphids, milking them for their secretions, and will eat anything. Other insects (dead or alive), any type of food scrap, and an occasional bit of water can be used to feed them.

Some ants, while fascinating to observe, can inflict very painful, severe bites. You should be aware of this variety of ant, and limit the ants kept in the center to those that do not injure humans.

## Earthworms

In addition to insects, children enjoy raising earthworms in the center, and they can serve a useful function in helping to feed other animals. Children can also be taught the value of earthworms to farmers and gardeners in aerating and fertilizing the soil. A container of fishing worms might be purchased to release in the children's garden. Worms can be found on the sidewalk or in the play yard after a rain, or a starter set can be purchased from a fishing camp or bait shop. The worms in the starter set will live and multiply in a container that can be tightly closed. Loam, fine earth, coffee grounds and/or corn meal, kept moist, provide an ideal habitat for raising worms.

## REPTILES, AMPHIBIANS, AND FISH

In some areas of the country, snakes, chameleons, turtles, frogs, and toads are plentiful. All are of interest to the children, and if not available in the play yard itself, can be collected during a field trip to a pond or purchased from a pet store for a small cost. Some fish can be obtained from rivers or ponds, and tropical fish and aquariums, of course, can be purchased from pet stores. These need not be expensive to provide valuable experiences for children.

## Snakes

Snakes are very clean and easy to care for. They need little water, are hungry only occasionally, and are enjoyed by the children. Although most snakes are totally harmless to man, and highly beneficial in that they eat rodents and insects that damage crops, children must be aware of the danger of some snakes. In an area of the country where poisonous snakes are abundant, children can be taught to identify them through pictures, books, and movies. In such an area it might be wise not to keep even harmless snakes as pets, for fear the children would confuse the harmless with the poisonous ones.

Safety measures should be introduced to all children. They should be taught never to touch, or even reach toward, a snake if they see one outside. They can be taught, upon seeing a snake, to stand very still until the snake moves away or, after standing still for awhile, to back slowly away and to tell the nearest adult about the snake.

Many harmless snakes—grass snakes, king snakes, black snakes, and garter snakes—are pleasant to hold and interesting to observe. Snakes must eat other living things, so small frogs, worms, or toads could be provided as food for them.

## Snails

Snails, less objectionable to many adults than snakes, are easily obtained. A pond will yield a collection of water snails that can be kept in an aquarium or a large glass jar filled with pond water. Some water snails lay their eggs on the side of the jar, while others give birth to living young. The container should contain a bottom of sand and a few pond plants. As snails eat either water plants or algae, it is important to use the pond water they were found in, and some of the plant life found in the pond.

Occasionally the children will find a snail in their garden or near a decaying tree stump. Land snails can be kept in a damp terrarium or a large food jar planted with a few wood plants, some moss, or a piece of rotting wood. A piece of lettuce or other greens might be fed to the land snails.

## Chameleons

Common in the South and Southwest and fun to observe are chameleons, the lizards that change their color to match that of the surroundings. Chameleons may be found outdoors, or ordered and purchased from a pet store. A terrarium for chameleons, a large glass jar, should contain a green plant and some brown branches. Plants should be sprinkled with water for the chameleons to drink, and many, many living insects provided for their food. A banana peel, placed inside of the jar, will attract enough fruit flies and other insects for the chameleons. Additional insects can be caught by the children and staff to keep the chameleons well nourished.

## Turtles

Many kinds of turtles can be found and kept in the preschool. However, there are state laws protecting the capture of a number of varieties of turtles that are on the endangered species list, and turtles purchased in a dime store or pet shop have been known to transmit disease. Baby pond or river turtles need a large pool of water to swim in, plus room to climb out of the water. A terrarium can be arranged with a shallow round or square pan of water set in the middle of gravel or dirt, or a terrarium, half full of water, can have a corner of rocks for the turtle to climb out and sun on.

Turtles eat worms, small live insects, and an occasional lettuce leaf. Bits of hamburger draped over a branch hanging over the pool of water, or dropped into the water, may be accepted by the turtle. Turtles must eat and swallow under water, so all food should be given to them near or in water deep enough to allow them to actually submerge and swallow food in.

## Frogs

Large bullfrogs need more room than an aquarium or terrarium can give them; hence, they are not satisfactory pets for a preschool. However, young frogs and tadpoles are just right for raising in the center. On a spring trip to a pond, the children may find a cluster of eggs, usually still in the water, that will hatch into

*The world is full of variety.*

tadpoles. Older children will not have any difficulty finding these clusters that look like tiny balls of clear jelly, each with a dot in the middle. The eggs can be put in a Mason jar and filled with the pond water in which they were found.

With a magnifying glass, the children can observe the center of the egg develop and grow. In a week or so, the tadpoles will emerge. Water plants and algae, from the pond the eggs were found in, should be provided as food. Later, as the tadpoles grow, tiny bits of raw hamburger, fish, or other raw meat, and small pieces of lettuce or spinach can be given for food. As the tadpoles change into frogs, a new home must be provided. The frog must be able to climb out of the water onto land. It is best to return developed frogs to the pond where they were found, for they demand large quantities of living insects to eat, and much more room that is often possible to give them in a terrarium or glass jar.

## Toads

Many parts of the country abound with toads. Usually they live entirely on land, although they often breed in water. A dry land terrarium can be a good home for toads. All toads, especially the larger variety, require large spaces in which to hop and huge amounts of living worms, slugs, and other insects to keep alive.

## Fish

A balanced aquarium is a must for each playroom. A goldfish bowl or dish does not serve well as a tank and is rarely successful with young children. A pet store operator, parent, or volunteer may be able to come to the preschool to assist the staff in establishing balanced aquariums.

Before purchasing fish, water plants, and snails, a clean tank should be prepared. No traces of soap or detergent should remain, and if the tank has been washed with soap, it can be left in the sun to air for several days. Next, clean sand should be spread in the bottom of the tank and clean water added. The tank should again stand for several days for the impurities to be eliminated from the water by the air and the sun, and the sand allowed to settle. The children can then take a trip to the pet store to purchase water plants, fish, and snails. After the plants have been placed in the sand, the fish should be very carefully lowered into the water, taking care not to injure them in any way. The aquarium should now be ready to enjoy.

A truly balanced aquarium requires little care or changing. Snails and other scavenger fish can help to clean up debris, and plants supply the necessary oxygen. The children should be cautioned not to overfeed the fish. Fish require very little food and should never be fed more than they can eat in a few minutes. They enjoy tiny bits of raw meat and small live insects. Commercial fish food can supplement the diet of insects and meat.

An aquarium, to prevent the rapid growth of algae, should be kept out of direct sunlight, but near enough a source of light to allow the plants and fish to grow. Specific fish can be purchased to eat algae if it becomes a problem. Some fish that are obtained from rivers and ponds are much more satisfactory than goldfish for young children. Common tropical fish, carefully selected, are much easier to raise than goldfish, although neither river fish nor the common varieties of tropical fish are as large and as colorful as goldfish.

*Mammals are of interest.*

MAMMALS   Mammals often promote more interest, conversation, and opportunities for learning in a preschool than do other varieties of pets. The children naturally can identify more closely with a warm, furry animal that possesses many human characteristics than they can, for example, with an insect, snake, or fish.

## Hamsters

Popular pets, hamsters can be purchased at a pet store. An old tank that was once used for an aquarium can be fitted with a snug top of heavy screen to serve as the hamster's home. Hamsters do love to chew, and anything of light wire or wood cannot provide an adequate home for them. A layer of cedar shaving on the bottom of the cage collects the nearly odorless droppings of the hamster and provides a bed. A water bottle for the cage can be obtained from a pet store and an exercise wheel might be included. Hamsters will eat carrots, lettuce, and other green vegetables and plants, in addition to purchased hamster food or seeds and grains. If conditions are favorable, a pair of hamsters will mate within their cage, and young will be born. Hamsters can successfully raise young in captivity. They are, however, nocturnal, much to the chagrin of the children who would like to watch them play rather than just sleep.

## Gerbils

These small desert rodents make delightful pets for the children to observe. Gerbils are playful, clean, and require little care. They are very similar to hamsters, but they mate and breed much more readily in a center environment and often are awake for more hours of the day. Gerbils can be reared in the same type of home as hamsters, with the addition of things they can chew— newspapers, tubes for toweling, boxes, anything of paper or wood. Gerbils do require some privacy; coconut shells, glass jars, flowerpots, or metal containers that cannot be chewed give them a place in which to hide.

Gerbils are extremely prolific, even in the noise of the center, and produce a litter every month or so. The male assists the female during birth and cares for the young as an equal with the female.

## Rabbits

A rabbit hutch may be established outdoors in the play yard for the entire center to enjoy. The hutch should consist of a screen cage, with a screen bottom, mounted off the ground. Rabbit droppings fall through the screening for easy cleaning. Rabbits eat a variety of vegetables and green plants, plus purchased rabbit pellets. They will also breed in captivity, and tame rabbits can be held, petted, and freed from the cage for the children to enjoy.

ECOLOGY   The interdependence of living things demonstrates to the children the precarious balance found in nature: the rabbit cannot live without living plants and vegetables to eat; the frog and praying mantis feed on living insects; and the snail feeds on algae—tiny living plants.

You should not allow children to keep an insect or pet that cannot live in captivity. Nor should you attempt to collect or cage those animals that, although they may live for a few days in the playroom, require freedom to survive. Many creatures can be observed by the children in their natural habitat. A bird eating food left for it by the children on the windowsill is just as much of a pet to them as if it were in a cage inside the playroom.

Your attitude toward harmless snakes and insects is very important and will be assumed by the children. Every snake, mouse, or insect has a unique function in nature. Allowing children to destroy one life, whether it be that of a worm, gerbil, or insect, may result in the destruction of a chain of life.

Plant life, as well as animal life, must be respected. Children can be taught in the preschool not to pick wild flowers indiscriminately or pull branches from flowering trees. They can be taught to take care to leave some seeds for next year and not pull up plants by their roots.

Children can also care for the environment and protect the lives dependent upon them by not littering. On a picnic or trip to a pond or park, help the children to leave the area in the same condition in which they found it, picking trash up and placing it in containers or taking care not to walk off the path. The concept of interdependence of living things is complex, yet it can be grasped by the young child through his actual experiences of caring for and observing living things in the classroom and by protecting the environment around him.

## CONCEPTS OF VARIETY

Selecting any topic that is of interest to the young child, you can foster the concept of variation in the universe. If four year olds become interested in their heights, you can help them to measure themselves, focusing on the individuality of each child. Some children may become intrigued with footprints left in the sand or mud of the play yard, and the variations of foot size may be pointed out.

In considering variation, you may lead the children in a discussion of their families. Some families include a grandmother, aunt, and cousin; others a mother, father, and child; and still others only a mother and a child, or a father and a child. In discussing the different family units, be cautious not to judge any one unit as preferred over another. All families should be respected; each serves a valuable function.

Talking about families could lead to a discussion of the variety among houses. How many children live in a single home? How many live in a mobile home, in an apartment house, in a duplex, a housing project, or a townhouse? Pictures of the various homes can be put on a chart, and the number of children living in each can be recorded by tally.

The pets, plants, and seeds in the center can also serve to foster the children's awareness of the great variety of life in their universe. Some pets swim and crawl; others hop, run, or fly. Some live in water; others must have dry land in order to live. Some insects eat other insects; others eat only leaves. Some reptiles eat other reptiles; some eat other animals and insects. In physical appearance, the animals vary. The fish, snake, and turtle are scaly; the rabbit, gerbil, and hamster are covered with fur.

The variety of toys in the playroom can be noted by the children. Wheel toys, alike in one respect, differ—some are made of plastic, others of metal, and still others are made of wood. As the children play with various toys, point out the characteristics of each one, asking the children to note any likenesses or differences.

Textures, colors, sizes, and shapes in the playroom and yard also vary. Even the two- and three-year-old children can have experiences feeling, sorting, and becoming acquainted with the variety in their environment.

Often, you can take advantage of a particular situation to teach young children about variation. For example, a four-year-old group of children, shelling peanuts to make their own peanut butter, became intrigued with the number of peanuts in each shell. One child would find only one peanut inside; another would find four, another two, and still another three. The fours could handle the association of one, two, and three, and made a game of counting the different numbers of peanuts found in the shells.

Five year olds noted variation in the number of chocolate chips in their cookies. Starting as an argument over who had the most chips, the children discovered that everyone's cookie had a different number. The teacher, picking up on this spontaneous interest of the children, counted the chips in the different cookies and recorded the information on a chart.

The variations in seeds captured the imagination of another group of children. One child collected every seed she could find and carefully enclosed each in a little plastic envelope. Other children, catching her enthusiasm, began collecting seeds, and soon an entire bulletin board was covered. Some seeds were black and red, some yellow, some furry, some sticky, some rough, some large, and others small.

Fostering an awareness of the variation within the universe can be thought of as helping to provide a foundation upon which to build human relationships. Accepting the wide variety that exists in the natural environment, the child is better able to accept the differences in the people with whom she is presently involved and in those people she will come in contact with in the future.

# CONCEPTS OF ADAPTATION _____

"Development, and therefore adaptation, implies a continuity of experience and the conservation of the past. . . . Adaptative change always involves a double understanding; understanding; understanding of the value of the past and understanding of the requirements of the present" (Forman & Kuschner, 1977, p. 26). The ability to adapt and to understand adaptation is necessary to develop.

Children have already experienced adaptations to their environment. Even though they may not think in terms of scientific adaptation, children change clothes and activities to suit the weather; they use machines and tools to adapt to their environment; and they live in homes, adapting to the climate.

A wide variety of pets and living things in the classroom and play yard helps children become aware of how animals adapt to their environment. The chameleon changes color to match that of the surroundings; the rabbit's coat thickens and may even change color as winter approaches; and the turtle and frog, when fall is over, burrow under ground in the terrarium.

Observing animals in their natural habitats is a valuable experience. Children can see how all of nature adapts to the environment. You can call children's attention to the pointed bill of the woodpecker cutting through the bark of a tree to capture insects, or you can focus their attention on the wide bill of the duck skimming the pond for small insects.

The development of machines marks one adaptation man has made to his environment. For all of human ingenuity, there are still only six basic machines today—pulley, lever, wheel and axle, inclined plane, screw, and wedge. Young children are familiar with these machines; they use them daily to adapt to their environment in the preschool. Familiarize yourself with the workings of the machines and construct some of them for use in the preshool to help children adapt to their environment.

Children can learn how these machines enable them to perform some otherwise impossible activity or game, or to do some task without as much effort. Pulleys can be useful to children outdoors in lifting dirt, sand, or water from the mud hole; indoors, children's paintings or clothing can be attached to them. Seesaws are actually levers, and even a two year old can have the delightful experience of going up and down on one that is low and safe. Older children may be introduced to the principles of the lever through their seesawing experiences. You may ask, "What will happen if Tommy sits closer to the middle?" or say, "Pam, move back so you balance." The shovel, wheelbarrow, nutcracker, ice tongs, scissors, and can opener also are based on principles of leverage. Discussions about levers and how they work are only appropriate with individual children or small groups as they actually play or work with them. Demonstrating a lever in front of a group is a meaningless activity.

Tricycles, wagons, and the like operate on wheel-and-axle principles. Children often become aware of the workings of these toys as they break or as they are being repaired. A volunteer may come to the center to repair wheel toys and talk with the children as she works. Often, the children spontaneously ask questions dealing with wheels and axles. At other times, you can point out to the children how they use these toys to adapt to the environment. The wheels permit them to travel, to carry heavy loads, or to move things from one place to another with ease.

When children want to move heavy boxes, blocks, or wheel toys up hills or over bumps and steps, you can show them the use of the inclined plane. When introduced in connection with their experiences, the idea of an inclined plane as a means of adapting to the environment becomes meaningful.

Screws are found in the woodworking area of the center. You can introduce children to screws by pointing out that they are tools that help join wood together, or you can show how screws help us adapt to the environment as they are replaced in chairs, tables, and other equipment in the preschool.

Children also use the wedge to adapt to the environment. Wedges, such as pins, needles, or knives, are used by people in the center. As they are used, the idea that these are tools that help us adapt can be introduced.

Some children are motivated to learn more about the machines in their environment; others are totally uninterested and merely ride away from an adult who attempts to introduce concepts of tools and adaptation. Yet, simple science books, science-kit materials, and their own experiences in the center can help children form initial concepts of machines, tools, and the way they are used to adapt to the environment.

# CONCEPTS OF ENERGY ————————————————————————

You will probably feel comfortable working with young children in the area of natural science. It's easy for most of us to observe plants and insects, and to provide children with these readily available, easily understood, familiar materials. But when it comes to concepts of energy, many of us shy away.

Our own inadequacies often limit the experiences we provide for children with concepts of energy. Even though we use electricity and energy daily, we often have incomplete concepts of these forces. Also, young children cannot handle abstractions, and energy is certainly an abstract concept.

Children must be able to observe, question, and act on a phenomenon in order to learn. Sometimes, when thinking of the concept of energy, this seems impossible for children to do. For this reason, Kamii and DeVries suggest that "a rule of thumb is to consider the objects that primitive people could act upon" (Kamii & DeVries, 1977, p. 11).

Children can and do observe and act on concepts of energy. For instance, a wind-up car uses energy, energy that they themselves control. Or their battery race car uses energy stored in a cell. They even experience energy as they bounce balls of different sizes and attempt to stop their tricycles on wet pavement.

Children do come in contact with other sources of energy; they feel the heat from the furnace on a cold day and enjoy the feel of the warm sun on their bodies as they play outdoors. They may even explore the force of the wind and use this wind as a source of energy to move their toys. They can explore the force of air as they blow up balloons and release them.

Electricity is still another form of energy that children experience daily. They can see that their food may be cooked and cooled with electricity, and their homes heated and lighted with it. Electricity often appears to be like magic to the young child—a touch of a switch and a light appears or disappears, and a press of a button and the beaters whir and the sweeper roars. Some simple experiments with electricity are appropriate for young children, and their interest in the science may replace the lost magic. A dry cell, some wire, and a small flashlight bulb give the children an opportunity to experiment with light. Dry cell batteries hooked up to a bell are a useful addition to the block building and housekeeping areas. You may wish to ask a volunteer—high school or college student or another teacher—to work with you and the children on some of these activities.

# —————————————————————— THE ROLE OF THE TEACHER

Thinking of key concepts of science and permitting children free exploration is not all that is required of a teacher. Throughout all of the children's experiences with science, you will want to foster their skills in the scientific method. As children explore any scientific concept, using any material, you can ask them to solve problems by observing, inferring, classifying, and communicating.

### Observing*

In observing, a child learns to use all or as many of his five senses as possible: seeing, hearing, smelling, tasting, and feeling. For example, he may observe a melting ice cube and make twenty or more observations based on what he sees, feels, hears, or touches. He may observe a burning candle and report what he sees and smells.

Some activities that might be used to help children observe and understand the use of observation are:

Seeing: Look at a lima bean growing; see the fish swim; watch the shadows on the play yard.

Smelling: Cut open a pineapple and smell the fruit; smell pine needles gathered on a walk; identify the vanilla the cook is using; smell the spices or the baking bread.

Touching: Touch the rough skin of the pineapple and feel the prickly leaves; touch the different textures at the woodworking bench—the smooth steel of the hammer, the rough sandpaper, the prickly boards; feel the smooth plastic and the fuzzy leaf.

Tasting: Taste the sweet pineapple, the vanilla cookies, and the baking bread; put a drop of spice on your tongue and tell how it tastes; close your eyes and taste a bit of onion, apple, pear, and radish, and guess what they are.

Hearing: Listen to the wind outside or to the sounds of the traffic in the street; listen to your own voice on a tape recorder; listen to the sounds in the kitchen, the center, and play yard.

### Inferring

When observations are limited, a child should learn to use the limited observations plus appropriate previous experiences to discover additional information or explain certain phenomena. It is useful for a child to understand the ways in which inferences are made, the limitations of inferential information, and how it differs from observation. The child must be willing to risk being "wrong" when he makes an inference; he gradually comes to understand that inferences are sometimes less accurate than observations.

Some activities that help children understand the meaning of inference are:

—————————————

* Reprinted with permission. D. Neuman,"Sciencing for Young Children," *Young Children*, 27 (1972), 218–20.

Mystery Box: Seal some object inside a box and pass the box around. Have the children guess what is inside the box without being able to see it.

Hands behind Back: Ask a child to put his hands behind his back. Place some small object in his hands—a button, spool, pen, bead, figurine—and ask him to identify it without looking at it.

Look Outside: Have the children look outside and tell whether it is hot or cold. Is the wind blowing or is it still?

Alive or Dead: Place an insect inside a jar and ask the children to decide whether it is alive or dead. Have them tell you why they think so.

Classifying

A set of objects may be classified by a child into a series of groupings or subgroupings. The child calls this "sorting," and even young children are able to sort a group of objects on the basis of one property or dimension such as color, hardness, or size.

Communicating

A child should be encouraged to tell how and what he observed, inferred, or classified in order to clarify his thinking and to build his skill of interacting with others. The child should be given opportunities to communicate with his peers as well as with teachers and adults in the classroom.

Some suggested topics and ideas to encourage children's communication are:

Living things: Ask the children, "How is a turtle like a fish?" "How is a kitten like a person?" "How do the kitten and turtle feel?" "What do they make you think of?"

Properties of Objects: Children can be encouraged to describe objects in their environment, using words such as "hard," "smooth," "soft," "large," "rough," "bright," "fat," "thin," "wide," "narrow," "shiny," "sticky," "loud," "mellow," "hot," and "cold."

Feelings: Children can be asked to describe how they feel, giving names to emotions. "How did you feel when you saw the birthday cake?" "How did you feel when that spider was on your arm?"

# IT'S UP TO YOU _____

"Science is a way of doing things and solving problems. It is a style which leads a person to wonder, to seek, to discover, to know, and then to wonder anew. It is a style in which good feelings of joy, excitement, and beauty accompany these active interactions with one's world. Not only children, but adults can experience science. It is a way of life" (Holt, 1977, p. 117).

As a teacher of young children, it's up to you to foster science as a way of life, a way of finding out and adapting to your world. This is not difficult to do with young children, for they are driven by a natural curiosity and desire to find out more about the world in which they live.

Knowledge of key concepts, however, gives you a framework for planning children's experiences and their environment. Children must have an environment rich with many things for them to experience, but the environment also needs to have a certain purpose and unity so children's encounters are not random and disjointed. The knowledge you, as a teacher, possess of scientific concepts provides this purpose and unity to the environment. With the framework of key concepts in mind, the arrangement of the environment, as well as the children's explorations within the environment, becomes clear.

Don't stop, however, by providing children with an environment rich in materials and free for their exploration. Continue in your role as a facilitator of children's developing scientific skills by encouraging them to observe, infer, classify, communicate, and draw conclusions. Then you and the children will experience the joy and excitement of being scientists.

## REFERENCES

Craig, S. *Science for the Elementary School Teacher.* Boston: Ginn & Co., 1947.

Forman, G. E., and Kuschner, D. *The Child's Construction of Knowledge.* New York: Wadsworth Publishing Co., 1977.

Holt, B. G. *Science with Young Children.* Washington, D.C.: National Association for the Education of Young Children, 1977.

Kamii, C., and DeVries, R. *Physical Knowledge in Preschool Education. Implications of Piaget's Theory.* Englewood Cliffs, N.J.: Prentice-Hall, Inc. 1978.

Neuman, D. "Sciencing for Young Children." *Young Children*, 27 (1972): 218.

Navarra, J. G., and Zafforoni, J. *Science for the Elementary School Teacher.* New York: Harper & Row, Publishers, 1960.

Science 5/13. *Early Experiences.* New York: Macdonald Educational, 1972.

Wann, K. *Fostering Intellectual Development in Young Children.* New York: Teachers College Press, 1962.

## RESOURCES

Science 5/13 series of books are excellent resources for teachers of young children. These include:
1. *Using the Environment: Early Explorations*
2. *Using the Environment: Investigations, Parts 1 and 2.*
3. *With Objectives in Mind*
4. *Change*
5. *Science from Toys*

These books are available from Macdonald Educational, 850 Seventh Avenue, New York, New York 10019.

## *PROJECTS*

1. Learn the principle of the wheel and axle. How can the concepts be presented to the young child? Use a wheel toy—a wagon or bike—and actively involve the child. What did he think made the bike move? Did his thinking change following your discussion? How?

2. Using the seven key concepts in science, record the daily experiences of the children pertaining to each concept.

3. Ask a nursery school teacher or a preschool teacher how she plans to teach science and how she introduces content to the children.

4. Observe children during play. What scientific concepts are they using? What terminology? How can a teacher introduce new concepts to the children?

5. Interview a two-, three-, and four-year-old child. Ask each one, "Are the clouds alive? How can you tell?" Ask about airplanes, trees, houses, and people. Record the children's responses and analyze them.

# MATHEMATICS FOR YOUNG CHILDREN

*It must be emphasized that it is futile to teach children to count by rote: in doing so they are not learning arithmetic. (Lovell, 1971, p. 35)*

# 11

*Children construct their own concept of number.*

Observing young children play, it soon becomes apparent that they experience number and mathematical concepts continually, and without the aid of a teacher. From the time the baby is only a few months old, he explores the world of objects and things, encountering big and little, near and far, discovering relationships, experiencing time, and using measurement.

There is no need to hurry the young child into symbolic representation of number. As Eileen Churchill points out, the fact that a child can, through imitation, use terms like "five" is no guarantee that he understands number concepts in the same terms as an adult. She says, "To teach a child to say words in a number series is not the same as teaching him to make a mathematical count, and teaching him tricks which enable him to find the right symbol to complete equations is not the same thing as teaching him addition or subtraction." (Churchill, 1961, p. 7)

Piaget (1965) has outlined and described the development of mathematical concepts in young children. He traces the beginning of such concepts to the time the baby discovers that objects have a permanence: that things do, in fact, exist, even when momentarily out of his sight. Until the child has reached this understanding, no mathematical attributes or relationships are perceived.

During the first two years of the child's life, which Piaget labels the "sensorimotor period," Lovell describes how the child puts an organization or structure on what he does, and on the sensations he receives through his sensory organs. Before the child can think, he has to be able to do things, such as grasping, moving, touching, and thought is evoked directly out of these skills be repeating them over again. In short, the thought of the young child is really internalized action (Lovell, 1971).

Between eighteen and twenty-one months of age, the child's awareness of relationships enables him to invent new behaviors and to see which actions will succeed and which will not without trying them out: the child begins to think. Symbolic play, imitation of other's actions, utterance of the first word— all occuring around the first birthday—enable the child, through images and words, to represent the word to himself without directly experiencing it.

The next stage of development, or the "preoperational stage," is characterized by the development of preconcepts in the child. What Piaget refers to as "conservation" is generally developed at this stage. Conservation refers to the idea that the mass of an object remains constant no matter how much the form changes. For example, if you give a five-year-old child two glasses, each half full of orange juice, the child will agree with you that the same amount of juice is in each glass. But if, before his eyes, the juice is poured from one of the glasses to a new one of a tall, narrow shape, the child will tell you that there is more juice in the new glass than in the remaining one. Or, to cite another example, he does not understand that a necklace stretched out in a straight line is no longer than an identical one laid in a circle, even when he has previously assured himself that both are of the same length. Finally, if two identical balls of clay are weighed by the child, he will admit that they are, indeed, identical in that they weigh the same. But when you flatten one ball of clay out, or roll it into a different shape, the child will believe that that clay is heavier, or more than it was before, even though no clay has been added. It is not until the average age of seven that the child begins to develop the conservation concepts that are basic to all other experiences with number and that underlie every principle of measurement.

## NO DIRECT TEACHING

Direct teaching cannot build concepts of conservation or of number in children. Children must develop these concepts for themselves, through their own experiences (Forman & Kuschner, 1977). Many teachers have tried to teach conservation and other number concepts to children prior to the age of seven, but most have only failed in these efforts. Although you cannot teach such concepts directly, you can provide the atmosphere and materials that will facilitate the development of concepts of conservation as well as number.

As a teacher, you will give children all of the materials and opportunities they will need to construct their own knowledge of number. Even the youngest children will require many things to see and to manipulate. As they grow they need opportunities to play with sand, mud, water, blocks, wood, and clay if they are to gain the ability to develop the conservation concepts underlying all of mathematics.

Children's number concepts are likely to be more accurate when they've had opportunities to play with a lot of materials. For instance, as children play with sticks, sorting them from shortest to longest, they are exploring the idea of seriation. As they sort doll clothes or blocks, make houses from wood or boxes, or make collages from twigs and leaves, they are experiencing for themselves concepts of seriation.

*Children can classify.*

Even though opportunities for children to manipulate and to explore objects are important in promoting mathematical skills, it is also necessary for children to have you as a teacher. If you understand the conceptual level of the young children and are sensitively attuned to their needs, you can introduce vocabulary as they play with materials. Or you can interject questions—"Why did you put these together? Which is longest?"—to lead children to greater understanding. You also provide additional experiences, with a variety of materials, as you continue to encourage discussion of the children's experiences.

## SOCIAL INTERACTION

Social interaction with other children is also essential for the child to clarify fully her mathematical concepts. The preschool, with its mix of older and younger children and the freedom for them to interact with one another in play, gives them the opportunity to try out their ideas about the world with their peers. With peers, a child can express differing ideas without fear of failure. This running head-on into difference of opinions during the social give-and-take of play is essential for the child's development of mathematical concepts.

# GENERAL MATHEMATICAL GOALS

In addition to providing materials, words, and language labels, and the social give-and-take of play, you may also want to identify key concepts and goals for mathematical understandings. This can help to guide the presentation and sequencing of materials and experiences. In considering general goals, the children's experiences might include the following:

1. Sorting and classifying collections of objects, leading to the comparison of groups of objects by matching, recognition of equal and unequal size of groups, and an understanding of sets and subsets.
2. Counting with cardinal numbers, promoting an understanding of one-to-one correspondence.
3. Measuring, first using arbitrary units, and observing such relationships as short/long, few/many, heavy/light, short/tall, and the like.
4. Explorations involving space and shapes in space.

These experiences can take place at many different levels in the preschool. Many of them will be continual, beginning with the young child in the crib, and extending through the age of five.

## SORTING AND CLASSIFYING

Children need many experiences in sorting objects, in recognizing particular attributes, in grouping the objects according to some attribute, and in perceiving relationships between objects. The greater the range of materials and objects available to the child, the more likely that he will grow in his ability to classify. Each day, all of the children in a preschool should be provided with as many of the following types of materials as possible to manipulate, sort, and group into categories.

1. A box of scrap material—velvet squares, tweeds, nets—cut into uniform sizes and shapes for children to feel, sort, and classify according to texture. A large enough collection of materials may lead the children to set up a yard-goods shop and play store.
2. A box or shelf of bells—cow bells, Christmas bells, decorative bells, sleigh bells—all inviting the children to sort and classify them according to sound, size, or shape.
3. A box of greeting cards—Easter, Christmas, Valentine's Day, Chanukah, birthday, or get-well cards. The children can use the pictures to decide

which category a card belongs in. They may begin to play card shop with a collection of these cards.

4. An old-fashioned button box, with buttons too large for ears and noses. Children sort buttons according to color, shape, size, design and other attributes.

5. A box of various textured papers, at first cut into uniform shapes and sizes, and later into many different shapes and sizes. Smooth papers, water-color papers, velvet papers, and many other types can be obtained from a local printing shop. At first children classify according to texture; later they also use shape, color, and size.

6. Individual boxes of shells, seeds, beans, macaroni, beads, or rocks.

7. Collections of nuts, nails, screws, and bolts to classify by shape, size, and function.

8. A box of marbles of many different sizes and colors.

9. A collection of rods or wooden dowels of various lengths and sizes.

10. A collection of pictures of animals, plants, cars, planes, boats, people, houses, and so forth, mounted on heavy cardboard for the children to sort and classify according to category—all zoo animals in one pile, all red cars together, and so on.

11. Commercial items, such as farm animals, plastic soldiers, birds, zoo animals, trains, toys, or trucks.

12. A collection of small, plastic doll dishes. These may be inappropriate for the housekeeping area because of their smallness and fragility, but they may be useful for the children's sorting and classifying experiences.

These materials, and many others like them, can be kept in the manipulative area where they will not be used in art projects or for housekeeping play. Boxes or sorting trays can be placed with the materials. These can be constructed either by attaching a series of metal jar lids onto a board or piece of heavy cardboard, mounting a number of clear plastic cups onto a board, dividing a board or tray into sections with colored tapes, or mounting small boxes onto a board or tray. The plastic sewing boxes or plastic boxes for storing nuts and bolts and fishing equipment also serve very well as boxes for sorting trays and stimulate the children to use materials in a mathematical way.

Children first should make their own groupings in any way they wish. They should be free to mix and match the materials, although you may want to put the materials back into their original groupings. Children under the age of five do not keep any one criterion in mind as they play with and manipulate the objects. They begin to put all pink buttons in one tray and, in the middle of sorting, decide to put all buttons with roses on them in the tray, or all big buttons, or all buttons with some other characteristic known only to them. At about five years of age, children group objects in terms of a set characteristic—all screws in one space, all nuts somewhere else, all red buttons in this cup, all round things in this box, or all the shells here.

In the next developmental stage of sorting, the children can group objects according to two or more properties—all of the small, yellow circles are put

*Children count.*

together, all of the large, blue trucks, all of the green, round buttons, all of the large, sticky seeds. Later, sets may be grouped around a negative concept—all of the toys without wheels, all of the animals that do not live in the zoo, all of the unpainted blocks. Still later, objects may be classified according to function—all of the things that are used to transport people, all of the things that are used to make something, and so on.

You should not guide the children as they sort their materials; whatever classification a child decides on should be accepted. As children reach the stage when aimless exploration has passed, you may ask why a collection of objects was sorted in a particular way. You may also ask a child to name the shape, color, or size of some of the objects, or you may ask a child to name the objects, promoting a consideration of categories.

In discussing the classifications with the child, emphasize the child's interests and experiences. Eventually, concepts of sets and subsets can be introduced, with any group of things labeled "a set," and any subgrouping called "a subset" (Payne & Rathmell, 1975).

COUNTING  Parrots do "count"—they can peck or squawk a specified number of times on command. But parrots, of course, do not have any concept of number. Young children can be taught as parrots to memorize number names and "count" on command; however, rote counting is meaningless to them, and bears no relationship to mathematical concepts. Meaningful counting implies that the child is aware of the fact that she is pairing the term "one" with the first object she is counting, the term "two" with the second object, and so on. When the child compares the number of members in two sets directly, one-to-one correspondence has taken place. As described by Lovell, the child has only to "count the number of members in the first set, remember the number name paired with the last object, count the number of members in the second set, and finally compare the final number names. Eventually he reaches the understanding that the words 'three,' 'seven,' etc., describe the property of a set containing a certain number of members. Developing at the same time is the notion that each member of the counting series is known to be one more than the one before it, and one less than the one that comes after it." (Lovell, 1971, p. 2)

In counting, number names are not numbers. Children have experiences with number names long before they have any concept of number. Your function is to facilitate the child's understanding of the meaning of number names and to develop her conceptualization of one-to-one correspondence.

Beginning with the baby in the crib, adults in a preschool center should take every opportunity to use number names. During infancy and toddlerhood the children should hear, over and over again, "One, Two, Buckle My Shoe," "One, Two, Three, Four, Five, I Caught a Fish Alive," and other nursery rhymes with numbers. The preschooler should be taught such songs as "Two Little Blackbirds," "This Old Man," "Five Little Chickadees," and such games as "In a Spider's Web." Stories, such as Gag's *Millions of Cats,* and the Holt, Rinehart & Winston Owl books of *Big Frogs, Little Frogs, Going Up, Going Down,* and *Captain Murphy's Tugboats* should be read repeatedly, giving children additional experiences in hearing number names and relating them to their lives.

Young children see and experience number names in the playroom, yard, and neighborhood. There may be number names on the mailbox, on and near the telephone, and even the rooms may be numbered. The child sees numbers on the recipes she uses in cooking or in mixing salt dough for play, and she observes the cook using numbers in measuring enough flour to make a cake large enough for everyone in the center to have a piece. The child watches with interest as you write the number name telling how old she is on her birthday, or the number name that describes her weight, height, or the number of fingers she has. She enjoys dictating her address to you as you write it on an envelope and mail it to her, and she is interested in finding the numbers on the mailbox or door of the center that tell the mailman where to deliver the center's mail. Hildebrand describes a birthday party for a four year old as a time for the teacher to count out four candles, the children to count four raisins to put on each cupcake, the birthday child to count four candles, and a time for making a sign with the number name "4" on it for the birthday child to wear on her day (Nixon & Nixon, 1971, p. 147).

Rote counting by the children each day often evolves into a rather meaningless chore; however, functional counting by the children is often necessary and can provide the children with a meaningful way to practice counting. The number of children who want to work with wood at a given time may be counted, or the number who have snow shoes and can go outside in the snow, or the number at a table who want another helping.

Depending upon the age and level of the children, they may count the number of round blocks, the number of books returned to the playroom, the number of boys who will go fishing with a volunteer, the number of children who have birthdays during the month, the number of cookies a group will need, the number of times a child can bounce a ball, or the number of children having blue eyes, red socks, or purple pants.

The child's individual manipulation of materials should receive major emphasis in developing his mathematical concepts. Games, however, may be designed to provide still additional counting activities and experiences in one-to-one correspondence. The following games should be used only by individual children, either on a self-selected basis or on your suggestion , and only as they serve to reinforce, clarify, and extend a child's own discoveries. None of the games is an appropriate group activity.

## Mystery Box

A set number of boxes is prepared by placing a different number of small objects in each and cutting a hole in one side. The child reaches in, feels the

*How many are there?*

objects in the box, and gives the number name to describe how many objects she feels. You should begin with one or two objects for young children and increase the number to seven, eight, nine, or even ten for the older children.

## Bowling

The child rolls a ball to knock down a group of objects—empty milk cartons, plastic squirt bottles, or empty juice cans. She then counts how many she has knocked down and how many objects are still standing. The child may play this game with a friend or two, with you, or by herself.

## Collections

The child makes a collection of objects to fit a number box. Boxes are labeled "1," "2," "3," etc. The child selects the specified number of objects from a scrap box or from outdoors and glues them in the box or box lid. It should be remembered that the objects in a set may not necessarily be exactly alike.

## Dominoes

Demonstrate to a child, or a small group of children, how to play dominoes, matching the domino with four spots with another of equal spots.

## Calendar Bingo

A calendar is mounted on a sheet of heavy cardboard. An identical calendar is cut up into individual number cards after mounting. The children match the individual numbers with the calendar that is uncut. This is a game for a single child.

## Button, Button

Working with one child or a very small group of children, you can give each child a handful of buttons of the same size, color, and shape. Then say, for example, "Move two buttons," and the children follow the direction by moving two buttons, as a set, away from the others. Children can then give directions to you or to other children. The number of buttons to be moved can be increased as the children are able to handle larger number concepts.

**MEASURING**  Authorities indicate that experiences in measuring should begin with arbitrary units with young children. The first relationships the young child develops often deal with size. You can help the children to identify the large or small blocks, the large or small pieces of paper, the large or small truck, or the large or small chair. You can reinforce the child, for example, to bring the large sponge to wipe off the table, or the small spoons to eat ice cream with (Payne & Rathmell, 1975).

*Meaningful activities with measuring are provided.*

As children play with mud, sand, and water, pouring from one container to another, they are filling and emptying three-dimensional space. These experiences eventually lead them to conceptualize volume and weight. A simple balance scale can be constructed for use in the sand pile to facilitate children's experiences with weight.

Providing children with a variety of buckets, plastic cups, bottles, and tins for use in the sand pile stimulates their measurement vocabulary. Often, young children use the terms "big" or "small" in their descriptions when other terms would be more accurate. Encourage the children to talk about the tall sand pile instead of the large one, or the shortest stick instead of the smallest, the enormous container, the longest bottle, the huge box, the highest pile, or the thick container.

Water play, as sand play, helps the children begin to realize that matter stays the same even if its shape is altered. Clear containers are suggested for sand and water play to allow the children to observe the level of matter within a container. You may initiate discussions as to how many times a small pail can be emptied into a large container; you may also introduce a set of measuring cups in the sand pile. Do not use such words as "pint," "quart," or "gallon"— water and sand play, at this stage, is only important as it establishes an experiential base on which to build future understandings of volume and capacity.

Concepts of linear measurement can be introduced as the children play. When a young child says, "Get me the big rope," respond with, "Here is the long rope." Measurement with linear units should also begin with arbitrary units. Children can, when the interest or need arises, measure the play yard, counting off the number of times their feet cover a given distance; or they can measure the height of a box by using their hands. A piece of string may be used to measure the desk, a table, a box or a chair, or a block may be used to measure the height of a block building. Introduction of such terminology as "inch," "foot," or "yard" at this point in time would only serve to confuse the children. The important thing is to introduce them to the concept of measuring and its usefulness (Early Experiences, 1972).

Other experiences with measurement occur when you and the children check the temperature outside before going out to play, the thermometer as they cook candy, or the thermostat to check the heat of their room. The children's own body temperatures can be taken and recorded, or the temperature of the water for water play may be taken. Children may actually observe the mercury rise and fall as a thermometer is placed in a pan of ice cubes or in a dish of warm water. From many experiences with measurement of temperature, young children should be able to determine the appropriate clothing to wear for any given weather condition. Some understanding of the measurement of temperature in cooking should also develop.

**EXPLORING SPACE AND SHAPE** Fostering geometric concepts in young children involves providing them with many opportunities to handle, use, and play with objects of various shapes. You should also provide the stimulation and the motivation for the children to become aware of the differences among the objects they play with. Children may be asked if the milk carton will roll like the ball, or how the rectangular block differs from the square one. Puzzles using geometric shapes such as circles, triangles, and squares are handy for children learning these shapes; they can compare the puzzle piece to the form in the puzzle board. A set of circles, triangles, or other shapes in graduated sizes can be used by the children in sorting, and many different-shaped blocks should be in each playroom for children to work with.

From repeated experiences with materials, children learn to identify the shapes of circle, square, and triangle. Teaching the child to label these shapes is not as important as presenting him with many opportunities to feel, touch, and play with them.

# IT'S UP TO YOU _____

The work of Piaget has contributed much to our understanding of how children develop mathematical knowledge. It is of critical importance that young children have plenty of opportunities to manipulate, explore, and test their environment. All young children need a great deal of perceptual, sensory experiences in order to form the foundation for later mathematical under-standings.

It is obvious, from the work of Piaget and others, that you cannot impose your knowledge of number onto children. It simply doesn't work. Each child must construct mathematical knowledge for herself.

This doesn't mean, however, that your role as a teacher is passive. On the contrary, your role is an active one. For it's you who must select materials for children's exploration, and then sequence these materials to foster their under-standing of number and mathematics. It's you who must plan specific experi-ences for both individuals and for the total group.

Then, too, you take full advantage of children's experiences and explo-rations with materials (Gibb & Castaneda, 1975). You do this by adding verbal labels to the children's experiencing, or by asking a thoughtful question, the "why" question, or by even redirecting children to another action they might take with the materials.

Kamii & DeVries (1978) describe this kind of teaching as being different from that of a traditional teacher. They believe this teaching means "drastic changes in the teacher's conception of the educative process. When the focus of teaching shifts from what the teacher does to how the child constructs his own knowledge, the center of the classroom will no longer be the subject matter or the method of teaching" (Kamii & DeVries, 1978, p. 310).

# REFERENCES

Churchill, E. *Counting and Measuring.* Toronto: University of Toronto Press, 1961.

*Early Experiences.* London and New York: Macdonald Educational, 1972.

Forman, G. E., and Kuschner, D. S. *The Child's Construction of Knowledge: Piaget for Teaching Children.* Belmont, Calif.: Wadsworth Publishing Co., 1977.

Gibb, G. E., and Castaneda, A. M. "Experiences for Young Children." In *Mathematical Learning in Early Childhood Education. Thirty-seventh Year-book of the National Council of Teachers of Mathematics,* edited by J. N. Payne. Reston, Va.: National Council of Teachers of Mathematics, 1975.

Kamii, C., and DeVries, F. *Physical Knowledge in Preschool Education.* En-glewood Cliffs, N. J.: Prentice-Hall, 1978.

Lovell, K. *The Growth of Understanding in Mathematics: Kindergarten through Third Grade.* New York: Holt, Rinehart & Winston, 1971.

Nixon, R. H., and Nixon, C. *Introduction to Early Childhood Education.* New York: Random House, 1971.

Payne, J. N., and Rathmell, E. C. "Number and Numeration," In *Mathematics Learning in Early Childhood,* edited by J. N. Payne. Reston, Va.: National Council of Teachers of Mathematics, 1975.

Piaget, J. *The Child's Conception of Number.* New York: W. W. Norton & Co., 1965.

## RESOURCES

Brearley, M. *The Teaching of Young Children.* New York: Schocken Books, 1970.

Kamii, C., and DeVries, R. *Piaget, Children and Number.* Washington, D.C.: National Association for the Education of Young Children, 1976.

The entire *Nuffield Mathematics Project,* and Science 5/13 series of books available from Macdonald Educational, 850 Seventh Avenue, New York, New York 10019 are excellent resources for teachers of young children. The Science 5/13 series includes 1) *Beginnings,* 2) *Early Explorations,* 3) *Science from Toys* and 4) *With Objectives in Mind.*

## PROJECTS

1. Read a book on Piaget, perhaps Hans Furth's *Piaget and Knowledge* or one by Piaget himself, such as *Origin of Number.* You must build your own understanding of this important theory.

2. Once you are familiar with the theory, try out some of the tasks with children. Remember, Piaget used these tasks simply to try to understand children's thinking, not as teaching tools. Some suggested tasks might be to:

   a. Ask a child to pour an equal amount of water into two containers that are exactly alike. Now ask the child to empty one of the containers into a container of a different shape. Now ask him to tell which of the two containers has more water.

   b. Give a child two pieces of clay that are just the same. Have the child verify that the clay balls are exactly the same, perhaps by weighing them. Now flatten out one of the balls and ask the child to tell which is more.

   c. Place five blocks in a row, and have the child place, in one-to-one correspondence, another five blocks in another row parallel to the first one. Have the child count the blocks in both rows. Ask him if both rows have the same number of blocks. Now move the blocks in the first row, spreading them farther apart, and ask the same questions.

   Each of these tasks will let you see for yourself that children need many experiences and much exploration with materials before hurrying on to formal mathematical learnings.

3. Observe children playing with sand or water. What terminology do they use? How could you introduce mathematical language without interfering with the children's play?

4. Observe children classifying a group of objects. How could you lead the children to an understanding of sets and numbers?

4. With a child, measure objects in the room. Use the child's hands or feet as arbitrary measures. What terminology does the child use? What concepts do you think are being fostered?

5. Compile a list of finger plays, nursery rhymes, or songs that introduce children to number names.

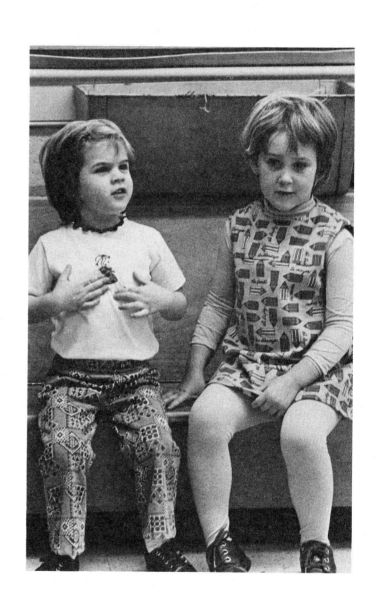

# THE YOUNG CHILD AND THE SOCIAL WORLD

*Actually, social studies include everything that enables children to better understand their world and their place in it.* (Seefeldt, 1977, p. 6)

# 12

*Children are social beings.*

Children are social beings, and as all humans, are born into a social world. As infants, children take their place in the social unit of the family. Later, as toddlers, children's social world expands to include other relatives and even close neighbors. By the time the child is just a few years old, she's fully immersed in the social systems of the neighborhood, school, and broader community.

Children's social world is broad. It includes not only family, neighbors, and classmates, but all of the social systems of our society as well. Think for a moment about how much of the young child's life involves the social systems of our society. For instance, children are participants in the economic system. Some save dollars for a treasured bike or other coveted item. Most are consumers, deciding which toy to purchase, what shoes they'll buy.

Today's children are geographers. Large numbers of children have traveled far from home, and if not, all have experienced the sand, mud, water, and dirt that cover the surface of the earth.

Children are historians. They experience time passing and eagerly ask about the "olden days" when you were young. Children take pleasure in their own history, wondering over baby pictures and items of baby clothing: "Was I really that small?"

And most of all, today's children are living and experiencing the values and attitudes inherent in a democratic society. Early in life, children begin to develop knowledge of the "rights" and "wrongs" of our society.

Because young children are socially active and do experience all of the social systems in our society, you have a responsibility to help them develop socially in at least three major areas:

1. Social skill development. Through all of the interactions with other children and adults at the preschool, children gain in social skills.

2. Development of knowledge of the social world. Through experiences, including field trips, children increase their understanding of the social world and the systems operating within that world.

3. Growth of attitudes and values that are consistent with those of a democratic society.

## SOCIAL SKILLS

Living in a group is not easy for anyone, but it's especially difficult for young children. Children have difficulty communicating with others. For one thing, their language facility is just developing; but for another, young children

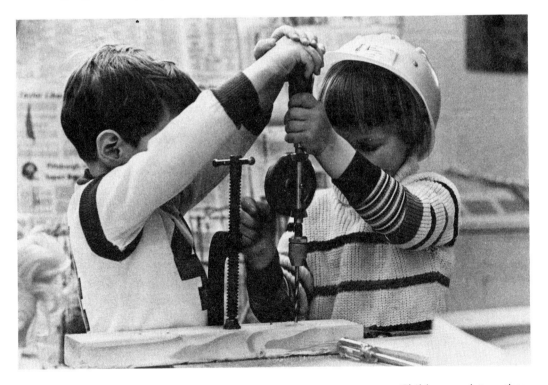

*Children work together.*

cannot put themselves in the place of another person. Social skills depend, in large part, on the child's ability to see how another person feels or thinks, and to take into account how the other person sees things.

Flavell (1970) has studied children's ability to put themselves in the place of another. He believes that before children can do this they must:

1. Understand that not everyone thinks, feels, or sees things alike.
2. Realize that they might have to analyze another's perspective.
3. Have the cognitive abilities to do this analysis.
4. Hold in their minds the results of this analysis.
5. Be able to translate this analysis into effective social behavior.

Certainly, these abilities are not easy, even for adults. But for young children they are most difficult. The preschool situation, however, offers abundant opportunities for children to develop and then practice these skills. Through play with others, especially dramatic play, where children do take on the role of another person, and through the normal give-and-take of the school day, children gradually begin to understand that others may think differently than they.

 The goals of the preschool are to enable each child to develop:

1. Confidence in himself.
2. Respect for self and others.
3. Skills of give-and-take that go with group living.
4. Acceptance and enjoyment of being with others.

These goals can be fostered by providing plenty of play activities for children, and by giving them opportunities to work together to solve problems. Dramatic play in the housekeeping area or other dramatic play area offers children unique opportunities to take on the role of others. They not only play as if they were a mother or father, doctor or teacher, but they must also hold in their minds the roles others take on—child, pupil, or patient.

Other activities also foster children's social skills. The building of a rabbit hutch, which requires children taking on different responsibilities to complete the project, or fixing a broken bike or wagon provides additional opportunities in working together.

Greif believes that more social development is fostered when children are free to choose their own playmates and when they can experience a sense of control over their world (Greif, 1977, p. 158). To provide for this, structure large blocks of time for children's play and permit children the opportunity to select their own playmates, as well as play materials and activities.

However, you will play an active role in helping children develop social skills. Both sharing and cooperative behaviors can be increased through specific teacher action. When you reinforce children's sharing and cooperative behavior by saying "How good of you to share" or "You worked well together," children know this behavior is valued and will repeat it.

You might find that simple yet direct instruction is effective in teaching social skills. Sometimes you might say, "Tell John you want the shovel," or "Susan is angry because . . . ," translating children's behavior for others. On the other hand, you might simply state the rules or the expected norms for the group: "There are ways to use the tricycle together. You can take turns—or you can ride on the seat and you can stand here" (Updegraff et al., 1948).

You will act as a model for children's social behavior. Children will want to be just like you when you are warm, spontaneous, and responsive. Another way you can model sharing behavior is by participating with children in their activities. There are a number of experiences you might share with children. You might take part in outdoor activities, rest with the children and participate in stories and games with them.

# ──────────────── KNOWLEDGE OF THE SOCIAL WORLD

Acquiring knowledge and concepts from the content of the social studies is an important goal of preschool education. As children increase their understanding of the world, their understanding of self and others increases. For example, children who know their way around their immediate neighborhood grow in feelings of self-confidence and are more likely to be able to relate effectively with others. Confident children, those who understand their social world, are able to develop interpersonal relationships with others.

Content from every area of the social studies, including geography, history, economics, and current events, can be introduced to young children in meaningful ways to provide them with a solid foundation on which to build an ever-increasing knowledge of the social world.

GEOGRAPHY   Through firsthand experiences of the immediate environment, and through the child's play, basic geographical concepts are introduced. Teaching geography to the young children is a matter of letting them become intimately acquainted with their environment and providing for ever-widening experiences with the world. Through their experiences with geography, children learn principles of measurement, the language of direction, the names of places and things, and the use of such symbols as maps.

In introducing young children to geography, you should consider their level of maturity, past experiences, play interests, and the misconceptions they possess. You can then select organizing key concepts as a framework on which to build understandings that will help the children learn about their immediate environment and serve as a foundation for their future learning. Key concepts in geography for young children might include experiences with maps and map making; concepts of living on the earth—the earth's size, shape, and motion; orientation and direction; location, scale, and distance; regional distinction; spacial interaction; and perpetual transformation.

## Maps

Many young children have seen their parents use a road map, or the weather-man on television trace his hand over a map of the United States. Within the preschool, experiences with maps and map making should be provided to acquaint the children with the purpose and function of maps.

Maps added to the housekeeping area or near the blocks or riding toys, both indoors and outside, can be used by the children as they ride around on their bikes, plan "trips," or play airplane. Manipulative map toys, such as "Block City" or "Play Village," with blocks and cloth maps of a pretend town, are enjoyed by children and provide an initial experience with the concept of mapping. Wall maps, poster maps, and large, simple maps of the children's community, city, state, and country can be on hand. When the occasion arises, you can show the children where they live or where the center is located. These maps can also be used to trace the route to be followed on a riding field trip to the place where each child was born, where their grandmothers live, or where you used to live.

Block play fosters mapping concepts as the children build representations of the things around them and the things they have seen on field trips or in their neighborhoods. Housing projects, airports, farms, and building sites can be depicted with block streets, highways, parks, and buildings. The concept of the map as a symbol is basic to understanding maps, and play with blocks is one very real way children can gain an understanding of representation. Maps in the block area seem to promote a greater concern for representational block building and can be added to the playrooms of four and five year olds.

Preschool children may be able to understand the concept of mapping out their playroom or yard with blocks. You may structure some problem to be solved; for example, "Where do you think we should put the new climbing bars?" or "How could we change the room around?" With the use of blocks and a map, attempt to reach a decision with the children. The symbolic nature of the block or map should be stressed during these experiences. You might say, "Let's put this block here to stand for the tree," or "These blocks will represent the fence," or "José, you put the blocks where the storage shed is. The blocks will stand for the shed."

One teacher drew a large rectangle on a piece of brown paper and cut colored construction papers to represent furniture in the playroom. She sat down at the table and began to arrange the pieces of paper. The children, curious and always wanting to imitate their teacher, asked her what she was doing. She explained to them that she was trying to think of a new way to arrange the playroom, and was using the papers to represent the furniture so she could tell where the things might fit. The children joined her in mapping out the room, and several of them constructed their own maps. After the class had decided on the room arrangement it wanted, the room was, in fact, rearranged. Following this experience, several of the children took paper home with them and constructed maps of their kitchens and bedrooms. Even pillows and teddy bears were represented by the papers.

The utility of maps is experienced as the children prepare to go on field trips. A map that you make of the neighborhood can serve as a frequent source of reference as the children take walking field trips. Relating the streets to those drawn on the map helps them to understand the concept of representation, as well as scale and distance.

## Living on the Earth

Even very young children in the preschool can begin to understand that the earth is where we live. They can begin to classify the things that are on the earth—trees, flowers, dirt, people, animals, buildings—and the things that are not—clouds, moon, sun, stars. Ask the children to name the things located on the earth and to collect pictures of them, or merely point things out to the children as they play outside.

Young children can observe the streets and sidewalks covering portions of the earth around them. They can be asked to name other things that cover the earth. Can the children identify the grass, the rocks, mountains, rivers, lakes, or valleys around them? Often, a stream, lake, river, or hill can be found near the center for the children to observe.

The children's awareness of the pattern of night and day and the seasons is the starting point from which they learn that the movement of the earth effects these changes. Young children are not ready for explanations of how the earth revolves around the sun, or even for role playing this phenomenon; however, they can observe the results of the earth's movement and relate them to their lives.

## Orientation and Direction

Each day the children go up and down the stairs, up and down the slide, or jump up and down. Such routine activities can help them become cognizant of the meaning of the words "up" and "down" in terms of location. You can sing to the children on the seesaw, "Now we go up. Now we go down. Up and down, and up and down," or to the children learning to walk stairs, "Up, up, up, climbing up the stairs." You can use "up" and "down" in connection with the child's experiences, pointing out the things that are up in the tree or up on the shelf, down on the ground or down on the floor.

Young children can also begin to comprehend such directional terms as "right" and "left." Playing the games of "Simon says" and "looby loo," playing policeman by controlling the bike traffic on the playground, or even shaking hands fosters a beginning understanding of "left" and "right."

Other directional and orientational terms of which the children should be aware are "under," "above," "below," "on top of," "on," "bottom," "between," "front," and "back." Their meaning can be demonstrated through the children's experiences. For example, say, "Joan, stand in back of Sue while she's sawing," or "Put this on top of the table," or "If you put the bike between you and the tree, your plan might work." A more structured activity can be conducted by asking the child to put a rag doll under, on, beside, between, in front, or in back of some other object.

Experience with direction and orientation also includes learning the names of the compass points—north, south, east, and west—and becoming familiar with street addresses. Children can learn their home street address and the address of the center. The children may dictate their address to you as you write it on the envelope to send home. They may take a field trip to observe all of the signs used to indicate addresses on the block, or to find the address of the preschool.

## Location, Scale, and Distance

"Which is nearer, the water tower or the apartment building?" "What is nearer, the boat or the tree?" "How far is it to the fence?" "On which trip did we walk the farthest?" "Who lives the nearest to the center?" "Who lives the farthest?" "How can we tell?"

Concepts of location involve measurement. A field trip by bus or car can be taken for the children to observe the speedometer record the speed of the vehicle or the odometer measure the distance covered. Perhaps a pedometer might be obtained and used by the children to measure the distance they walk in one day at the center, or to measure the distance they walked on a field trip.

## Regional Distinction

The concept that regions are parts of the earth with similar physical and cultural characteristics can be introduced to the very young child through direct experiences. On field trips, the children can be asked to compare the buildings, streets, trees, and plants in the city, in a heavily industrial area, near the preschool, and in the country. A trip to the farm, the country, or a seashore provides an opportunity to ask the children to compare the different geographic areas.

Some vicarious experiences might be necessary, and indeed useful, in teaching young children about regional differences. If mountains are not located anywhere near the center, use slides, books, or pictures to introduce the children to mountains—or to seashores, valleys, forests, or hills. Books, such as *The Story of Ping, Nine Days to Christmas,* or *Playtime in Africa,* can help children to understand other people and cultures and their differences pertaining to their geographic locations. These books also make children aware that, although people live differently in different parts of the world, they all have the same feelings, needs, and desires.

## Spatial Interaction

The concept of people interacting over space can be introduced to the children through their direct experiences involving such examples as trade, transportation, and communication. Visits to a shopping center to observe produce being delivered fosters a discussion of where food comes from and how it gets to the store. After returning to the preschool, the children may discuss the food they eat for lunch: "Where did it grow?" "How did it get to us?" "Who helped to get it to us?" "Did it come by truck, airplane, or boat?"

Transportation is of interest to young children; they love to watch the street traffic or airplanes trail across the sky. The center's large collection of wheel toys, floating boats and ships, riding wheel toys, and wooden machines and tractors provides them with opportunities to play with the things related to transportation. Children may enjoy observing the traffic, noting the different types of cars and trucks that pass the preschool.

The different ways in which children and staff travel to the center can be listed on a chart. The different modes of transportation within the center can also be noted, and the older children can collect pictures of people walking, running, riding bikes, roller skating, or traveling in wagons or doll carriages to paste under the captions.

Air transportation is fascinating to the children, and many of them will have had the experience of riding on a plane. A trip to the airport can give all the children some familiarity with the size of airplanes and the procedures involved in flying. And a trip to the moon can be taken vicariously by reading accounts of the astronauts or viewing films.

Various means of communication are directly experienced by the children in a center. One teacher took the children on a trip through the center to seek out all the communication devices utilized by the center staff. The children noted a telephone and intercom, a typewriter, a duplicating machine, and a mail box.

## Perpetual Transformation

Children can gain initial understandings of the concept of perpetual transformation as they observe the ways in which man changes the environment as well as the ways in which nature causes man to change. They can watch men tearing down buildings, scraping up roads, and building highways or shopping centers. A book such as Virginia Buston's *The Little House* describes the process of change in a way that children can comprehend. A rainy or cold day may cancel the scheduled peanut butter and jelly picnic, so that the children actually experience how natural phenomena force men to change their behavior.

Children may participate in changing their environment by smoothing the ground for a garden or digging a hole in the earth to fill with water. They may help to cut the grass around the center, plant some seeds, or remove the branches from an old tree. In almost any city, they can observe the constant digging up of streets, paving over them, and digging them up again next spring. Such activities give children additional experiences with the reality of perpetual change.

## Field Trips

The study of geography cannot take place entirely within the confines of the preschool. The children must be able to go on trips away from the center to experience their larger world. Learning psychologists caution, however, that field trips do not always develop into learning experiences for young children. Trips can be too global, too full of distracting stimuli, and often too exciting or frightening for young children to gain anything from them. Clearly, when children are herded onto huge buses, transported for hours, and taken to see a place of little real interest to them or relevant to their way of life, field trips are practically useless—a waste of time, money, and energy.

On the other hand, well-planned, carefully selected field trips do give the child in a preschool real experiences with the wider world and geographical concepts. They can provide opportunities for him to:

1. Relate to others in the community.
2. Learn new words associated with the new places and things he sees.
3. Plan cooperatively for the trip.
4. Clarify his ideas or concepts.
5. See something new or something familiar with his friends.
6. Experience change from the routines of the center.
7. Learn something new through the stimulation and motivation provided.

Trips can also be useful in strengthening the emotional ties between the center and the child's family and home. Taking a trip with friends to visit his mother at work makes a young child feel important, respected, and loved by both center and family. A trip to the gas station on the corner, the same one daddy goes to, supports the mutuality of the center's activities and those of the home.

When a mother asked one teacher why in the world she was going to take the class to a grocery store when the children went there every day anyway, the teacher explained that they would not be going with the purpose of buying groceries for a week; instead, they would be learning to identify the different types of fruit—fresh, frozen, and canned—that are found in the store. Furthermore, experiencing the trip as a group would give the children a more common basis for their play, fostering dramatic and cooperative group activities. Information gathered on the trip could be shared when the children returned to the center, helping to create a feeling of unity and oneness.

**Planning a Trip** Even infants go on trips when their attendant or care giver carries them to the kitchen, play yard, or other playrooms. Toddlers are probably most comfortable on trips confined to the center itself, or on those within a block of the center that are neither elaborate nor complicated. By the time the child is three, four, or five years of age, weekly, increasingly complex, and extensive trips can be planned and taken. These trips can be of immediate value to the preschool child.

In planning trips, you should determine the past experiences of the children and their existing concepts and interests. If all of the children have been to the fire station and exhibit little or no interest in firemen or engines, a trip somewhere else might be of more value. However, if the children are still excited by fire engines and playing fireman, and are seeking additional information about fire engines even though they have taken four trips to the fire station within the past two years, another trip might be of great value.

Two preschool children were taken on a tour of Cape Kennedy and, to the great disappointment of their parents, were not at all interested in the Cape. The only thing of interest to these two children, who had never experienced a bus ride, was the large bus that transported the tourists around the Cape. At their stage of development, and with their past experiences and interests, these children probably could have benefited more from a simple bus trip than from an elaborate trip to Cape Kennedy.

Sometimes the planned purpose of a trip is changed by the children's interests. A group of middle-class children went on a trip to a dairy with the express purpose of finding out where milk came from. However, the children were only interested in the amazing phenomenon of a cow "going to the bathroom." Although it did not involve the children in discussions of milk, that trip did stimulate much discussion and wonder as to the process of elimination.

Another group was taken to the airport to have the opportunity to sit on a plane and to be served a soft drink by the stewardess. But the children became entranced with a floor scrubbing machine in the lobby of the airport that spewed out soapy water, scrubbed it around on the floor, and then, ever so magically, sucked it all up. The children did get to sit on the airplane and have their soft drink, but on the return to the center the only topic of discussion was the scrubbing machine. The children talked, played, and wondered over floor cleaning. They even constructed their own machine out of a box and a broom handle, and the white sailor hat from the housekeeping corner was converted to a cleaning person's hat. So pervasive was the children's interest in this machine, that the group returned to the airport with the sole purpose of observing it once again and interviewing the person who managed it.

With young children, field trips taken by an individual child, or by a small number of children, may be more feasible and more valuable than trips involving the entire group. When field trips are common events in the center, children understand that they might not go on every one. Volunteers can be trained to transport a small number of children on a trip. With just a few children involved, opportunities for vocabulary development, concept formation, and learning are increased. In addition, the questions and the comments of each child can be considered more completely.

**Before the Trip** It is during the planning time that the children can be prepared for the trip. The reasons for going on the trip should be discussed, and some familiarity with the content developed. Children might indicate the questions they want answered as a result of the trip, or the things they especially want to see. Safety rules, established by the children themselves, can be listed and reviewed. Pictures of the place they will visit, or books and films about the experience they will be having, can also be shared by the children before the trip. Children might also dictate a letter to the person in charge of the place to be visited, asking for permission to come.

Prior to any trip, you or another staff member must visit the site selected. In this way, safety hazards can be identified and eliminated, unusual details planned for, and arrangements made with the people in charge. A Head Start group faced a disappointing experience when they arrived at a department store to ride on the escalator, only to be met by the floor manager, who would not allow the children to ride because of the liability risks involved.

Preschools planning many trips can develop a card file of places of interest in the community, eliminating the need to identify safety hazards, plan for unusual details, and contact personnel every time a trip is taken. A volunteer, as his contribution to the center, visited every probable field-trip site in the area. On a form he recorded the contact person, the phone number and address of the place, a map of the easiest route to take (with alternate maps indicating special interest sites such as a bridge, a river, train tracks, or a factory), parking areas, safety hazards, free or inexpensive materials given to children, and other special things of interest they might see at the place. The cost involved, if any, any special clothing required, and things to look for and ask about were also recorded. This file was periodically updated and saved each teacher much time in planning for field trips.

**Permission Slips** Permission slips should also be obtained prior to trips. These permission slips do not remove the responsibility of the center in case of accident, but do serve to keep the parent involved and informed as to the preschool program and whereabouts of his child. A blanket permission slip, covering walking field trips in the immediate area, might be signed by the parent on a yearly or monthly basis. Special trips, those involving a bus, or any trips farther than the immediate neighborhood should require individual parent permission slips.

**Immediate Trips** We tend to forget that the entire world is new and exciting to young children and overlook many things in the immediate neighborhood that could stimulate and motivate them. Even within the preschool trips can be taken to the director's office, the nurses' office, the mailbox, the kitchen, the yard, or to another classroom to see the babies. There can be a trip to trace the water pipes from the bathroom to the basement, to identify all of the machines used in the center, or to record every sound the children hear in the center. Other trips can be taken outside of the school to fly a kite, watch the moths fly, see the trees in the wind, wait for the mailman, watch the garbage men, count the number of windows in the school, observe repairmen, watch the clouds, see the sunshine, or observe the shadows.

Walking trips are popular with children; and children have the stamina to walk a great deal farther than imagined. Plan a walking trip for the shady side of the street, or at a time when the sun is not too hot. You can also schedule stops under a tree for a drink of water, or rest stops in the park, helping to make the walking field trip pleasant and easy for the children. These short walking field trips allow the child to focus on one or two concepts without the distraction or excessive stimulation of a long bus trip. Some children who are frightened about leaving the preschool are often reassured if they can see it in the distance or follow a homemade map of the area, always keeping the school in mind.

Some of the things children might do on a short walking field trip include seeing a neighbor's flower garden, visiting a grandfather in the neighborhood, reading the signs on the streets, counting the number of trees, watching a police officer at work, watching workers build or tear things down, counting the number of red lights, or counting the number of houses on a hill. Children can also observe the different types of clothing people are wearing, imagine the whereabouts of the people whose cars are parked along the road, or see how many different types of flags they can find.

As valuable as the walking field trip is to the children, occasions arise when they must be transported by bus, car, or some other means. The first riding field trip of lasting value to the child is to observe his mother and father at work. Such a trip can include a few of the child's selected friends, or just the child and a staff member may go alone.

Nearby stores, shopping centers, and market places offer endless possibilities for trips. The three year old enjoys the "behind the counter" trip, where he can actually go behind the counters to observe the merchandise. The grocery store, supermarket, and butcher store never lose their appeal to the young child who can observe produce being delivered or unpacked or meat being cut and placed in refrigeration units. A field trip to the nearest gas station acquaints the child with the smells of oil, tires, and gasoline. And the employees at the station do so many interesting things to cars with machines, pumps, lifts, and tools. Other places that may be of interest are shoe repair shops, radio and television repair shops, bakeries, laundromats, beauty parlors, hamburger stands, boat dealers, printers, sign shops, paint stores, and photographic studios.

An integral part of social studies, knowledge of community services, can receive attention during field trips. The post office, police station, firehouse, library, or water plant will often make special arrangements for young children to observe their work.

One field trip that is essential for each child attending the center is a visit to your home. There he can see that his teacher sleeps in a bed—but, amazingly, not at the center. "Look, she has a TV, and here's where she hangs her clothes!"

Occasionally, a large-scale trip can be scheduled. However, such a trip requires more planning and careful consideration as to purpose. Is the circus really appropriate for the young children? What will they learn? Will they be more frightened than curious? Would a trip to a nearby planetarium be better for the school-age children? What additional provisions for safety will be necessary? How can excitement and confusion be kept at a minimum? Such trips are often more valuable and successful if parents attend with the children, so the center should make an effort to schedule them for weekends when families can participate.

**During the Trip** An adequate number of adults is necessary for any trip with young children. Possibly one adult to every three or four children might be called for. The adults, especially the volunteers, must be certain of their responsibilities, the purposes of the trip, and the safety rules to be followed.

Montessori, when taking her children on a walking field trip, used a long rope which was knotted at intervals. Each child held onto a knot, making a train of children. This is an effective means for keeping children safely together when walking across a busy intersection or on the side of a busy highway. You carry the rope and, before crossing the street, the children line up with each one holding onto a knot. Once across, the children are free to walk informally in small groups or to skip along with an adult.

Singing or chanting marching songs or poems helps a group to stay together without one of the adults constantly having to enforce numerous rules. Along the way, the adults can spontaneously direct the children's attention by asking questions, commenting on various points of interest, and even directly reminding the children of the things they came to see.

**After the Trip** Returning to the center after the trip is usually the time to provide the children with rest, relaxation, and refreshments. Tired from walk-ing and visiting, the children need time to assimilate their experiences before recounting them, drawing about them, or building with blocks to represent the things they saw. This part of the trip is often described as a letdown. The excitement is over, weariness has set in, and the children seem uninterested in the entire project.

By the next day, or after rest or juice, the children are usually ready to "read" books about the trip or to express their feelings and ideas about it through play or art materials. The children may be able to dictate a thank-you note to the neighbor who let them see her flowers or construct an airport with the blocks. Props can be provided for the children to act out the things that impressed them on the trip, and slides, movies, or snapshots taken during the trip can be developed and shared with the children, giving them something to talk about for months to come.

**A Reverse Field Trip** Reversing the typical field trip, many preschool centers bring social studies experiences into the center by inviting visitors. The fireman can come to the center in the truck with his hose and some of his equipment, or the policeman can come in his impressive uniform with his gun and other equipment. The parents, with their own special skills and talents, stories to tell, and things to share, are always deeply appreciated visitors.

Just as a field trip must be planned with the children, so must the visitor's plans be discussed with them. The visitor himself also needs information before he visits the center. If he is going to talk with the two- or three-year-old children, it is often helpful to inform him as to the listening skills and attention span of the children. It might be mentioned that he is not expected to "talk to" the children, but rather talk "with them." He should also be encouraged to bring items to show or demonstrate. Rather than requiring the children to sit through a formal presentation, they might benefit more from being able to play with the longshoreman's rope, to hold the fireman's hat, or to feel his heavy hose.

Children should be actively involved in preparing for the visit. They may decide who will greet the visitor, where he will sit, who will take his hat and coat, and where they will serve him juice and cookies. They may dictate a list of questions that they want answered.

Following the visit, the children can dictate a thank-you note to the visitor, and can either sign their names, if able, or draw a picture to attach to the note. You can use the information shared by the visitor to foster children's play, art, and music activities. You can also provide the children with additional infor-mation through books or other resource materials.

**HISTORY** How can a young child of three or four, who does not know today from tomorrow or yesterday, be taught history or study the past? History, in the preschool, is "the story of what we did today. Yesterday is already far away, but what was done yesterday seems to have a power over today that is new and peculiar to this age" (McMillan, 1919, p. 297).

In the preschool, the study of history does, indeed, begin with the present. Some time might be set aside, either for small groups or the total group of children, to discuss the day's happenings. "What did you do today?" "What did you like about today?" "What made you laugh, cry, or sing today?" Questions such as these help the children develop a memory of the events of their immediate past. Later, the discussions can include remembering the fun last week when a real cowboy twirled his rope, or the fun at the Valentine's Day party. The end of the week might find fours and fives discussing the events of the past week and planning for the upcoming week. These older children may even remember a Valentine's Day party as they plan a spring party, naming the things they want to repeat and those they will eliminate.

You can keep a history of the year for each child in your class, including art projects, notes of the things the child said, records of her physical growth and development, recordings of accomplishments, and other anecdotal records. Photos taken of the children at the beginning and close of the year can be included. These highly personal "history" books are favorites of the children and are talked over by parent and child, as well as you.

Four and five year olds may even compile their own books. They can dictate to you the things they enjoyed doing best at the center, the things they think they have learned, how they have changed, or the field trips they have taken. One group of children dictated an entire book about the field trips taken over the year, recalling every place visited and everything that happened. They illustrated the book themselves, and it was placed on the library table for the enjoyment of all.

## The Family

A child feels proud and important when she and her family are the subject of the history lesson. Children may be able to bring photos of themselves as infants to the center to show the other children. You can discuss how they have changed and grown and ask them if they remember when they could not even walk or talk. For a child without access to baby pictures, the staff can begin to build a history of her growth in the center by taking frequent pictures and keeping records.

Some children have fathers, mothers, grandparents, or great-aunts or uncles who can recall some of the family history. Of course, not every family can provide the child with a family tree with several generations listed; however, every parent can state his own birthplace and that of the child, and mothers and fathers can describe what they did as children. They can tell the child a favorite game or the things they liked to eat best when they were little, or they can describe the tricks they played on their parents.

You must talk to the children about their families, "[not] merely to collect the data of people's lives, but to give them what is best in their own family histories." (McMillan, 1919, p. 297) You might send a note to the parents informing them of how you are attempting to deal with history to assist them in talking to their child about events of the past.

Groups of fives may be interested in hearing about the history of their preschool, finding out who lived in or used the building they now occupy. School-age children may become interested in the history of their school—the person for whom it was named, what stood on the site before the school was built, or how the area has changed.

Accurate concepts of time and of the past are not developed in young children. They can, however, understand that some things happened a long time ago. They were babies a long time ago, and their father was a baby "a really long, long time ago." In this context, they can deal with the idea that America was discovered a long time ago, the Civil War was fought a long time ago, and dinosaurs lived on the earth a long time ago. It is not important that the children comprehend exact time lines. "A long time ago" is enough for them to deal with at this stage in their lives.

## Holidays

Each day is a special day in a preschool; however, some days are particularly special because of their historical significance. Through holiday celebrations, children can have direct experiences with religious and historic customs of their families and their community, and they can build a foundation for later understanding of the culture and customs of others.

The diversity of backgrounds of the children and staff within a school are valuable in selecting the holidays to be observed. The children's parents, grandparents, or neighborhood volunteers may all serve as resource persons to the center in planning to present celebrations authentically. The activities involved should be consistent with the children's developmental level, concepts, and interests. Generally, the most successful holiday celebrations are those that only vary the activities within the preschool's set routines and schedule. Eliminating rest time or changing the lunch hour can make the day a disaster. The usual schedule should be followed with added attractions. Green and red sparkle dust may be added to the art tables during the Christmas celebration, or pastel easel or finger paint may be provided during the activity time to celebrate a spring festival. Some special art project, perhaps threading ribbon through a berry basket at Easter or making a collage Valentine's Day card, might be added. Children can sing their favorite holiday songs during music time and hear their favorite holiday poems and stories during story time. They can also participate in preparing the holiday snack or in adding some special decoration to the tables.

Holiday celebrations are more meaningful to the children if they are participants rather than observers. Cutting open a pumpkin at Halloween, scooping out the seeds, feeling the slimy inside, making pumpkin pie from the meat, and later planting the seeds involve all of the children in the activity of the celebration. Each age group participates in celebrations at its own level.

A one-year-old child may enjoy the lights on a Christmas tree and the tissue paper his gift was wrapped in, but a celebration can hold little meaning for him. The two year old may have some notion of what the word "party" means; but he is still not ready to participate in a sophisticated celebration or for changes in schedule or routine. Icing his own graham cracker or cookie and dropping sugar candies on it may constitute a Christmas celebration for a two year old, and a cupcake with a candle on it and the singing of "Happy Birthday" may be more than enough for a two-year-old's birthday party.

Three year olds can begin to enjoy planning a party a few days ahead of time, but they still require informal celebrations—a few surprises to eat, a special song or story. By the time the children are four years of age, they can listen to stories about the holiday, sing songs, or participate in simple ceremonies. Fives can take an active part in preparing their own foods, planning their own party, giving plays, and learning songs and poems.

**Columbus Day** Children could not care less about the controversy over who discovered America, or when it was discovered. But they do enjoy popping corn and hearing the story of how the Indians taught Columbus about corn a very long time ago. They like to hear how Columbus sailed such a far distance, just to bump into America. Some children may be able to construct boats and float them in a tub of water, leading to a discussion of what will sink and what will float.

**Halloween** Very young children do not understand the art of masks and may become frightened by wearing them or by seeing others in them. For children under the age of five, other aspects of Halloween should be emphasized. The children can grow pumpkins or purchase one from the neighborhood stand or farmer's field. Tasha Tudor's *Pumpkin Moonshine* can be read and enjoyed by two-, three-, four- and five-year-old children, and *Brownie's Hush* by Gladys L. Adshead is excellent at Halloween time. Children might enjoy dropping splashes of orange and black paint on a piece of paper and folding the paper in half, creating a ghost, witch, or pumpkin. Pumpkin cookies and pie, applesauce, apple cider, and apple cookies are appropriate goodies for this fall celebration.

Halloween is an excellent time to introduce concepts of safety. A policeman can be invited to speak with the older children, informing them of safety rules, methods of crossing streets, and other special Halloween precautions.

**Thanksgiving** The historical aspects of Thanksgiving are not meaningful to the young child, but the idea of giving thanks and getting together with friends to share a special meal can be very meaningful. The children can watch as the cook prepares the huge turkey for the oven. They can even help to chop the vegetables for the stuffing or make cranberry sauce or bake bread for the meal.

Thanksgiving may be a good time to introduce concepts of ecology. A forest ranger, park naturalist, or fish and game warden can be invited to talk with the children about the forests, streams, and woods. The children might even take a trip to a nearby woods or farm to gather their own food. If they are lucky, they can pick cranberries from a bog or gather corn from a field to prepare for a snack.

**Christmas** Perhaps the most overdone holiday, and one that children sometimes enjoy least, is Christmas. Young children, exhausted from waiting for the day to come and concerned over Santa and gifts, often fail to enjoy the pleasure of the occasion. You should make a deliberate effort to avoid unnecessary pressure on the children, so as not to destroy their fun.

Christmas poems, music, and stories can be shared with the children. Artwork might consist of making decorations for a tree from the scrap box or, for the fives, stringing cranberries and popcorn. Three- and four-year-old children might enjoy stuffing a pine cone with peanut butter and birdseed to hang outside of the window. A Mexican piñata can be filled with toys and candies and broken by the children.

*Children can experience division of labor.*

**Chanukah** Chanukah, usually occurring about the same time as Christmas, is a Jewish celebration of faith. Invite parents to the preschool to demonstrate the lighting of the candles and to describe the significance of the holiday to the children. A number of Chanukah games can be played with the children.

**Easter** Springtime and the rites of Easter and Passover indicate the renewal of life. Children can take a walking field trip to observe the signs of spring and to contrast living from dead things in their environment. This is a good time to bring in the young of any species—to observe tadpoles grow and change, to watch kittens play, or to see chicks hatching. Children can see how many different types of eggs they can collect—frog, turtle, chicken, snail, or fish eggs—and they can fry, boil, or poach some of them. They also might eat a spring salad collected from their very own garden.

**National Holidays** Learning to sing "This Land Is Your Land" or "Flag of America" or having a troop of scouts present the colors and recite the pledge could be meaningful experiences for young children celebrating national holidays.

**Birthdays** A child's own birthday is, for her, the most important holiday celebration of all. There should be a uniform way for all children in the preschool to receive expressions of happiness on their birthdays, and no child should be asked to perform conspicuously in front of the group. A special birthday book with a cheerful picture from all of the children can be presented to the birthday child. A photograph of the child can be taken and mounted on a board for all of the class to see, and some special activity can be arranged for her.

**Valentine's Day** The children can make valentines from scrap materials and mail them to their parents at work. They can cook red Jell-o or cut out heart cookies for a treat, or frost a cake with pink or red icing. You might mail a valentine to each child at his home, but children should not exchange cards in the preschool until they are four or five years of age. Even then, each child should bring enough cards for all the other children in his class, without attempting to address one for every child in the center.

**Other Holidays** Occasionally, such other holidays as Japanese Boy's Kite day, when everyone flies a kite, or a special Spanish celebration can be observed in the preschool. Korean holidays, the Chinese New Year, or the Brazilian carnival signifying the beginning of Lent might be of interest to the children if someone in the neighborhood or someone they know can describe the holiday for them.

# ECONOMICS

A beginning awareness of economics can also be fostered in the preschool. Young children in their daily lives do experience the economic concepts of material needs and supply and demand, diversity of jobs and division of labor, consumers and producers, and decision-making procedures.

## Material Needs

All children want "more"—they want more turns at the easel, more time in the new riding toy, more cookies, or more time to play outside. In the preschool, where endless wants are very real, budget cuts probable, and finances strained, children should be taught to conserve materials. Paint, paper, and paste, although readily available to the children, should never be wasted. Paper scraps should be picked up and placed in a box to be used for collage the next day. Rims of paste jars should be wiped clean to preserve the paste, and the favorite color paint that is limited in supply should be shared and treasured by all of the children.

Care of property is not a middle-class concept. All people, from whatever income level, want their material things cared for; and children, at a very early age, can be taught to care for and respect their own property and that of others.

The phonograph, which may be available for the children to use by themselves, must be handled in a certain way. If it is misused, the preschool will have to repair or replace it, perhaps using funds with which new records could have been purchased. The idea that the school must replace the same things over and over if the children or staff fail to care for them properly, and that the constant replacement of the same things negates purchasing other, more attractive things, should be developed in the children.

Books, records, rhythm instruments, manipulative toys and objects, and housekeeping toys should all be handled properly and returned to their proper places when the children are finished with them. Clothing should be hung in a designated area—never left lying on the floor for someone to trip over. You can establish a lost-and-found box to exhibit your concern over lost or missing property. You can help children understand that if Althea's mittens are lost her mother will have to buy her a new pair, leaving no money to buy a toy or something else Althea would rather have.

## Division of Labor

Each person in the preschool has a specific job—the nurse, physician, social worker, janitor, educational supervisor, teacher, and aide each has his own specific work to do. Children can informally interview the people in the preschool, finding out the nature of their jobs, how and why they perform them, and who helps them carry them out. You can help the children become aware of the diversity of jobs by asking, "What would happen if everyone in the preschool were a nurse? Who would teach? Who would clean? Who would cook? Who would repair the building?" The importance of each and every job to the functioning of the school can be stressed, so that the children develop the understanding that work is divided to accomplish many things at one time.

Older children can form their own system for dividing labor as an experiment. A day may be set aside for each child to assume a certain responsibility in the school. One child may be assigned to care for the pets, another to clean the paintbrushes, and another to pick up blocks. Generally, during the normal course of the daily activities, these tasks are shared by all of the children. Some children may elect to assume responsibility for a certain task because they enjoy doing it, or have special skills, or feel especially confident taking on a certain responsibility.

The children can also be made aware of the division of labor in their homes. With both parents working, responsibilities in the home are divided among all family members. Ask the children to list their household duties and those of their siblings, mother, and father.

## Consumers and Producers

Young children, on a trip to the store, become aware of the purchases they can make. Discussions can center around the things they and their families buy. You can identify the service people in the school—physician, dentist, plumber—and help the children to realize that they also purchase service rather than material goods from certain people. The school itself might be involved in the production of some items, or parents might produce marketable goods or provide services at their homes.

## Decision-Making Procedures

Decision making is a part of every activity in the preschool, with infants selecting their own schedule and toddlers their own diet. Older groups of children, with much experience in deciding what they will do and how they will do it, can participate in group decision making. The fours and fives can decide on the menu for the Valentine's party, the games to be played, and the people to be invited to share their fun. Groups of children can also decide on a piece of equipment for the center to purchase, poring over catalogs and determining the amount of money each thing costs.

Children who have been encouraged to make decisions for themselves from an early age will, as adults, be less likely to allow others to make their decisions for them. They will be prepared to participate as active citizens in a democracy, selecting their own leaders, voting, and determining their own rules and regulations.

## CURRENT EVENTS

Young children, surrounded by TV, newspapers, and radio, have little choice but to become aware of and involved in current events. The preschool should foster the children's natural interest in news, utilizing current events in the program whenever possible.

## Newspapers

Rather than subscribing to a child's weekly newspaper, the preschool might do better to subscribe to a daily adult newspaper, preferably one chosen for its human interest stories or the variety of news pictures it uses. Specific sections of the paper can be shared with the children. Some sections may be placed in the housekeeping area for the children to look at "after a hard day's work." The news magazine section may be placed in the library area.

The paper, in its entirety, is rather unwieldy for young children to handle; however, divided into sections, it becomes a much more viable resource. At times, news stories and pictures can be clipped from the paper and posted for the children to see. A picture of a child who had been bitten by a dog led one group of children to discuss what to do in the presence of a strange dog and how to care for their pet dogs. A story of a man who claimed that a ship from outer space had landed in his back yard, and who had pictures of "spaceman footprints to prove it," was shared with another group of children. They were asked if they believed the man or the scientists at the university who stated his claims were false. The children, based on their perceptions of outer space, decided that the man was really making up the story just to get his picture in the paper.

A single news picture or story can stimulate the children to question the happenings around them, and the resultant discussion may help to clarify their concepts. Such news items as the new baby monkey at the zoo, the arrival of the pandas from China, the baby ducks hatched under the bench in the park, or the snowstorm that hit the city are particularly enjoyed by the children.

The preschool's own newspaper, sent to the parents, can include items dictated by the children or stories about the children. This newspaper, with definite meaning to the young child, can develop her concern for the news of others.

## Television

Rather than using television in a center to watch specially prepared shows for children, use it only on special occasions for news items. A weather report on television or radio could help the children decide whether to plan a picnic or an indoor party for the next day; it could also help them determine what to wear. If four and five year olds are interested in space, they may enjoy watching the blastoff of a new space venture. A circus coming to the city, the visit of a president, or the news of a ship docking or a building being torn down might also be viewed by the children for brief periods of time.

# DEVELOPING ATTITUDES AND VALUES ————————————

Attitudes and values develop early in life. They remain as rather stable guides for behavior all through life. Children pick up attitudes from those around them. Everyone can recall a young child imitating his father making pancakes on a Sunday morning, or imitating a teacher scolding a group of children. Just as children imitate and pick up these overt behaviors, they pick up and imitate the values and attitudes of those they admire and live with.

Children first imitate and take on the values and attitudes of their parents. They do so because being like their parents offers children a measure of security. It's good to be like those who take care of you; it's good to have your parents' approval. Parents are the most significant persons in children's lives, and therefore, children strive to become like them.

Once children enter into the neighborhood or the preschool, other models are present. Now you, as well as other peers, are sources of children's values and attitudes. Even when you or other members of the staff try to hide your values and attitudes, you are not successful. Values and attitudes are subtly communicated and just as subtly picked up by others.

Because attitudes and values are so easily picked up by children, it was once believed that children were born with a set of "rights" and "wrongs." Research does show that children, even as young as two and three, do have set values and attitudes, but that they have acquired these from others (Goodman, 1952; Seefeldt, 1977).

If attitudes and values do appear early in life, you have a large role to play in the formation of children's attitudes. You need to understand how values and attitudes develop, and hold clearly in your mind those that are universal to a democracy, and those that will be promoted in the school.

The universal values consistent with the rights and responsibilities of living in a democracy include:

1. Valuing the dignity of each individual.
2. Universal participation in establishing rules.
3. Permitting each person freedom of speech.
4. Reinforcing the rights of each individual for protection and happiness.
5. Seeing that everyone has a part in the school society and that everyone has some responsibility to others.

These values and attitudes can be translated into a concern for others, the freedom of speech, as well as the need to be responsible for self and others.

It is inappropriate to actually teach children values and attitudes concerning such things as religion, politics, love, marriage, or sex. These are the attitudes and values that the home and church have primary responsibility for conveying; yet it is equally inappropriate for you to ignore your responsibility in fostering those attitudes consistent with living in a democracy.

You, as well as other staff members, will want to work toward fostering an understanding and appreciation of the beliefs and viewpoints of all of the children in the center. In a preschool, where there are children representing a wide variety of ethnic groups, nationalities, and socioeconomic levels, you have a unique opportunity to develop basic attitudes of citizenship in a democracy.

The belief in the worth and dignity of each individual should be consistently demonstrated. If you scold a child for spilling paint, you are demonstrating to all that you value the paint more than the child or the child's feelings. If you encourage children to make decisions for themselves and give them the freedom to act on their decisions, you are reinforcing the idea that each child is a worthy human being with rights and responsibilities as well as freedoms.

You should be aware of your own values and be willing to reorganize them if need be. You might ask yourself (Raths, 1962, p. 39):

1. Do I know where my values came from?
2. Why do I feel the way I do?
3. Did I always value this?

These questions have been suggested by Raths to help children in the process of value clarification, but they are equally useful for you in clarifying your own value system. Raths believes that a secure classroom atmosphere is necessary in order for you to help children clarify values. Children cannot express their values in words or actions unless they feel secure and comfortable. The preschool must be a place where children can feel psychologically safe to talk about their feelings and beliefs. You can listen to children expressing their beliefs and then ask questions to help them clarify these beliefs. Raths suggests that the following types of questions are useful in helping children to clarify their values: "Are you glad you feel that way?" "Have you thought of any other ways of doing that?" "Have you felt this way for some time?" "What are some examples of what you have in mind?" "What are some things that are good about the way you feel?" "Is this idea so good everyone should feel that way?" "Who else do you know who feels that way?"

# IT'S UP TO YOU ——————————————————————————

As a preschool teacher, you will have a large responsibility for introducing children to the entire social world. Much of a child's initial understandings has taken place in her home and immediate neighborhood, but in the preschool these learnings are clarified and expanded.

The preschool is a social system in itself. Through interactions with other children and adults, children gain social skills and increase their ability to work and cooperate with others. Through the experiences of the school, including holiday celebrations, field trips, and visitors to the class, you can foster children's understanding of the complex social systems we all depend on. Concepts from history, geography, and economics are introduced to children.

Undergirding all of these experiences, however, is an awareness of children's values and attitudes. Although you will not directly teach children values and attitudes, you do have a responsibility to foster those values and attitudes that are consistent with those in a democratic way of life. Children should learn to respect themselves and others, and to take their share of responsibility for the welfare of the total group.

## *REFERENCES*

Flavell, J. H. "Developmental Studies of Mediated Memory." In *Advances in Development and Behavior,* edited by H. Reese and L. Lipsett, New York: Academic Press, 1970.

Goodman, M. *Race Awareness of Young Children.* Cambridge, Mass.: Addison-Wesley Publishing Co., 1952.

Greif, E. B. "Peer Interactions in Preschool Children." In *Social Development in Childhood: Day Care Programs and Research,* edited by R. A. Webb. Baltimore, Md.: The Johns Hopkins University Press, 1977.

McMillan, M. *The Nursery School.* London: J. M. Dent & Sons., 1919.

Raths, J. "Clarifying Children's Values." *The National Elementary Principal* 42 (1962): 35–39.

Seefeldt, C. *Social Studies for the Preschool/Primary Child.* Columbus, Oh.: Charles E. Merrill Publishing Co., 1977.

Updegraff, R., Chittenden, G. E.; Dawe, M. C.; and Gutteridge, M. "Research and the Curriculum." In *National Society for the Study of Education: Forty-Sixth Yearbook. Part II.* Chicago: University of Chicago Press, 1948.

## RESOURCES

Robinson, H., and Spodek, B. *New Directions in the Kindergarten.* New York: Teachers College Press, 1965.

*Social Studies for Children.* Washington, D.C.: Association for Childhood Education International, 1956.

## PROJECTS

1. Interview a two-, three-, four-, and five-year old child. Ask each child what his mother and father do during the day. Ask, "What is money?" "What do you do with it?" "Where does it come from?"

2. Attend a field trip with a group of children, or take a child on a walking field trip. Notice which things interest the children. How can you follow up on their interests?

3. Plan a celebration for young children around some holiday theme and state your goals and objectives. What resources will you use? How could the celebration foster understandings of other people?

4. Observe young children at play. What difficulties do they have in getting along with each other? What social skills do they lack? What social skills do you see developing? How should you assist the children in developing relationships and understanding of others?

# THE HEALTH OF THE YOUNG CHILD

## PART FIVE

Healthy living, with nutritional, medical, and dental needs met, is necessary to the total development of children. They should be encouraged to develop wholesome attitudes toward their bodies, learn the basic principles of safety, and to gain skills in movement and balance. Not only will these activities serve to build healthy bodies, they will stimulate the child's intellectual functioning as well. A combination of healthy living, physical activity, and a balanced curriculum fosters in the child physical as well as mental health.

# NUTRITION EDUCATION _____

*Many children are not knowl-
edgeable about their nutritional needs or at least are not
sensitive to them.*
(N. B. Smith, 1975, p. 143)

# 13

Serving themselves, the two-, three-, and four-year-old children efficiently pass dishes filled with steaming chunks of meat, then, buttering bread they themselves baked that morning, happily begin eating. A cook, moving about the small tables, each seating four or five children and an adult, refills serving dishes and joins the children in conversation. The children eat, giggle, and talk about their favorite foods, often discussing important nutrition concepts in the process.

Mealtimes such as this are repeated daily in schools for young children across the nation. They are among the most important times in the day. Food while fulfilling a basic physical need also provides psychological comfort and satisfaction. The calming effect and pure sensory pleasure of eating during snack and mealtime heighten possibilities for attitude formation and concept development.

Snacks and mealtimes are a major vehicle for sensitizing children to nutrition needs and concepts. Some goals for nutrition education that can be fulfilled as children eat together might include:

1. Helping to meet the total nutritional needs of the infant and child.
2. Providing food with consideration for the cultural patterns, food practices, and social needs of the child and his family.
3. Encouraging the development of healthful food habits.
4. Providing meals in a safe, clean, and pleasant environment.
5. Providing a continuing nutrition education program for the children, the parents, and the staff of the center.
6. Helping children to learn to enjoy a wide variety of foods.
7. Building the understanding that good food is necessary for strong bodies and minds.
8. Developing feelings of self-assurance by encouraging children to make many choices and take appropriate responsibilities.

## MEALTIMES

Carefully planned mealtimes can facilitate the realization of the goals for nutrition education in preschools. Mealtimes should be calm times—times to eat together, to share good feelings, to talk, to plan. In any preschool program, meal and snack times should be occasions for the children to be near an unhurried, relaxed, and responsive adult.

Usually the number and type of snacks and meals served in a preschool depend on the length of time children spend there. The scheduling of meals and snacks also depends on the facilities available for food preparation, storage, and service, as well as the accepted food customs of the home and the community. A suggested schedule for meal service is:

*Mealtimes are important times.*

| Length of Program | Minimum Number of Snacks and Meals |
|---|---|
| Four hours or less | One snack, usually midway through. |
| Five to seven hours | One midday meal and a snack in the midmorning and midafternoon |
| Eight hours or more | Two meals and two snacks |

Menus, of course, should be carefully planned by a qualified nutritionist, and the food prepared by competent persons in sanitary, safe kitchens. Menu planning should consider each child's eating patterns. You must communicate closely with the parents concerning the child's eating habits, her likes and dislikes and changing needs. Menus should include food from each of the four basic food groups daily.

1. Dairy Group—milk whole, evaporated, or skim, and cheese and cheese products.
2. Meat—meat, poultry, fish, eggs or alternatives of beans, peas, cheese, or peanut butter.
3. Vegetable-Fruit—fruit and vegetables of any kind.
4. Bread-Cereal—whole grain or enriched breads and cereals.

In preparing food for young children, their peculiar likes and dislikes must be considered. For example, young children often do not like foods cooked together, or even touching one another on their plates. For this reason, meats could be served with gravy in a separate dish and vegetables not mixed together. Children are partial to food that can be eaten with their fingers. Raw vegetables, cut into bite-sized pieces, could often be substituted for cooked vegetables, and meats cubed or sliced into small pieces for easy handling and eating.

Often, how the food looks determines whether or not the young child will like it (or even try it). A variety of colors at each meal is important, along with a variety of textures. Children are sometimes more sensitive to strong flavors and spicy foods than are adults, so that a balance at each meal between strongly flavored food and bland food should be maintained. Bread that is cut into diamonds, squares, or strips; carrots cut into circles or strips; or potatoes cubed, sliced, or ridged are all more interesting to young children than are foods served in the same shape over and over again. Children eat very small helpings. For instance, young children usually manage best with:

1. ½ to 1 cup of milk
2. ½ to 1 ounce of meat
3. 1 to 2 tablespoons of each vegetable or fruit
4. ¼ to ½ slice of bread

Children's appetites vary from day to day. Second servings should always be available for those who want them.

Most important to successful mealtimes in programs for young children is the atmosphere. The room itself must be clean, cheerful, and well organized. The adults should strive to set the stage for a happy, calm, unpressured time. Generally, if menus are carefully selected, food wholesomely prepared, and a responsive atmosphere maintained, few children will feel negative about eating. If eating problems do persist after the child has been in a program for a period of time, you might want to consult with the child's parents and physician. You could find out what foods the child likes best, or if the child is, in fact, eating sufficient foods at home. It may be that something could be changed to help the child feel more comfortable in the program.

## MEALTIMES WITH INFANTS

Infants gain most of their feelings of trust by being fed when they are hungry. As the infant's basic need for food is met, he begins to develop the feeling that the world is a safe place and that people in the world can be trusted. If the baby's hunger is not satisfied, or if he is not held and comforted during feeding, he becomes increasingly fretful in his frustration.

Ideally, infants in preschools should be breast-fed. According to the Department of Health, Education, and Welfare, "Every effort should be made to accommodate the special needs of the mother who is breast-feeding so as to minimize disruption of nutritional care and of the mutual developing mother-child relationship. In some instances it may be possible for an infant to receive one bottle of formula during a four to six-hour interval in the preschool and to breast-feed during the remainder of the twenty-four hours." (*Nutrition Kit: Project Head Start,* 1970)

If breast-feeding an infant is not feasible, the center must strive to duplicate adequately the closeness, warmth, and love of a breast-feeding mother. In exemplary preschool programs, this is accomplished by having a nursery attendant, specifically trained for her position, in total charge of four, or at the most five, infants, allowing each infant the freedom to determine his own schedule.

Before feeding, the infant should be changed and made comfortable. Each infant should be held during the feeding, and for as long as he desires afterward. Formula can either be brought in by the mother or prepared at the center. During the feeding, you should be relaxed and unhurried—smiling, chatting, and responding to each infant as you feed him. Some infants gulp their food quickly, as if hurrying to get on to some other more exciting happening; others savor each suck, in no hurry to end the enjoyable activity. Some infants stop and play with you or the bottle, sucking a few minutes, resting, and then starting again; others are no-nonsense suckers, out to complete a task, crying if they lose the nipple. Whatever the feeding style of the infant happens to be, you should match your behavior to it.

The introduction of solid foods varies and depends on the individual child. "It seems desirable to follow in the preschool those practices carried out in the home. Thus, infants receiving table foods at home should be offered similar foods in the center" (*Day Care: Serving Infants,* 1972, p. 10).

By six or seven months, the baby is able to sit in a highchair for short periods of time. Appetites vary greatly at this age, as does the ability to wait for food. These babies should be fed when they dictate, but you may feed two or three of them at one time. It is at this age that babies begin to demonstrate individual food preferences, and food should be selected to agree with their tastes. Various finger foods should be placed on the highchair tray for the baby to explore, and you should respond to his smiles, tears, or other actions during the feeding. Any attempt the baby makes to feed himself should be reinforced. A spoon may be provided for the baby, or he may be given a crust of bread, carrot stick or hard cookie or cracker to chew on. The baby usually gets little food in his mouth, but he is learning to feed himself, learning that he can do things for himself, building a sense of confidence in himself.

From a year of age to around two, the child increasingly assumes responsibility for self-feeding. His search for autonomy makes him insist on doing things for himself, but his inability to handle cup, spoon, fork, and plate with accuracy can make this a difficult period in feeding. The child should be allowed to do as much of the feeding as he can; you should unobtrusively guide a cup that is being held nearly upside down, or, as the child is feeding himself, place a spoon of some food in his mouth. Again, all children are individuals, and each will establish his own method of eating. Some will spend hours slowly and neatly eating their food; others will eat quickly and without concern for neatness, wanting to get on with the next activity. You should make every effort to converse with the children during mealtime, using the food and the child himself as topics of conversation.

## TODDLERS' AND PRESCHOOLERS' MEALS

Every meal should be special to the very young child in a preschool program. Meals for the two- to five-year-old children must be served "family-style." This method allows each child to select her own food, to be responsible, and to feel confident and proud. Family-style meal service involves the following elements:

## Preparations

Quiet activities should take place directly before mealtime. Hands and faces should be washed individually while some children set the tables, listen to stories and records, or cuddle on your lap. Books to read, puzzles to work, pictures to look at, or a place to sit with a friend should all be available before meals.

Even the very youngest children should be given some responsibility for setting tables. Napkins can be put in place by the children and dishes and silver arranged. The older children can count the number of glasses needed and place one at each setting. All children can be involved in selecting a centerpiece for their own table.

## Adult Participation

The participation of adults at mealtimes is crucial. Family-style meal service means that you and the aides eat with the children. One adult should eat with every four or five children, and the same food should be served to all. Some teachers of young children rationalize their coffee, tea, or colas by saying, "Adults have special privileges children do not have." If, however, you hope to develop sound nutritional concepts in young children, you, as a model, should seek to limit yourself only to those foods the children eat. If you are on a diet, learn to limit the size of your portions, rather then bringing in special foods.

Conversation should flow freely during mealtime and it can center around the food itself. You can informally name the foods served and discuss food concepts: "Is the food sweet or sour?" "Do you like eggplant fixed this way?" "Do you remember what the eggplant looked like before it was cooked?" "What colors are on the table today?" "Where do you think these beans came from?" "Would you like a little more?" "What is your favorite vegetable?"

## Serving

During family-style meal service, food should be served in small bowls, complete with serving spoons. Children can pass the serving bowls to one another, helping themselves to the portion they wish. Small serving bowls can be managed by very young children, and older children and teachers are always nearby to assist if necessary. Cooks can circulate, refilling the bowls, or children can be given the very special task of taking an empty serving bowl to the kitchen for refilling.

Pitchers should also be available for children's use. They learn to pour their own milk, juice, or water. When the pitchers are kept small, and the amount of fluid in them limited, children have successful experiences with pouring, fostering their self-confidence, dignity, and worth.

New foods should be introduced often, but no child should be expected to eat any food she finds objectionable. Desserts, which the child also can select and serve herself, should never be denied to a child for any reason.

## Responsibility

Just as the responsibility for setting the table should be shared by the children, so should the cleaning-up activities be shared. As the children finish, each one should assume responsibility for her own dishes and table. Silverware and dishes can either be taken to the kitchen or to a waiting cart. Plates can be scraped into one can, paper products disposed into another, plates stacked, and silver put into a can of soapy water. When everyone has finished, tabletops should be sponged with soapy water. The pleasures derived from participating

*Snacks should be nutritious.*

in a group activity, plus the fun of sloshing with soapy water, make cleaning up an exhilarating experience.

INTRODUCING NEW FOODS    New foods should be introduced to children gradually. To do this, specific experiences can be planned. These might include the following:

1. Involving children in the preparation of new foods before they are presented at mealtime. Peas can be shelled, beans cut, corn husked, and cauliflower washed and broken into pieces.
2. Introducing children to new foods at snack time. Bits of turnips, brown bread, oranges, or whatever food is new to the children can be first presented as a snack.
3. Encouraging children to taste new foods through tasting parties. New foods can be presented in bite-sized pieces on fancy trays.
4. Having children participate in feeling a "mystery bag" containing a new fruit or vegetable. After each child has felt the bag and whispered her guess to you, the bag may be opened and the fruit or vegetable examined and tasted.
5. Having children share in the preparation of a special holiday food. Cranberries can be washed and cooked at Thanksgiving or asparagus cut and cooked in the spring.
6. Giving children the responsibility of preparing the snack for the day—fixing enough of the new food for everyone to have a taste.
7. Sending some of the new food home for the children's parents and other family members to share.
8. Asking parents or neighborhood volunteers to share their cultural or ethnic dishes with the children in the preschool by giving the cooks their recipes.

# SNACK TIME

Snacks can be formal or informal. Sometimes it makes sense to have the entire group of children stop their play, clean up, and come together for a snack. Holidays, birthday parties, and other such occasions warrant children sitting down together for a formal snack. When snacks are served informally during the week and more formally for a holiday, excitement and sparkle are added to even the simplest holiday celebration.

Formal snack times, with everyone sitting together, can be used to introduce children to a new food or idea. With all of the children together, sharing the same food, it's easy to focus discussions on how foods are alike or different, where they grow, or how they were prepared. This time may be used to discuss future plans for the day or to review the morning's events.

Informal snack times, however, are enjoyed by the children. At informal snack time the food is prepared and available for the children. Small pitchers of juice, with cups and napkins close by, are strategically placed in the room or play yard. When they are thirsty or hungry, children can help themselves. In this way children can decide when they need nourishment and develop self-sufficiency as they serve themselves.

Some children may not even take time from their work for a snack. Fully involved in completing a booklet, one girl took her juice and cracker to a table and ate while working. Other children like to take their snack into a secret fort under some trees, or make their own "tea party" in the dramatic play area.

Informal snack times can conserve valuable play time. They also avoid excessive adult direction and give the children the opportunity to learn for themselves. When informal snacks are served, children must make the decision as to when they will eat. In one kindergarten program, the teacher noticed that one child ate his snack as soon as activity time began. Knowing he had large breakfasts, she asked him to think about his decision. "If you eat your snack now, will you get hungry later in the day?" She helped him to think about the choices he had to make, and to consider the consequences of his decisions.

Contrary to popular belief, snacks or desserts need not be sweet or high in calories and low in nutrition. Snacks may come from any of the four food groups, and should be planned with the child's total diet in mind. Think of all of

*New foods are introduced gradually.*

the foods children enjoy instead of cookies, candy, or cake. You might serve the children:

raisins and nuts
carrots and celery sticks
pieces of apples
orange segments
dry cereal
tomato wedges
cucumber wedges, sticks, slices
strawberries
pineapple cubes
grapes
peas in a pod

popcorn
radishes
peaches
cabbage leaves
cauliflower bits to dip in sour cream
broccoli bits to dip in sour cream
melon balls
green pepper sticks
tangerines
cheese chunks
crackers to spread with cheese, tuna spread or peanut butter

# LEARNING THROUGH COOKING _____

"We're going to 'speriment with dough, hurry up!" called Robert to his friends when he saw his teacher bringing out the baking utensils. No matter what the age of the child or the type of preschool program, cooking and children just seem to go together. Whether children view cooking as an adult activity or as an experiment, it can be a wonderful activity for them. As they cook, children become acquainted with concepts of food, food production and preparation, as well as with many other concepts. Concepts of measurement, chemistry, and ideas from the social sciences—where food comes from, who brings it, how it is paid for—can all be fostered as children cook.

Any cooking activity must be carefully planned and the goals of the experience clarified. How you use language to label the children's experiences, as well as how you focus attention to important details and later integrate the experience into other learnings, determines the values of the activity.

Prior to the cooking experience you should take some time for planning. Weikart suggests that the cooking activity be planned to foster a specific goal (Weikart et al., 1971). Rather than using the activity to determine the goals as you go along, plan the goal prior to the activity. For example, cooking pudding could be useful in fostering a number of goals, and children's questions and interests should be considered during the activity; but the experience will be more profitable for the children if you know what your goals are beforehand. If you select the goal of introducing children to concepts of sequencing, then you can focus the children's attention to the first, next, and last things required to make pudding. You would label the activities: "First you must . . . ," "Next you stir . . . ," "The last thing to do is . . . ," Then you would use these words as children experience other things throughout the day and week. Relating the cooking experience to other activities reinforces the concepts introduced and

*Cooking can be fun.*

helps to integrate these into children's total learning: "Remember when we made the pudding, we first had to . . . ," "Today we must do this first," or "The last thing we will do is . . . ."

Many concepts can be introduced, reinforced, or extended as children cook. Some possible learnings are:

1. Concepts of physical change. Foods will melt, liquefy, solidify, and change form, sometimes many times, as they cook.

2. Mathematical concepts of measurement, number, and weight. "We need two cups of . . . ," or "Let's take a pound of apples . . . ." Time concepts are also possible: "Let's set the oven for 375° and bake the cookies for one hour."

3. Vocabulary. New words like "simmer," "dissolve," "melt," "knead," "broil," and others can be introduced.

4. Reading. When you cook, print large recipes for the children to follow. You might use pictures or sketches to illustrate the words. Read the printed word as you cook, letting children see the usefulness of reading.

5. Cultural awareness. Cooking can introduce children to the customs of people. Matzos could be made for Passover, stollens or Mexican Christmas cookies for Christmas, or black-eyed peas for New Year's Day.

6. Cooperation. The children learn to work together as a team to produce something.

7. Self-Esteem. Children learn to value themselves as they cook. Actually producing something that they and others can eat is a very satisfying experience.

8. Concepts of food. As you cook, you could introduce children to any number of concepts of food. You might focus on how the food feels, tastes, smells; what names different foods have; colors, food groups; what specific foods do for our bodies; or which foods could be eaten raw as well as cooked (Jameson, 1975, p. 149).

Deciding on the goal of the cooking activity is but one thing you do prior to cooking. Once the goal is decided on, you must also consider the following:

1. What is the age and maturity of the children? What skills of coordination do the children have? Will they actually be able to stir, cut, pour, and measure? What knowledge of food do they currently have on which to base this experience?

2. How many children can take part in the activity at the same time? If you pour ingredients into a bowl in front of the children, you are not cooking with them—you are only cooking in front of them. Select recipes or activities that permit a number of children to work at one time, or arrange the cooking activities so children can work in small groups. One teacher brought five small pumpkins to school. Small groups of two or three children and an adult volunteer cut and cleaned each pumpkin and later prepared it for a pie. Another teacher set up tables of equipment for making gelatin, so each child could participate in preparing dessert.

3. How safe is the activity for the children? Care must be exercised with frying pans, hot plates, or stoves. Children should be told, in a matter of fact way, of the dangers and safety measures that must be followed. It is not necessary to alarm children or teach them to fear heat; they merely need to understand it and respect it.

   The sharpness of knives and the potential dangers of other kitchen utensils should be explored and examined with the children. When they are aware of the proper methods of handling equipment and knowledgeable of potential dangers, young children exhibit an amazing degree of self-control and responsibility.

4. Sanitation must also be considered. Before any cooking project begins, children's hands should be washed, and cooking surfaces such as tables and counters should be scrubbed with soapy water. These sanitary measures quickly become routine when children are frequently involved in cooking activities.

## BEGINNING

Beginning with simple cooking projects can be a successful experience for young children. Spreading as much peanut butter as possible on a quarter slice of bread is very satisfying, and the product is a nutritious snack. Stuffing cream cheese into celery sticks is another simple, yet appealing, cooking activity for young children; and spearing pineapple chunks and cheese cubes on toothpicks gives a real sense of accomplishment.

Many teachers use the preparation of gelatin or pudding as a beginning project. One hot plate, either to boil the water or cook the pudding, is all that is necessary. Some instant puddings or desserts require no heat whatsoever, but the measuring involved makes their preparation a fine activity to start with.

Other cooking activities for beginners are popping corn, cooking rice or beans, or boiling a vegetable. The children are delighted to see how much rice results from a half cup of uncooked rice. Vegetables change in texture, smell, color, and taste when boiled.

With an oven, you can always bake bread. If you have never baked bread, you may be fearful of such a project with the children. Practice first, remembering that the only secret to baking bread is being certain that the liquid added to the yeast is truly at a lukewarm temperature. Bread is actually easy to bake as no exact measurements are really necessary.

Holidays are special occasions in a preschool, and many foods associated with them can be prepared by the children. Birthdays, of course, require attention and a special treat. Two year olds may enjoy frosting and decorating their own cookie or cupcake. Older children can make their own ice cream.

Cooking activities are even more advantageous and exciting when children participate in the production of the food. One nursery school delights in periodically growing a sprout salad. The teacher selects and brings to the school a large variety of edible seeds that have not been treated with a fungicide. Beans, peas, mustard, and watercress seeds are some that are commonly used. The seeds are placed in large food jars with screw tops, watered, and kept in a darkened place. To avoid molding, the seeds are rinsed off daily. They sprout in several days, and when they have grown to about one-half inch, the children, flavoring them with oil and vinegar dressing, eat their sprout salad. A most nutritious meal, enjoyed by all!

Several string bean plants will produce enough beans for each child to have one or two with her meal. One tomato plant can produce enough fruit to serve an entire center. Tomatoes can be started inside, and then transplanted outdoors after the ground has warmed in the spring. Radishes, lettuce, carrots, and beets grow quickly and produce freely.

## RECIPES

The following recipes require simple mixing and measuring but little or no cooking. They can easily be prepared in a preschool.

*Snow Balls*

4 cups mixed dried fruit
Rind of ½ orange (orange part only, stripped with vegetable peeler)
1½ cups almonds or any grated nut or coconut

*Toss together fruit, rind, and ½ cup of nuts. Prepare meat grinder by pouring hot water through to prevent sticking. Force mixture through grinder. With moistened hands shape into ¾-inch balls. If using nuts, chop remaining cup. If using coconut, grate finely. Roll balls in nuts or coconut to coat. Store in covered jar. Makes about six dozen.*

### Peanut Butter Banana Pops

1 cup milk
1 ripe banana, cut into chunks
½ cup creamy peanut butter
½ teaspoon vanilla

*In a blender purée milk and banana until smooth. Add peanut butter and vanilla.* Blend well. *If a blender is not available, mix ingredients together and mash and blend with an eggbeater. Pour into freezer molds and freeze until firm. Unmold and eat.*

### Banana Milk

1 banana
1 cup milk

*Mash the banana. Add milk and whip with an eggbeater for a thick, fruit drink. Increase portions to serve more children. Makes enough for two small glasses for small children.*

### Uncooked Candy

1 cup honey
1 cup peanut butter
2 cups dry milk

*Mix well and roll into small balls.*

### Coconut-Raisin Drops

1½ cups chunk-style peanut butter
3 tablespoons maple syrup
¾ cup dark seedless raisins
Flaked coconut

*In a bowl, blend together peanut butter and maple syrup. Stir in raisins. Drop mixture by rounded teaspoonful into the flaked coconut. Roll mixture in the coconut to coat, and then shape with the hands into balls. Chill until firm in a covered container in the refrigerator.*

### Cheese-Nut Celery Sticks

1 3-ounce package cream cheese
¼ cup chunk-style peanut butter
3 tablespoons milk

3 or 4 cleaned celery stalks, cut into
   3-inch lengths
2 tablespoons chopped peanuts
Few grains of salt

*In a bowl, combine cream cheese, peanut butter, milk, and salt. Beat until blended. Fill celery pieces with cream cheese mixture and sprinkle with nuts.*

These recipes require some cooking or baking, but are simple enough for children to participate fully in their preparation.

### *No Bake Oatmeal Cookies*

*Put together in a mixing bowl*
   3 cups quick oats
   4 tablespoons cocoa

*Mix thoroughly and put into a saucepan*
   2 cups sugar
   ½ cup milk
   ½ cup peanut butter
   ¼ pound butter or margarine

*Mix together and boil the saucepan ingredients one minute. Pour syrup over oat mixture and mix until oats are moistened. Drop from spoon onto wax paper.*

### *Applesauce*

8 large apples (3 pounds)
½ cup water
½ cup (or less) sugar
1 tablespoon lemon juice

*Set out a 2-quart saucepan with a tight cover. Wash, quarter, and core apples. Put apples in a saucepan with water. Cover and simmer for 15 to 20 minutes or until tender when pierced with a fork. Stir occasionally and add water if needed to keep from scorching. Mash apples with potato masher. Add sugar and lemon juice. Stir until sugar dissolves.*
   *For spicy applesauce, substitute brown sugar for the granulated sugar and blend in ¼ teaspoon cinnamon.*

### *Mexican Cream Candy*

4 cups sugar
½ pound butter
2 teaspoons vanilla
3 tablespoons white syrup
1 large can evaporated milk

*Melt butter. Add sugar, milk, and syrup. Cook, stirring constantly, until it forms a soft ball in cold water. Set aside to cool, then beat until creamy. Add nuts and vanilla. Drop by teaspoonfuls onto wax paper.*

### Cranberry Sauce

2 cups cranberries
1 cup water
1 cup sugar

*Wash cranberries. Simmer with sugar and water for about 15 minutes.*

### Meat Balls

*Let the children make their own cracker crumbs. Mix 1 cup of cracker crumbs with 1 pound hamburger. Add salt and 1 chopped onion. Mix by hand. Roll into balls. Fry in electric frying pan.*

### Apple Batter Pudding

1 cup milk
1½ teaspoons baking powder
1 beaten egg
1½ cups flour
6 apples (sliced)
Cinnamon or nutmeg

*Add milk to flour slowly, stirring to keep out lumps. When smooth, add other ingredients and mix. Don't beat. Arrange slices of apples about 1 inch deep into a buttered baking dish. Sprinkle cinnamon or nutmeg over them. Pour batter mix over apples and bake ½ hour in 375° oven or until top browns. Good with hard cheese.*

Don't forget the fun of preparing simple foods. Children could scramble eggs, hard boil or fry eggs, juice oranges or lemons, toss a salad, make a fruit salad, make apple or carrot sandwiches from slices of either, make oatmeal, grits, or rice, and cook hotdogs.

**AFTER THE COOKING** After children have made the food, it can be eaten and enjoyed. Occasionally, foods may be prepared for other children, parents, or the staff. Foods may also be prepared for holiday gifts or treats. For the most part, however, cooking is most rewarding for the children when they are able to consume the foods they prepare at snack or mealtime.

While enjoying the foods they have cooked, children can recall the cooking experience. Guiding the discussion, you can encourage children to remember the things they did, and the changes that occurred in the food, or to think about the way the food tastes. You could also focus the discussion on the goals you established for the experience. If you wanted children to gain concepts of sequencing, then the conversation might include discussions of what was done first, next, and last.

After you have finished eating, you might introduce a song, finger play, or story about the food that was eaten. Or you could show the children pictures of the food they prepared being grown, processed, or harvested. Their personal involvement with the food will bring meaning to the vicarious experiences of looking at pictures.

# _____ LEARNING ABOUT FOOD

Direct experiences with food are the best way to introduce children to nutrition concepts. "We feel that small children learn more by doing, by touching, tasting, and working with real food, or coming in contact with the food sources, rather than just seeing pictures of food or hearing about food and where it came from" (*Nutrition Kit: Project Head Start,* 1970).

Yet, not all nutrition education must be conducted in connection with children's actual experiences. At times vicarious experiences can be useful in reinforcing and clarifying children's actual experiences. It may be that you can use the following to reinforce and extend children's experiences with food.

STORIES   Many stories stimulate discussions about food or could lead to other activities with food. It seems natural, after reading Robert McCloskey's *Blueberries for Sal,* to eat blueberries and find out how and where they grow. The sound of a blueberry dropping into an empty bucket is fun to hear: "That is the same sound Sal heard!" You might ask, "What did Sal's mother do with all of those blueberries?" At school blueberries can be eaten uncooked or cooked in muffins, pancakes, or as a sauce.

A. A. Milne's *The King's Breakfast* is a favorite poem of young children. The king would not even taste marmalade, but insisted on having butter with his bread. Children can taste marmalade and compare it with butter. "Did the king use good judgment?" "What is marmalade?" "How is it made?" "Can we make marmalade?"

You could enjoy the stories of *The Gingerbread Boy, The Biggest Bear, The Three Bears, Johnny Appleseed* or *Little Miss Muffet* and then taste the foods described in the story. There are many other stories, poems, or nursery rhymes that revolve around foods children could taste and enjoy.

PLANTING A GARDEN   Planting, maintaining, and then harvesting a garden gives children many opportunities to increase their knowledge of food, as well as a feeling of accomplishment. You can collect and then plant seeds from foods eaten in the school, or purchase seeds for planting.

As children plant and care for their garden, they might consult books to find out the best way to care for plants or to produce the best yield. Children might be interested enough in the garden to make comparisons between their garden and that of farmers. As the children plant corn by hand, you could ask them to speculate how a farmer plants corn. Then consult a farmer or reference books, or view a movie to find out how farmers do plant corn. The same type of experience could take place as the harvest is completed.

**FIELD TRIPS**  Field trips are also useful in learning about food. You can visit a farm, observe the machines planting or harvesting. If it's not possible to visit a farm, a farmer might visit the class. Bringing some of the tools or a sample of food, he could explain to the children how eggs are produced, corn grown, or other food prepared for market.

Visit a supermarket. At a store the children can find out how many different ways corn, peas, or beans are found. They can observe fresh, frozen, canned, or dried foods. The group can observe delivery trucks and the process of transferring the food from trucks to the shelves.

Visits to food-processing plants—kitchens of fast-food restaurants, bakeries, or canneries—might be possible. The children can observe large quantities of food being prepared for distribution.

**PLANNING MENUS**  After children have had many experiences with food, they might be asked to decide on a menu for their lunch or snack. The cook could be consulted for help in "menu" planning, and she could tell the children of the need for foods from the four basic groups. You can give the children cutouts of food and paper plates, and have them plan a "menu" using these cutouts. Discussions on the values of different foods and the need for a balance between the four basic food groups can take place.

**MAKING BOOKLETS, CHARTS, AND MURALS**  Children could cut pictures of food from magazines and make scrapbooks or wall charts. They could make booklets in which they classify different foods. Some booklet ideas are 1) *Food That Grows on Trees,* 2) *Food from Animals,* 3) *Food That Grows under the Ground,* 4) *Food That Grows in Water,* 5) *Foods I like,* 6) *Foods for Breakfast,* or 7) *A Good Meal.*

**PUBLISHING COOKBOOKS**  As you cook, you can compile the recipes into booklets for children to take home and share with their parents. You could also include sample menus, so parents will have a better idea of the foods their children eat at school.

**DRAMATIC PLAY**  Food cutouts obtained from The Dairy Council or made from magazine pictures of food mounted on heavy paper can be placed in the dramatic play area. Children can use the cutouts to serve meals to one another at home or in a restaurant. Empty or full canned goods and empty food boxes can be used by the children to play store, food shopping, or house.

**LEARNING STATIONS**   Puzzles of food or flannel boards with food cutouts are enjoyed. Learning stations can be constructed. A fine learning station can be made with a large paper plate or a flannel board divided into four parts to represent the four basic food groups. Cutouts of food are used with the plate or the board. Children sort the cutouts into one of the four places. The backs of the cutouts are color coded so children can check their choices. Before children use these games, they should be familiar with the idea that there are four basic groups of food. The fact that foods fit into one of the four groups—dairy, meat, fruit and vegetables, and bread—can be pointed out as children actually eat or prepare foods. Understand, however, that knowledge of the four groups is not usually present in children below the third grade (Jameson, 1975, p. 149).

_____ **IT'S UP TO YOU!**

To make children knowledgeable as well as sensitive about nutrition should be a serious goal of all preschool programs. There is a great advantage in teaching children good food choices while they are young and before eating habits are entirely fixed. Surveys show that eating habits of children become fixed, and that they become poorer as children grow older (Cronan, 1969). As children cook and eat in a preschool setting, and learn more about food in other ways, they are developing knowledge and sensitivity about food that may help them establish sound nutritional habits that will last a lifetime.

Because young children are especially vulnerable to the effects of malnourishment (Birch, 1970), schools must also be concerned with providing children with nourishing foods. "Children, as growing organisms, are dependent on what they eat to a more immediate extent than are their elders" (Birch, 1970, p. 221). Many children in our country have been found to subsist on poor diets that have been labeled as shocking or starvation.

Malnourishment is directly related to impaired intelligence and school failure (Birch, 1970). If you want children to succeed in school, you must realize that children develop in relation to the total environment. It's not enough for you to plan cognitive activities for children; you must also be sure that children's health and nutritional needs have been met. If children do not receive adequate nutrition, their brains will not grow and develop normally; and all of the carefully planned, enriching, and cognitive experiences of a preschool will not change this fact.

Providing for nourishing foods and building knowledge of nutrition are still not sufficient. Children must also feel good about food, able to make wise food choices and try new and different foods. You can build these good feelings about food. From sitting together and chatting and eating to experimenting with dough, the activities in a preschool should be designed to foster positive attitudes toward food as well as to promote food knowledge. Children who are knowledgeable about food, who are establishing sound eating habits while young, and who are developing positive attitudes toward foods will have a better chance of growing, learning, and fulfilling their total potential.

## REFERENCES

Birch, H. G., and Gussow, J. D. *Disadvantaged Children: Health, Nutrition, and School Failure.* New York: Harcourt Brace Jovanovich, 1970.

Cronan, M. L. "The Role of the School in Providing for Nutrition." In *Nutrition and Intellectual Growth in Children,* edited by S. Sunderlin. Washington, D.C.: Association for Childhood Education International, 1969.

*Day Care: Serving Infants.* Washington, D.C.: Department of Health, Education, and Welfare, Office of Child Development, 1972.

Jameson, D. "What Do They Know from Bacon and Eggs?" *Childhood Education,* 51 (1975): 146–49.

*Nutrition Kit: Project Head Start.* Washington, D.C.: Department of Health, Education, and Welfare. 1970.

Smith, N. B. "Child Nutrition in a Changing World." *Childhood Education* 51 (1975): 142–46.

Weikart, D. P.; Rogers, L.; Adcock, C.; and McClelland, D. *The Cognitively Oriented Curriculum.* Washington, D.C.: ERIC and The National Association for the Education of Young Children, 1971.

## RESOURCES

Cohl, V. *Science Experiences You Can Eat.* Philadelphia: J. B. Lippincott Co., 1973.

Croft, K. B. *The Good for Me Cookbook.* San Francisco: R and E Research Associates, 1971.

Goodwin, M. T., and Pollen, G. *Creative Food Experiences for Children.* Washington, D.C.: Center for Science in the Public Interest, 1974.

Pictures, nutrition information, puzzles, food books, and even cookbooks can be obtained either free of charge or for a small fee from the following organizations. Write them to request information about their nutrition materials.

Florida Citrus Commission
Lakeland, Florida 33802

National 4 H Foundation
7100 Connecticut Avenue
Washington, D.C. 20015

Nutrition Education Materials Catalogue
National Dairy Council
1511 K Street N.W.
Washington, D.C. 20005

Society for Nutrition Education
National Nutrition Education Clearinghouse
P.O. Box 931
Berkeley, California 94701

UNICEF U.S. Committee
331 East 38th Street
New York, New York 10016

U.S. Department of Agriculture
Washington, D.C. 20006

Other agencies that can be contacted include your health department, health associations, university agricultural extension service, and consumer protection agency.

## PROJECTS

1. Identify foods from the four basic food groups. Plan a menu designed for four year olds in an eight-hour preschool program. Check your plans with a nutritionist or person who prepares meals for young children.

2. Observe young children of different ages eating. What likes and dislikes do you notice? Can you tell which foods children seem to enjoy the most? How do the children eat? What role do the adults—parents or teachers—play in children's eating?

3. Nutrition education isn't only for the classroom. You have a responsibility to share nutrition information with parents and staff. Begin a collection of resource materials on nutrition, food preparation, and purchasing that might be helpful for adults living or working with children. You could begin with the list of resources for this chapter.

4. Plan a cooking lesson for young children. Clarify your goals. If possible, conduct the lesson with young children.

# HEALTH AND SAFETY___

*It is widely accepted that good health is necessary for the optimal development of children.* (Review of Head Start Research since 1969, 1977, p. 38)

# 14

Children need to have sound physical and mental health in order to develop, grow, and learn. When children enter a preschool, they must be provided with a physical environment that is safe and healthy, as well as with a program designed to foster attitudes, skills, and concepts of health.

Healthy, safe living and health education are closely related in a preschool center. Teaching health and safety concepts cannot be separated from daily, ongoing experiences in the health and safety routines that are a part of any preschool. Health and safety education activities are not scheduled for ten minutes each day or as a once-a-week activity. They are ongoing activities, taking place continually as children actually experience the concepts being introduced.

As children brush their teeth, giggling at one another as the toothpaste foams about their mouths, they are participating in a routine required to sustain health. At the same time, however, the opportunity is present to introduce concepts of health, as well as to develop sound attitudes toward care of the body.

## HEALTH AND SAFETY GOALS

Health and safety education can better the lives of children, families, and communities. Promoting sound physical and mental health and structuring a safe environment are goals of all preschools. Good health is defined as complete physical, mental, and social well-being, not merely the absence of disease or infirmity. Therefore, the goals of health education could include the following:

1. Promoting physical and dental health.
2. Structuring a safe physical environment.
3. Preventing accidents and illnesses.
4. Developing children's knowledge of growth and development.
5. Providing for exercise and rest, toileting and washing.
6. Promoting sound mental health and social development.

Because health and safety education is so all-encompassing, the children's families and the total community should become involved in fostering the goals of the center. To be effective, health and safety education can be based on the following principles:

1. Health education should be directed to children and parents, as well as to the preschool staff, health professionals, and the total community.
2. The focus of the goals should be on action. Goals can be defined in terms of what children or adults will do as a result of their experiences in the preschool.

*Happy children are healthy children.*

3. Health education should emphasize skills that children can develop immediately. Knowledge gained by the children should not apply to only a few situations, but be general enough to lead to further learning in the future.

# PROMOTING PHYSICAL HEALTH

When nursery schools and preschools were first proposed, physicians were horrified at the idea of so many young children in close contact with one another. Spread of infectious diseases, they believed, would be rampant, and many young children would be exposed to serious or even fatal illnesses. Health precautions, however, were taken by the first nursery schools, and safety measures enforced. Children were not admitted to the playroom until they had passed a health inspection.

Today, immunization programs have markedly decreased the threat of childhood illness, and the availability of antibiotics has removed the fear of childhood illnesses being passed from child to child in a preschool. There is evidence that when preschools do follow health and safety measures, and provide a program in health education, children in groups can and do remain healthy. Children in groups do not experience any more serious incidence of illness than children not in groups, nor do they experience any illnesses that differ in nature from what occurs in the general community (Eldardo & Pagan, 1971, p. 26).

## PHYSICAL EXAMINATIONS

Both the staff and the children in a preschool should have regular physical examinations. Many state and county regulations recommend that anyone coming in contact with the children should have a physical examination. Even when local regulations do not suggest this, it is a good idea for the adults who work with and care for children to be certain they are not carrying any infectious disease that could possibly be passed on to the children.

Children are frequently required to have a physical examination prior to their entrance into a preschool center. The majority of states now require that children be immunized before they enter school in order to prevent the spread of potentially dangerous childhood diseases. Many times the physical examinations of the children can be conducted in the center and provide an excellent opportunity to introduce children to concepts of health and safety.

A preschool might be able to arrange routine examinations at the center. The local health department or a private physician may be able to conduct the examinations. When the physician or dentist is able to conduct routine screening examinations in the familiar environment of the preschool, the examination becomes an integral part of the daily activities rather than an unusual and possibly traumatic procedure to be feared.

If examinations are to be conducted at the center, parents must give their permission and should be present when possible. Children are more comfortable when parents are present, and the physician can relay information about the child directly to the parent. Parents are also necessary in order to provide the physician with useful information about the child.

Even when physical examinations are not a part of the center's program, you can do much to help children utilize the exam as a learning experience. Young children should be told what will happen during an exam; once the unknown becomes known, the fear is removed and apprehension lessens. You might arrange to have a physician talk with the staff before the examinations, informing teachers of the procedures that will be followed and how best to prepare the children; or the physician might be able to speak with the children herself prior to the examinations. In this way, the children become familiar with the physician and have some idea of what procedures will be followed.

You must at all times be honest with children, telling them simply, but factually, what to expect. Some children may, as a result of some previous experience, need more assurance than others. If a child seems particularly anxious, you or the parent may wish to hold him while the physician is conducting the examination, or engage him in reassuring conversation.

If children can have some experience with the physician's instruments before the examination, the entire process becomes more familiar and acceptable to them. For a small price, an actual stethoscope for use by the children can be purchased. The children can listen to their own chest sounds or the heartbeats of other children or the rabbit. You might introduce such other instruments as the tongue depressor or the light used to look in ears, noses, or throats.

Because play activities permit children to show competence in otherwise unfamiliar, potentially threatening situations, some recommend that children be permitted to play with medical equipment as a part of the regular play experiences in the preschool (Klein, 1979, p. 14). Klein recommends that syringes be used in water play and other medical equipment in doll or house-keeping play in order to stimulate children's conversation, yet offer a comfort-able approach for the fearful child.

Unfortunately, immunizations are often a part of the physical examina-tion, causing many children to fear or dread health care. However, if the young child is prepared for the immunization matter-of-factly and truthfully, she can often handle the event more calmly. Young children do not need extensive preparation, nor should they be prepared too far in advance. Discussion about the immunization on a one-to-one basis may be effective, or role playing the process of immunizations can be used to prepare children for necessary "shots."

Following the examinations, you could encourage the children to talk about their experiences or to engage in dramatic play. Questions such as "What did the doctor do?" "Did anything really frighten you?" or "What did you like the best?" help the child to express her feelings, clarify her concepts, and ask additional questions. Props in the housekeeping area, or in a special part of the room—a coat, a stethoscope, a tongue depressor—may stimulate the children to play out the doctor-patient relationship. Books such as Berger's *A Visit to the Doctor,* Leaf's *Health Can Be Fun,* and the Menninger Foundation book *My Friend the Doctor* could serve to stimulate follow-up discussion of the physical examination or to promote dramatic play. Children may also want to dictate their own books about the doctor that would more accurately reflect their personal experiences.

## DENTAL HEALTH

The most common health defect of preschool children is tooth decay; therefore, you should take every oppor-tunity to introduce concepts of dental health to children and parents in coordi-nation with actual experiences. The approach must be an active one, in which children learn by doing (Essa & Edwards, 1977).

The distribution of new toothbrushes provides a natural way to initiate a discussion on the care of teeth. "Why do we have teeth?" "What do we use them for?" "How do we keep them clean?" Brushing should be done after every meal in the preschool—it is easily and quickly established as a routine with the children. With the very young children, you might assist in squeezing the proper amount of toothpaste on a brush, but toddlers and preschoolers should be able to manage the entire operation without your supervision. Toothbrushes may be stored in their original containers or in individual toothbrush racks, with the child's name above each brush. Individual tubes of toothpaste are also recommended. Some centers distribute one toothbrush for use at the school and another for use at home, in order to promote continual dental hygiene. When necessary, centers can also provide toothbrushes for other family members.

A nurse, dental hygienist, or dentist may be asked to visit the preschool to demonstrate correct toothbrushing and flossing techniques to the children. A trip to the dentist's office for treatment, especially a first visit or one following emergency or painful treatment, can be a frightening experience. However, when children can visit the dentist's office prior to their first treatment, or meet the dentist in the preschool, the experience becomes less traumatic. If this is not possible, structure some other experience with dental treatment before the first visit. Informal talks, a demonstration of the use of dental mirrors, role playing, or films and books such as *My Friend the Dentist* provided by the Menninger Foundation may all help to prepare the child.

Following a visit to the dentist, children enjoy dramatic play. A simple chair, a flashlight, and a white shirt are useful props. The flashlight allows the children to examine one another's teeth or new fillings, and the shirt serves as the dentist's coat.

Losing a baby tooth is a dramatic occasion in the life of a preschooler and can be an effective learning experience. The tooth that fell out can be shown to the younger children; it can be examined and discussed: "Why did it come out?" "What will happen next?" Robert McCloskey's *One Morning in Maine*, in which little Sal loses her tooth, can be read to reassure the children that a new tooth will come in.

Dental health is closely related to the child's nutrition. In addition to providing well-balanced meals, snacks served to the children should be selected with care. Such foods as fresh fruits, vegetables, unsweetened fruit juices, cheese cubes, nuts, and popcorn can all be enjoyed by the children as wholesome snacks.

# STRUCTURING A SAFE ENVIRONMENT _____

Although each infant and young child in the preschool is an individual and no rigid group scheduling is workable, some establishment of flexible routines is necessary for safe living and the emotional stability of the entire group of children and adults.

Good housekeeping techniques can be established throughout the preschool, with the children assuming a great many of the responsibilities. Although you have little control over the selection of the physical facility, you can see to it that the playroom and yard are clean. Very young children, mouthing everything they come in contact with, require extremely clean places in which to live and play. Toddlers and preschoolers, who spend a great deal of their waking time on the floor, also need clean surroundings. You and the young children alike can clean up spills as they occur, put toys and other objects away in designated places when not in use, and pick up scraps and other refuse.

Habits of personal hygiene should be introduced to the children and practiced routinely. Many such habits are effectively taught through imitation and example. Children observing adults use tissues, wash their hands, and brush their teeth want to copy these practices. When water, soap, towels, and tissues are convenient and readily available to the children, they are fully utilized. A child who is positively reinforced for getting a tissue to wipe his nose, or for washing his hands after play or before eating incorporates these habits into his life.

Other health measures can be directly taught to children. As children fall or cut themselves, they can be shown how to wash wounds with soap and water. They can also be cautioned not to put things in their ears, noses, or mouths. You may demonstrate to small groups of children the proper way to obtain a drink from the water fountain. Small paper cups in dispensers allow children to drink whenever thirsty without contamination.

ACCIDENTS   Accidents do happen in the most carefully planned environments and are a major cause of illness and disability in young children. (See Table 3, pp. 337–39 for a description of the major accident hazards at the various stages of development and for measures required to prevent such accidents.) It follows that all personnel should be familiar with the policies for handling an accident or sudden illness. Basic knowledge of first aid, including procedures to control bleeding and artificial respiration, should be required of all persons working with children. The local Red Cross sponsors training courses that can be utilized by preschool personnel. When you feel competent as a result of first-aid training, accidents can be handled efficiently, in a matter-of-fact, calm manner.

In their training procedures, the staff may role play some common types of accidents, discussing among themselves how to handle each type. The staff may also practice and role play alternative measures that could be taken. For instance, Plan I for a child injured on the playground might include the aide going to the phone to call for assistance while you stay with the child. Plan II should also be developed in case the aide cannot be freed to call or is occupied somewhere else in the preschool.

All preschools should make very specific plans in case of fire. The local fire fighters will help you to plan for emergencies and suggest ways of improving the general safety of the center. When planning fire emergency procedures, be certain to:

1. Plan two or more ways to exit from each room of the center in case one planned exit is blocked by smoke or fire.
2. Pick a place to meet outside of the center and develop a method of counting children, or otherwise accounting for each person and child.
3. Practice the fire plans with children and staff.
4. Learn how to use fire extinguishers.

First-aid supplies should be located in each playroom and within easy access to the play yard. The phone number of the local poison control center should also be readily available. You should attend to the injured child first, and then deal with the feelings of the other children. Following an accident, you can discuss with the children what caused it, how to prevent it in the future, and how best to help the injured child.

ILLNESS    What do you do with a sick child in a preschool? For many years, the policy was to send a child who was ill home or to isolate him in a "sickroom" or "nurse's office." Now, however, other methods of dealing with ill children are being tried, often with positive results. At Mary Elizabeth Keister's center and at the Frank Porter Graham center, children who are ill are kept in the center rather than sent home. In Dr. Keister's center, special care for the ill child is provided: "Interestingly, we believe that having the sickbay has reduced, rather than increased, the incidence of illness in the nursery. We regard our provision of sickbay as one of the most important facets of the program" (Keister, 1970, p. 34).

Experiences in the sickbay can be useful in teaching health education. Dr. Keister states further, "We find gratifying our young ones' friendly accepting attitudes toward persons who wear white uniforms and stethoscopes, their positive attitudes toward taking medicine, their interested cooperation in physical examinations and in first-aid treatment" (Keister, 1970, p. 34).

In discussing the Frank Porter Graham center's policy of not isolating sick children, Dr. Frank Loda indicates that he does not believe it to be radical or unusual: "We simply point out the fact that children shed viruses before they become clinically ill. . . . We have tried to answer the problem, not by isolating the sick child, but trying to provide for both the sick and the well child. In a sufficiently healthful environment there is not the threat of causing excessive illness because we keep sick and well children together without causing excessive illness in our environment" (Eldardo & Pagan, 1971, p. 31).

Some states prohibit the dispensing of any medicines by anyone other than a nurse or the child's parents for children in group care; other states have more liberal policies. Some preschools designate one staff member to administer all prescribed medication to eliminate confusion over whether or not the child received the medicine and when. Of course, no medication whatsoever, including aspirin, should be given any child in any center without the authorization of the physician and parents.

# UNDERSTANDING GROWTH AND DEVELOPMENT ————

Experiencing the routines of naps, exercise, and toileting, the young child in a preschool can begin to develop a positive body image and to understand concepts of growth and development.

REST PERIODS AND NAPS    Children in a group must balance their active, boisterous times with quiet, restful periods. They seem naturally to follow a period of very active outdoor play

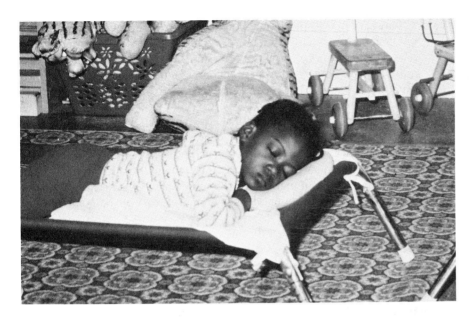

*Young bodies need rest.*

by resting under a tree, playing quietly in the sand, or even going back into the building to read or rest on their cots. One teacher even tried an experiment in which she did not call the children in from play to take their usual morning nap. Around thirty minutes after the regularly scheduled rest period, all but four of the children had wandered into the room and stretched out on their cots.

Not all children in preschool rest in the same way or require the same amount of resting time. All, however, must take some time to relax in whatever manner they choose. Some children demand long naps in quiet, darkened rooms; others are content to read a book, listen to a record, or play with toys on their cots rather than actually sleep. Every child should be allowed to select whatever type of resting situation she desires, as long as it does not disturb others.

When children are allowed to select their own quiet type of activity, the battle between you ("I know what's good for you") and the child ("You can't make me") is eliminated:

> Planning for a period of cessation of noise and discord may mean a storytime with everyone sprawled comfortably on the floor, or a record time with the children in similar comfortable positions. One teacher collected a wide assortment of small gadgets, mechanical and magnetic toys, locks and keys, pipe cleaners, erasers and colored pencils, small pencil sharpeners, shoe polish, fingernail polish, and whatever else normally appears first in kitchen catchall drawers and later in children's pockets. These were kept in several boxes which were constantly refilled with new items as she found them and cleared temporarily of old ones. At rest time the children could take one thing they wanted from these boxes, or a puzzle or a book to their cots. For the forty-five minute rest in this

all-day school the children played quietly for part of the time, stretched out peacefully for part of the time, and heard a story or music for the last part. They got up from rest quite toned down, as was evident from the quiet relaxed conversation that accompanied the putting away of cots (Rudolph & Cohen, 1964, p. 345).

Several rest periods a day should be provided in the preschool. There should be short, quiet breaks, that might even include juice or milk, and a nap time when children can actually fall asleep if they desire. Children in an all-day center require room to stretch out on a cot, usually in the afternoon, to sleep. Half-day programs might find the use of floor mats satisfactory for short resting periods; however, folding cots or beds are preferable for both half- and full-day programs.

Children, knowing that rest time is coming, naturally begin to put their toys away, and prepare to nap. Even the two year olds, once the routines of brushing teeth, washing, changing clothes, and settling on a cot are established, can take primary responsibility in caring for themselves.

Some young children in groups may find it difficult to relax, even when the room is quiet, the shades drawn, and soothing music played. These children can be helped to rest in individual ways. Some may be provided with screens around their cots; others can have their backs rubbed, or enjoy the company of a favorite blanket or stuffed animal.

Occasionally, a child may come to a preschool with a fear of resting or sleeping. You can help to reassure her, listening to her fears but not accepting them. If you scare away the bugs from under a cot, you lend credence to the child's fantasies. You are convincing her that there surely is the possibility of many bugs under her cot; after all, you are going through the motions of chasing them away. Tell the child that there is nothing to be afraid of, that there are no bugs, or whatever, and that as she grows she will learn not to be afraid.

Children should be allowed to sleep as long as they desire unless schedules demand that they be wakened to prepare for going home. Just as the children naturally sense the need for rest, they naturally wake up when their need for sleep has been met. Children who have had sufficient rest during the day are better able to relax and sleep during the night, so you and the parents need not fear that if the child takes a long nap in the center he will not sleep at night. On waking, the children can be led to the bathroom for toileting and face washing, and helped to dress. A snack, often consisting of something refreshing to drink, is usually appreciated by the children as they wake up.

The adults supervising rest time should also assume a posture of rest. Record-keeping and other work should be left to do at another time. The staff member can stretch out on a cot herself, setting an example for the children, or relax in a chair and enjoy the restful atmosphere herself.

## EXERCISE

Developing muscles need exercise. Equipment in and outdoors to encourage both small- and large-muscle exercise is, of course, present, and children should have the freedom to explore and experiment as they desire. However, additional experiences may be planned to help the children become more aware of their bodies and how they move.

Body awareness can begin with the infant as you dress and undress him: "Let's put your arm here. Now we'll put the other arm through here." The toddler may be helped to differentiate body parts: "Pull the sock up over your calf." "Put this ribbon around your waist." "Put your hands on your hips." Mirrors in the center also assist the child in becoming familiar with his body and the things it can do. Wall mirrors, mirrors by cribs and dressing tables, mirrors in the bathroom, hand mirrors, and even mirrors that magnify should be provided.

Photographs of the children that are mounted on heavy cardboard and placed on bulletin boards help them to see exactly how they look. Such games as "Simon says" and "Looby loo" can be played to stimulate knowledge of body parts. Children can explore body movement using ankle bells, hoops, or balloons as they dance or move to music. A drum can often be used to pick out the child's spontaneous rhythm as she moves in the center or play yard. Starting with a child's own rhythm stimulates her interest in learning to move to music or to the beat of some other thing or person.

Young children can be led in their exploration of body movement. You can provide problems for the children to solve and help them to discover how to respond. Two types of problems are involved in "movement exploration": 1) those designed to encourage each child continuously to explore and discover a variety of movement responses and 2) those designed to encourage exploration and discovery of limited movement responses. The first type of problem, free exploration, is more appropriate for very young children; however, the second type, guided exploration, which is centered around both you and the child and is involved in promoting and refining skills, can be introduced to four and five year olds. Problems or tasks may be stated in a number of ways in order that all children grasp their meaning. Each child's response is a correct one and should be reinforced with praise. Thus, every child succeeds.

In exploring movement, a group of children might be asked to show how many different ways they can move across the room:

Can you walk in place? Forward; sideward; backward?
Walk on your tiptoes; on your heels.
Can you walk without touching anyone else?
Walk quickly and quietly.
Walk slowly; with long steps; with tiny steps.
How would you walk if you were walking up a hill?
How would you walk on a rainy day? A snowy day; a hot day?

On another day, children could explore running:

Can you run quickly, without touching anyone?
Run lightly; run heavily.
Run, but stop when the drum beats.
Move your arms while you run.
Run following a leader.

These activities give children the opportunity to improve their body control. Running in itself is a difficult task for young children. And to be able to exercise the control of not touching someone else while running, or to be able to stop running on a given signal, requires much skill and repeated practice. In movement exploration, children compete only with themselves, and each time they note their increasing ability to control their own bodies, they gain in feelings of success and confidence.

As they mature and have many experiences in moving, children can also be taught to explore such various movements as leaping, jumping, hopping, sliding, galloping, and skipping:

> Can you leap into the air?
> How high can you leap?
> How many different ways can you land?
> How high can you jump?
> Can you jump and land quietly?
> Jump like a bouncing ball; jump low; jump high.
> Jump forward; backward; to the side.
> Jump in and out of circles drawn on the floor.
> Hop on one foot, then on the other.
> Hop quickly; hop slowly.
> Hop high; hop low.
> Slide slowly; slide quickly,
> Slide to one side, then to the other.
> Move your arms while sliding.
> Gallop forward; backward.
> Gallop slowly; gallop quickly.
> Skip forward; high; low; lightly; heavily.
> Skip around obstacles or marks drawn on the floor.
> Do something with your hands while you skip.

These movements often do not come easily to young children. By holding a child's hand as the music plays and jumping, hopping, or galloping with her, you can help the child to master the movement. Many five year olds cannot gallop or skip, and they should not be made to feel inadequate because of it. By experimenting with movement and music, the child eventually will gain these skills.

General movements can be explored by asking each child to find her own special place in an open room. The children should be far enough apart so that their outstretched arms do not touch anyone else's. Again, you give directions, but each child gives her unique response at her own developmental level.

> Find your home spot; move away from home in any way you want; return when the drum beats or the bell rings.
>
> Look around to avoid collisions; run away from home; run back on the signal; do not touch anyone else when running.
>
> Find a way to get from home to any other space while moving close to the ground.
>
> Walk like a bear, frog, horse, or any other animal.

Move from home without walking or running.

Reach out as far from home as you can without moving your feet from the floor.

These exercises begin to develop the child's awareness of body movements and of control of the moving body. Hackett and Jensen point out:

> One of the greatest values of movement exploration is the simplicity of the concept. Movement indicates that some action is used in seeking a solution to a problem. Each child is separately engaged in analyzing the problem, and seeking a solution within the limitations of his own physical and mental abilities. By having to concentrate on the solution of a problem, rather than solely on himself, the child becomes completely involved in the activity (Hackett & Jensen, 1967, p. 2).

Each child's responses to a problem are correct, each child performs as an individual, each child is challenged, and each experiences success. Movement exploration in the preschool provides children with a background in motor development before they become engaged in activities that demand advanced skills.

## TOILETING

"Where's the bathroom?" ask the four and five year olds on their first day in a preschool. The bathroom to young children is still a very important place, and toileting a very important part of their day in the center. Bathroom time, as with every other routine in the center, is an individual matter with young children. No two children, or no two teachers, can schedule their need to use the bathroom at the same time.

Ideally, bathrooms should have child-sized facilities that can be managed by the children independently. They also should be located within the play-room, so that young children do not have to leave their play to travel the length of a hallway, or go downstairs. Although preschoolers can "go to the bathroom" without your direct supervision, they must feel secure in the knowledge that a concerned adult is nearby, ready to help if necessary. When aides or volunteers are present, one adult can always be available to help individual children with buttons, zippers, or panties that must be pulled up or down.

Before and after lunch, and again after nap, are often busy bathroom times. They can become very social occasions, with children soaping hands, playing in the water, brushing teeth, chatting, and even singing together. Such times also provide the opportunity for further discovery of the body, and the differences between boys and girls. In a preschool center, boys and girls under the age of five use the same bathroom facilities, and they begin to note their differences in a natural way. Comments and questions of the children should be handled matter-of-factly with such statements as, "Boys stand and girls sit," or "Girls are different from boys." Adult terminology should always be used in reference to sexual organs.

Infants and children under the age of two do not have sufficient neuromuscular development to be "toilet trained" in any true sense. The best

332 of young child

procedure is to change these babies frequently rather than allowing them to stay in soiled diapers. Around the age of two—sometimes a little before, sometimes after—is an appropriate time at which to begin to toilet train the child. The process must always be coordinated with that of the home, as two different methods would confuse the child as to what is expected of her.

When a child is ready, you can observe her for signs that she needs to use the toilet and respond by placing her on it for several minutes. A few words of praise will reinforce a successful experience. Children in a center, observing others use the bathroom, usually are easily trained; they are eager to imitate the older children. Putting a child in training pants rather than diapers often signifies to her that a new type of behavior is expected.

Accidents happen and should be accepted as a normal course of events with a quick cleanup, a fresh change of clothing, and some comforting words to the child. Many young children, even after they have reached the ripe age of five, become so involved in their play and activities that they leave the bathrooming until the last possible moment. Then, much to their chagrin, they are too late. Never shame them for such failures; rather, take a comforting, matter-of-fact attitude to help them regain feelings of adequacy and confidence. Accidents also may occur if a child is ill, or they may be a response to an emotional upset that you should seek to identify.

*"I'm small now, but I'm growing."*

# PROMOTING MENTAL HEALTH

"I'm small now, but I'm growing." "I don't know if I can do it, but I'll try." "I can do it!" Such comments come from children who know who they are, feel good about themselves, and who are eager and ready to learn and try something new. Research indicates that the very early experiences of a child influence his feelings about himself for the rest of his life. The child's future mental health depends, in part, on the adults with whom he interacts in the preschool.

The entire program in a preschool center must be geared to fostering feelings of self-worth, dignity, and self-esteem in each child, leading to the development of a healthy self-concept. In a preschool, it is essential that each child be recognized as an individual, and that each experience contribute to building feelings of adequacy and competence. Developing children's self-concepts, the foundations on which they will build all future relationships with others, is a continual process which begins at birth.

**INFANTS** Self-discovery begins with the infants' first exploratory behavior as they begin to manipulate their bodies and develop images of it. This exploration of self and the differentiation of self from the environment are the first steps in developing a concept of self (Elkind, 1978). Until about eight months of age, an infant treats his fingers and toes as if they were not a part of him; it is not until later that he recognizes the baby in the mirror as himself.

When infants are in a center program, opportunities should be provided for them to explore their own bodies. Clothing that restricts their exploratory movements, such as gowns with mitts to cover the hands, may limit first attempts at self-discovery. All babies should have some time without clothing, perhaps before bathing, in order to provide for self-discovery.

As you care for the babies, play with them. When babies are awake, and in a happy, playful mood, you can play with them using a mirror. Holding the baby so he can see in the mirror, say, "Here's your nose," "Jim's toes," "Sue's feet," and so on, naming various body parts. The baby should always be called by name—the same name used at home. You can say, "Where's Jeffie?" and answering yourself, respond, "Here's Jeffie!" With a lot of experiences of this type, the baby begins to recognize his own name and learns more about himself.

Babies, in order to develop sound mental health, must know that they can influence their world. They can make you laugh or even squeal when they've mastered the technique of grabbing a hunk of your hair or your glasses. Babies cry, and when their needs are met as they cry, they also learn that they count in this world. You do not spoil the baby by responding to his cry; rather, you help him know that he is important and respected.

Respect is important. Each baby must be cared for as an individual. His own schedule must be considered. His interests, likes, and dislikes are also used to determine the schedule of the center. According to Read, "Respect for a child must begin early. Respect him for trying to pull to sitting even though he falls over; for trying to walk even though he falls every time he takes a step; for being eager to learn about the world even though he messes things up doing it; for desiring to grow at all times even though he may try too hard and overreach his present abilities" (Read, 1966, p. 75).

TODDLERS    During toddlerhood, children's efforts to care for themselves should not only be supported, but strongly encouraged and fostered. In order to know who they are, toddlers must be allowed to participate in the realistic situations of dressing, washing, cleaning up, or even setting tables.

Independence is the key to the toddler; in order to gain independence, he wants to do everything for himself. It is no doubt easier for you to take complete charge of dressing these young children; however, aware of the importance of each child's need for autonomy, you should help the toddlers to dress themselves. This requires patience on your part, and some rather subtle guidance. You can hold the sleeve open while the toddler puts his arm through, or you can start the sock by pulling it down off his heel and let him pull it the rest of the way off. Toddlers must always be allowed to feed themselves and participate in any other care-giving experience.

A place of the toddler's own should be set aside in the preschool. A cubby with his name above it, or even a discarded ice cream container with his name, could be used as his special place in which to keep his own things. When the child has a separate place for his toothbrush and washcloth, for his personal possessions, and for his cot, a sense of identity results. The name label, which tells him that he is a separate and important person, should include a picture or symbol that he can recognize.

Toddlerhood is not the easiest time for adults to be with children; it is a period of development often involving negativism and rebellion. Toddlers quite often say "No!" to everything and defy adults in every possible way. Rather than stopping such behavior, you can make every effort to allow toddlers to express themselves, giving them many choices, but structuring the choices and the environment in such a way that permits you to maintain control over the situation.

PRESCHOOLERS    Growing in independence, with a fairly accurate self-concept, children aged three to five are now able to relate to other children. Cooperative group experiences foster feelings of confidence, independence, and understanding of himself in relation to others in the preschool child. He needs experiences that will help him control his emotions in order to play and work with others and to accept responsibility for himself.

Preschoolers must see themselves as successful. Repeated failure, criticism, or discouragement tend to lower a child's self-esteem to the point where he may become unwilling to attempt new activities. Children need many success experiences and recognition for tasks well done. Exploring and experimenting with various materials and achieving mastery over them helps the preschooler to feel successful.

You can foster a sense of self-worth and dignity in the preschoolers by using their names as often as possible and in such various ways as the following:

1. Always call the children by name and use their names frequently as they work and play.
2. Use the children's names in songs: "Mary Wore a Red Dress" or "Here Is a Friend That We All Know." Or substitute their names in poems and stories.
3. Write the children's names on objects that belong to them, saying, in effect, "This is your name. This belongs to you."
4. Keep sets of name cards for the children to handle and play with, sorting them into groups.
5. Affix the children's names to their art products, saying "This is a part of you. You created it. We are proud of you."
6. Put names on the children's cubbies and clothing, assuring them that things belong to them.
7. Make lists of children's names for the playroom.

Preschoolers, in order to feel good about themselves, must be given responsibilities and challenges they can meet. If a child's responsibilities are constantly assumed for him by you, an aide, or a volunteer, his feelings of worth and dignity are undermined. There are many responsibilities in the center that preschoolers can assume:

1. They can clean up after themselves.
2. They can care for their own personal materials.
3. They can care for pets or plants in and outdoors.
4. They can participate in preparing their own work materials—mixing paint, preparing salt dough, and the like.
5. In cooking activities, they can assume adult-like responsibilities.
6. They can make personal decisions and be encouraged to think for themselves.

Preschoolers in group care, for sound mental health and self-awareness, need to be able to express their emotions in acceptable ways. Play activities; art experiences; sand, water, and mud play; and movement and dance can all provide emotional outlets for them. They should also be encouraged to verbalize their emotions, and can dictate stories to you with such titles as "Three Wishes" or "Sue Was Mad."

You can help change preschoolers' concepts of themselves. Some children may come to the school feeling rejected, unloved, undesirable, or bad. Such children can, through positive experiences, begin to develop a sense of self-worth and dignity and a feeling of belonging. One child who ate little or nothing, and who was used to hearing his parents, grandparents, brothers, and sisters call him a picky, fussy eater, was turned into an "eater" by an astute teacher. One day when the child did happen to put some food in his mouth, the teacher snapped his picture with a Polaroid camera, exclaiming, "Look, Jim is

*Jim is an "eater."*

an 'eater.' " She showed Jim and the other children the picture over and over again, convincing the child that, yes, he was an "eater" after all. As a result of the experience, Jim's eating patterns continued to improve. Other children could have their pictures taken as they climb, run, or execute other skills. The pictures could then be labeled, "Jim can run," or "Sue can read," illustrating to the child his abilities and successes.

The more adequate a child's mental health and the stronger his feelings of self-confidence, the more certain it is that he will be able to form meaningful relationships with others. Children with healthy self-concepts, who can lose a little and still maintain their pride in themselves, are those children who are bound to succeed in later life.

## IT'S UP TO YOU! _____

Fulfilling the goals of health and safety education is up to you, the teacher. Based on your knowledge of babies, toddlers, and preschoolers, and the needs of a particular center or community, identify the goals for fostering children's knowledge of health and safety, and at the same time, take steps to insure that the preschool does, in fact, provide children with a safe and healthy physical environment.

*Table 3*

| age | characteristics | accident hazards | measures for prevention |
|---|---|---|---|
| Birth to 4 months | Eats, sleeps, cries | Bath-Scalding | Check bath water with elbow. Keep 1 hand on baby. |
| | Rolls off flat surfaces | Falls | Never turn back on baby who is on table or bed. |
| | Wriggles | Toys | Select toys that are too large to swallow, too tough to break with no sharp points or edge. |
| | | Sharp objects | Keep pins and other sharp objects out of baby's reach. |
| | | Smothering | Filmy plastics, harnesses, zippered bags and pillows can smother or strangle. A firm mattress and loose covering for baby are safest. Babies of this age need *complete* protection. |
| 4-12 months | Grasps and moves more | Play areas | Keep baby in a safe place near attendant. The floor, full-sized bed, and yard are unsafe without supervision. |
| | Puts objects in his mouth | Bath | Check temperature of bath water with elbow. Keep baby out of reach of faucets. Don't leave him alone in bath for *any* reason. |
| | | Toys | Large beads on strong cord and unbreakable, rounded toys of smooth wood or plastic are safe. |
| | | Small Objects | Keep buttons, beads, and other small objects from baby's reach. |
| | | | Children of this age still need *full-time protection*. |
| | | Falls | Don't turn your back on him when he is on an elevated surface. |
| | | Burns | Place guards around registers and floor furnaces. Keep hot liquids, hot foods, and electric cords on irons, toasters, and coffee pots out of baby's reach. Use sturdy and round-edged furniture. Avoid hot steam vaporizers. |

*Table 3 (cont.)*

| age | characteristics | accident hazards | measures for prevention |
|---|---|---|---|
| 1-2 yrs | Investigates, climbs, opens doors and drawers; takes things apart; likes to play | Gates, windows, doors | Keep doors leading to stairways, driveways, and storage areas securely fastened. Put gates on stairways and porches. Keep screens locked or nailed. |
| | | Play areas | Fence the play yard. Provide sturdy toys with no small removable parts and of unbreakable material. Electric cords to coffee pots, toasters, irons, and radios should be kept out of reach. |
| | | Water | *Never leave child alone in tub, wading pool, or around open or frozen water.* |
| | | Poisons | Store all medicines and poisons in *locked cabinet*. Store cosmetics and household products, especially caustics, out of reach of child. Store kerosene and gasoline in metal cans and out of reach of children. |
| | | Burns | Provide guards for wall heaters, registers, and floor furnaces. Never leave children alone in the house. Close supervision is *needed* to protect child from accidents. |
| 2-3 yrs | Fascinated by fire. Moves about constantly. Tries to do things alone. Imitates. | Traffic | Keep child away from street and driveway with strong fence and firm discipline. |
| | | Water | Even shallow wading pools are unsafe unless carefully supervised. |
| | Runs and is lightning fast. Is impatient with restraint | Toys | Large sturdy toys *without* sharp edges or small removable parts are safest. |
| | | Burns | Keep matches and cigarette lighters out of reach of children. Teach children the danger of open flames. Never leave children alone in the house. |

| Age | Characteristics | Type of accident | Prevention |
|---|---|---|---|
| | | Dangerous objects | Lock up medicine and household and garden poisons. Store dangerous tools, firearms, and garden equipment in a safe place out of reach of children. Teach safe ways of handling appropriate tools and kitchen equipment. |
| | | Playmates | Accidents are more frequent when playmates are older—the 2 year old may be easily hurt by bats, hard balls, bicycles, and rough play. |
| 3-6 yrs | Explores the neighborhood, climbs, rides tricycles. Likes and plays rough games. Frequently out of sight of adults | Tools and equipment | Store in a safe place, out of reach and locked. Teach safe use of tools and kitchen equipment. |
| | | Poisons and burns | Keep medicines and household products and matches locked up. |
| | | Falls and injuries | Check the play area for attractive hazards such as old refrigerators, deep holes, trash heaps, construction and rickety buildings. |
| | | Drowning | Teach the danger of water and start swimming instruction. |
| | | Traffic | Let him learn rules and dangers of traffic. He must learn instant obedience where traffic is concerned. |
| 6-12 yrs | Away from home many hours a week. Participates in active sports, is part of a group and will "try anything once." In traffic on foot and bicycle. Teaching must gradually replace supervision | Traffic | Drive safely as an example. Use safety belts. Teach pedestrian and bicycle safety rules. Don't allow play in the streets or alleys. |
| | | Firearms | Store safely, handle carefully, teach proper use. |
| | | Sports | Provide instruction, safe space, and equipment, and supervise any competition. |
| | | Drowning | Teach swimming and boating safety. |

*Accident Prevention*

Reprinted, by permission, from *Health Services: A Guide for Project Directors and Health Personnel* (Washington, D.C.: U.S. Department of Health, Education and Welfare, 1971), p. 37–39.

Remember that health means freedom from illness and includes mental and social health as well as physical health. Because health is so important to children and encompasses their total life, parents and community members should be involved in fulfilling the goals of a preschool program.

Teaching health and safety takes place as children experience health care. Concepts of teeth and dental hygiene are introduced while children are brushing their teeth or concepts of physical health are stressed during physical examinations.

A program that is concerned with health and safety is also one that provides a balance between exercise and rest. As children participate in both exercise and rest activities, they begin to develop concepts of the need for both for health living.

## REFERENCES

*Day Care: 6 Health Services: A Guide for Project Directors and Health Personnel.* Washington, D.C.: U.S. Department of Health, Education, and Welfare, 1971.

Eldardo, R., and Pagan, B. *Perspectives on Infant Day Care.* Orangeburg, S.C.: Southern Association for Children under Six, 1971.

Elkind, D. *A Sympathetic Understanding of the Child: Birth to Sixteen.* Boston: Allyn & Bacon, Inc., 1978.

Essa, E. L., and Edwards, M. F. "Preventing Tooth Decay." *Voice for Children* 10 (1977): 12–14.

Hackett, L. C., and Jensen, R. G. *A Guide to Movement Exploration.* Palo Alto, Calif.: Peek Publications, 1967.

Keister, M. E. *The Good Life for Infants and Toddlers.* Washington, D.C.: National Association for the Education of Young Children, 1970.

Klein, D. "Rx for Pediatric Patients: Play While You Wait." *Young Children* 34 (1979): 13–20.

Read, K. *The Nursery School: A Human Relations Laboratory.* Philadelphia: W. B. Saunders, 1966.

*Review of Head Start Research since 1969.* Washington, D.C.: U.S. Department of Health, Education, and Welfare, 1977.

Rudolph, M., and Cohen, D. *Kindergarten: A Year of Learning.* New York: Appleton Century Crofts, 1964.

## RESOURCES

The following organizations have many materials concerning health that are either free of charge or available for a small fee.

The Administration for Children, Youth and Families
Box 1182
Washington, DC 20013

The ACYF has a number of free materials concerning the health and safety of children. Among them are *Day Care 6: A Guide for Project Directors and Health Personnel.*

American Automobile Association
8111 Gatehouse Road
Falls Church, Virginia 22042

The AAA offers free teaching materials for children. Ask for copies of *Ten Guides for K-Grade 3* and *My Own Safety Story.* These will be free of charge through your local AAA club.

National Safety Council
425 North Michigan
Chicago, Illinois 60611

U.S. Department of Health, Education, and Welfare
Washington, DC 20201

The U.S. Department of HEW can be contacted to obtain much free material on the health and safety of children. You might ask specifically for the following materials:

*Your Child from One to Six*
*Infant Care*

*You might also contact your state department of education for health and safety materials.*

# PROJECTS

1. Interview a teacher of young children. Ask her what the goals of her health and safety education program include. Ask her how these goals are implemented.

2. Tour a preschool center. Note the way the environment is arranged. What things are present that show accident preparedness? What things should be provided? (Telephone numbers of fire and hospital services near the phone, fire extinguishers, etc.)

3. Interview a child of four and another five years of age. Ask them some questions designed to evaluate their self-concept. "Who are you?" "What can you do?" "Where are you?" "What would you rather be?"

4. Observe in a preschool during nap, lunch, or play time. How do the teachers use the ongoing activities of the center to teach health? What additional learning experiences could be introduced at these times?

# SUGGESTED
## RESOURCES

Association for Childhood Education International
3615 Wisconsin Avenue, NW
Washington, DC 20016

Bank Street College of Education
610 West 112 Street
New York, New York 10025

Black Child Development Institute
1028 Connecticut Avenue, NW
Washington, DC 20036

Bureau of Child Development and Parent Education
New York State Department of Education
Albany, New York 12224

Bureau of Education for the Handicapped
U.S. Office of Education
Department of Health, Education, and Welfare
7th and D Streets, SW
Washington, DC 20036

Child Study Association of America
50 Madison Avenue
New York, New York 10010

Children's Defense Fund
1746 Cambridge Street
Cambridge, Massachusetts 02138


Child Welfare League of America
67 Irving Place
New York, New York 10003

Education Commission of the States
Early Childhood Project
300 Lincoln Tower
1860 Lincoln Street
Denver, Colorado 80295

ERIC Clearinghouse on Early Childhood Education
805 West Pennsylvania Avenue
Urbana, Illinois 61801

Family Service Association of America
44 East 23rd Street
New York, New York 10010

International Catholic Children's Bureau
65 Rue De Lausanne
CH-1202
Geneva, Switzerland

Mental Health Materials Center
419 Park Avenue, South
New York, New York 10016

National Association for the Education of Young Children
1834 Connecticut Avenue, NW
Washington, DC 20009

National Association for Mental Health
1800 North Kent Avenue
Rosslyn, Virginia 22209

National Association for Retarded Children
2709 Avenue E. East
Arlington, Texas 76011

National Congress of Parents and Teachers
700 North Rush Street
Chicago, Illinois 60611

National Health Council
1740 Broadway
New York, New York 10019

Play Schools Association
111 East 59th Street
New York, New York 10022

Public Affairs Committee
381 Park Avenue S
New York, New York 10016

Society for Research in Child Development
University of Chicago
5801 Ellis Avenue
Chicago, Illinois 60637

The United States Children's Bureau
Administration for Children, Youth and Families
P.O. Box 1182
Washington, DC 20013

U.S. Department of Health, Education, and Welfare
Washington, DC 20402

U.S. Department of Labor
Women's Bureau
200 Constitution Avenue, NW
Washington, DC 20402